SO-CPD-184

The
South
Atlantic
Quarterly
Fall 2006
Volume 105
Number 4

Visit Duke University Press Journals at www.dukeupress.edu/journals.

Subscriptions. Direct all orders to Duke University Press, Journals Fulfillment, 905 W. Main St., Suite 18B, Durham, NC 27701. Annual subscription rates: print-plus-electronic institutions, $166; print-only institutions, $150; e-only institutions, $148; individuals, $35; students, $21. For information on subscriptions to the e-Duke Scholarly Collection through HighWire Press, see www.dukeupress.edu/edukecollection. Print subscriptions: add $12 postage and 6% GST for Canada; add $16 postage outside the U.S. and Canada. Back volumes (institutions): $150. Single issues: institutions, $38; individuals, $14. For more information, contact Duke University Press Journals at 888-651-0122 (toll-free in the U.S. and Canada) or 919-688-5134; subscriptions@dukeupress.edu.

Permissions. Photocopies for course or research use that are supplied to the end user at no cost may be made without explicit permission or fee. Photocopies that are provided to the end user for a fee may not be made without payment of permission fees to Duke University Press. Address requests for permission to republish copyrighted material to Permissions Coordinator, permissions@dukeupress.edu.

Advertisements. Direct inquiries about advertising to Journals Advertising Coordinator, journals_advertising@dukeupress.edu.

Distribution. The journal is distributed by Ubiquity Distributors, 607 DeGraw St., Brooklyn, NY 11217; phone: 718-875-5491; fax: 718-875-8047.

The *South Atlantic Quarterly* is indexed in *Academic Abstracts FullTEXT Elite, Academic Abstracts FullTEXT Ultra, Academic Research Library, Academic Search Elite, Academic Search Premier, America: History and Life, American Humanities Index, Art Index Retrospective, 1929–1984, Arts and Humanities Citation Index, Corporate ResourceNet, Current Abstracts, Current Contents/Arts and Humanities, Discovery, Expanded Academic ASAP, Historical Abstracts, Humanities Abstracts, Humanities and Social Sciences Index Retrospective, 1907–1984, Humanities Full Text, Humanities Index, Humanities Index Retrospective, 1907–1984, Humanities International Index, International Bibliography of Periodical Literature, Literary Reference Center, MasterFILE Elite, MasterFILE Premier, MasterFILE Select, MLA Bibliography, News and Magazines, OmniFile Full Text V, OmniFile Full Text, Mega Edition, Research Library, Social Sciences Index Retrospective, 1907–1984,* and *Student Resource Center College with Expanded Academic ASAP.*

The *South Atlantic Quarterly* is published, at $166 for (print-plus-electronic) institutions and $35 for individuals, by Duke University Press, 905 W. Main St., Suite 18B, Durham, NC 27701. Periodicals postage paid at Durham, NC, and additional mailing offices. Postmaster: Send address changes to *South Atlantic Quarterly*, Box 90660, Duke University Press, Durham, NC 27708-0660.

ISSN 0038-2876

The Last Frontier: The Contemporary Configuration of the U.S.-Mexico Border

SPECIAL ISSUE EDITOR: JANE JUFFER

The
South
Atlantic
Quarterly
Fall 2006
Volume 105
Number 4

Jane Juffer

Introduction

Our citizens have new responsibilities. We must be
vigilant.
—President George Bush, address to the nation,
November 8, 2001

Vigilantes at the Last Frontier

In the August heat of the New Mexico desert,
fifty miles north of the border with Mexico,
homeland security has become a pressing local
issue. The question posed is this: If the U.S. government can't do the job of policing the border,
who will?

The Dickerson Auction Barn in Las Cruces is
gradually filling up. Two young men, skinheads,
looking disaffected. A couple in their sixties,
dressed as if they've just come from church,
the woman with a large bouffant hairdo. A man
playing Daniel Boone, shaggy hair, gun holster
at his waist and knife in a sheath strapped to
his leg, with his wife and preteen son, clearly
disgruntled by this Sunday afternoon outing.
Dozens of single men, young to old, mainly
white, many ranchers dressed in cowboy boots
and hats fill the aluminum chairs. A small group
of protesters, many of them Latino students and

South Atlantic Quarterly 105:4, Fall 2006
DOI 10.1215/00382876-2006-001   © 2006 Duke University Press

faculty from New Mexico State University, stand along the wall. Local police officers mill around. They await the words of Bob Wright, who has called this meeting to establish the Las Cruces chapter of the Minuteman Civil Defense Project, a border watch group that is gaining strength along the border as well as in other parts of the United States.

"President Bush after 9/11 asked America to be vigilant," says Wright, a lanky man in a cowboy hat. He says that the Minutemen in Arizona, who ran a well-publicized campaign in April 2005, have assisted the Border Patrol in thousands of arrests. In urging people in the audience to sign up to patrol the New Mexican–Mexican border, he calls on the audience to do their "civic duty" in helping their country, to be "another pair of eyes" in these "extraordinary times."

Hundreds of people along the border have responded to the Minutemen's call. Many arrive at designated border spots in their RVs, pulling out their lawn chairs and settling down to watch for "aliens." It's a new leisure activity, one that doubles as civic duty. In taking up President Bush's post-9/11 call for all Americans to be vigilant, they are practicing a "kinder, gentler" form of vigilantism. In a time of national crisis, Bush calls on citizens to do their part to protect the nation by reporting any unusual activity and constantly being prepared, thus protecting their own households and property as well as their communities. Answering this appeal, border vigilantes have entered the mainstream: In 2005, the Minutemen earned the praise of the Bush administration as well as the invitation to speak to congressional committees, prompted the head of the Border Patrol to call for the formation of a volunteer civilian patrol based on the Minutemen model, and were represented on NBC's popular show *The West Wing*. Chapters sprang up throughout the country; border security became an issue in Tennessee, Minnesota, and Maine. Nearly every national news outlet has done features on the group.

The Minutemen's mainstreaming speaks to the current state of the U.S.-Mexico border: Long considered a peripheral, marginalized zone, the border has now become central—indeed, the model site of neoliberal governance. As both national governments withdraw, private organizations and individual citizens must take up the slack. The relationship between citizen and state is mediated by the free market (in the form, for example, of NAFTA) and its articulation to private property. Many of the Minutemen are ranchers along the border, as angered by trespassing on their property as they are by the threat of terrorists entering from the south. The citi-

Figure 1. Minutemen break-away group patrols California-Mexico border, July 2005. Photo © 2005 David McNew/Getty Images News; used by permission.

zen/consumer/subject acts responsibly, with enterprise, to constantly produce membership in the nation. The Minutemen operate by a code of ethics that distances the group—at least rhetorically—from the nasty history of vigilantism along the border: lynchings of Mexicans and African Americans in the South by border vigilantes and white supremacists. They claim not to "take the law into their own hands," meting out punishment as they see fit, but rather to call the Border Patrol and even assist undocumented people in need of water and medical assistance. They rearticulate the individualism of frontier justice; they offer a communitarian ethic of protecting their communities and the nation during a time when the national government can't (or won't, some argue) do the job. Whereas some vigilantes don't care at all about the judicial system or due process, the neoliberal vigilante actually perceives himself to be a solid citizen. Volunteerism is one important component of the neoliberal agenda, as can be seen in the Bush administration's call for religious organizations and other private entities to do the work of the welfare state.

Yet a withdrawal of the state doesn't completely capture the current climate on the border. Neoliberalism is complicated by the post-9/11 pressures to build up the Border Patrol and secure the nation, even while keeping the borders open to ever-expanding trade with Mexico. Although the heightened attention to the border as a site linked to global terror began immediately after 9/11, it became particularly intense when, in the summer of 2004, the Justice Department leaked news to the major media outlets that a Saudi pilot named Adnan El Shukrijumah—rumored to be an al-Qaeda operative—was spotted in an Internet café in Tegucigalpa, Honduras, possibly recruiting, possibly planning attacks or entry into the United States. The FBI issued a border-wide alert for Shukrijumah, Attorney General John Ashcroft offered $5 million for information about him, and Latin America was named "the potential last frontier for international terrorism."[1] That makes the U.S.-Mexico border the most likely point of entry for "terrorists" to enter the United States.

None of the rumors were verified, but it was more than enough to make the Minuteman mission seem perfectly reasonable and necessary, perhaps even to lay the groundwork for acceptance of more extreme variations of the vigilante. There are already those elements in the group—not the watchful citizen doing his volunteer duty but rather the violent, gun-toting renegade racist determined to take the law into his own hands and punish the "illegal aliens" who can be easily lumped together with terrorists. The Minutemen occupy not only a physical borderland but also a political borderland, an ambiguous space between adhering to the law and proclaiming its ineffectiveness and thus irrelevance. As national founder Chris Simcox said at a meeting in March 2003—before the Minutemen went mainstream—"So far we've had restraint, but I'm afraid that restraint is wearing thin. Take heed of our weapons because we're going to defend our borders by any means necessary."[2] There was just a hint of that sentiment at the Las Cruces meeting, when Simcox, the rally's featured speaker, emphasized his belief in the law but his frustration with "Washington": "We must force our government to do their job by threatening to do it for them."

This issue of *South Atlantic Quarterly* examines conditions along the border in a post-9/11 world. As several essays demonstrate, the border has become a paradigmatic site of neoliberal governance in both economic and political terms. In economic terms, Alicia Schmidt Camacho argues that the "forms of exchange and consumption that have underwritten neoliberal development have come to depend on the social relations institutionalized in the border region: in particular, an economic caste system that demands workers well-versed in both service and low-skilled labor, whose weak social integration assures that they make relatively few demands on either state." In political terms, U.S. governmental officials sanction the Minuteman movement even as Mexican officials disseminate brochures on how their citizens who cross the border might survive the hazards of the desert and other perils that threaten lives (see Schmidt Camacho)—both governments thus acknowledging that the Border Patrol cannot stop people desperate for work. Vigilantes step into the space between the state and the market, representing community values, providing humanitarian assistance, and acting as neighborhood/border watch groups. They appeal to a U.S. population that is growing accustomed to thinking less in terms of guaranteed securities and rights and more in terms of individual responsibilities and desires.

These communitarian and consumerist impulses work with rather than against a military buildup along the border. If the Minutemen are recognized and represented as "just doing their civic duty," and if the Border Patrol acknowledges that they need the group's assistance, and if together they still can't do the job, then calls for more technological and military resources, new deployments of Border Patrol agents, and constantly expanding detention centers where undocumented immigrants are held for long periods of time without representation or hearing dates are accepted by the American public as an acceptable and even expected development. The Minutemen proclaim their adherence to the law, but, in turn, their claim that the law is not being upheld as more "illegals" and "potential terrorists" cross the border becomes the reason for deploying exceptional measures that exceed the law but are accepted by the lawmakers and the public. In this sense, the border is no longer a strange, exotic, and dangerous space but rather one of the primary sites where the particular kind of neoliberal yet militaristic governance of the post-9/11 era can be exercised. The border is characterized by what Giorgio Agamben called a state of exception—the condition that obtains when governing bodies legitimate the suspension of certain rights in the name of national security, or the greater good of the nation, or the global war on terror.

Along the border, this state of exception has a particular physical arrangement, delineated by heightened surveillance at border checkpoints, more Border Patrol vans cruising the streets with officers that are better armed than ever, and calls to build actual walls along some stretches of the border (such a wall already exists in Tijuana, as Santiago Vaquera-Vásquez describes in this issue). Stretches of the border have become like Agamben's camp: "the space that opens up when the state of exception starts to become the rule. In it, the state of exception, which was essentially a temporal suspension of the state of law, acquires a permanent spatial arrangement that, as such, remains constantly outside the normal state of law."[3] The state of exception allows, indeed requires, exceptional measures—yet these measures no longer seem exceptional but rather a commonsense aspect of the post-9/11 world; as Agamben says, "Faced with the unstoppable progression of what has been called a 'global civil war,' the state of exception tends increasingly to appear as the dominant paradigm of government in contemporary politics."[4]

In the permanent state of exception that makes the border paradigmatic, senators from border states become experts on global affairs. Says Republican senator John McCain of Arizona: "I am worried about our border. We now have hundreds of thousands, if not millions, of people who are crossing illegally every year. And we are now seeing a larger number of people crossing our southern border who are from countries of interest as opposed to just Latin America."[5] McCain thus links the history of the border as one that is porous to the South with the post-9/11 fear of the East, making his state a central node in the global war on terror. This is a savvy move, for it allows McCain to both draw on the history of demonization of Mexicans and other Latin Americans who enter to look for jobs and also to seamlessly connect this group of Others to a new group of Others—terrorists from "countries of interest," the new border lingo for the Middle East and other sites linked in the U.S. imaginary to al-Qaeda. In this demarcation of the Other, Mexicans may become less threatening, due to their very proximity and familiarity. Indeed, as I discuss below, even the Minutemen support the creation of a guest worker program, referring mainly to Mexican workers. On the other hand, the continual production of a category of Others based largely on race may be easily adjusted to include any brown person, given the "appropriate" circumstances.[6] Such was the case in London in the summer of 2005, after the subway bombings there, when police chased, shot in the head five times, and killed an innocent Brazilian, Jean Charles de Menezes, purportedly because he was wearing a bulky coat in the summer, but surely also because he was brown. Similarly, the Spanish government produces a category of undesirable Others as it patrols its border with Morocco—a narrow and deadly strip of the Mediterranean Sea—in an attempt to keep Africans from entering, as Ana Manzanas Calvo argues in her article comparing the U.S.-Mexico and the Spanish-Moroccan borders.

Despite its dominance, the United States is not having any more success "winning the war" on the border than it is winning anything in Iraq. Migrant deaths have reached new highs (Manzanas, Sadowski-Smith, Camacho Schmidt), murders of women continue unabated and unresolved in Ciudad Juárez (Wright), environmental conditions remain worrisome to many (Hill, Sadowski-Smith), and the drug cartels are more powerful than ever. Ironically, says Tony Payan, the "four major cartels have become increasingly efficient and flexible hierarchies, ready to respond to the contingencies of the drug war and the technological innovations at the border instigated by the Department of Homeland Security." And the effects of "free trade" in Mexico are to keep pushing its people north to find jobs, even as they maintain their attachments to home, as shown in Laura Lewis's discussion of the transnational ties forged between Mexican communities in Winston-Salem, North Carolina, and San Nicolás, a rural community on Mexico's southern Pacific coast.

The Last Frontier?

What moment does the Bush administration invoke when it refers to countries south of the border as "the last frontier"? The time of Manifest Destiny, when Anglo frontiersmen pushed their way west, incorporating land that belonged to Native Americans and Mexicans, a push that culminated in the U.S.-Mexico War and the signing in 1848 of the Treaty of Guadalupe Hidalgo, which forced Mexico to cede half its territory to the United States? The time when nation building required gaining control over territory and marking that control with the transformation of frontiers into borders? The time after 1848 when native Mexicans, the *Tejanos* of Texas, rebelled against the loss of land and the failure of the treaty to grant them rights of citizenship? The rebellion prompted "frontier justice," as practiced by the Texas Rangers, who formally organized in 1873 to protect the land of ranchers from incursions by its previous owners. The Rangers committed numerous atrocities, producing the very unrest they claimed to squelch as native Mexicans rebelled. Bush, the parodic Texan in his cowboy hat and too-tight jeans, is perhaps nostalgic for these days when the Rangers reproduced the frontier that was so critical to the production of masculinity even as the frontier threatened to disappear. (Bush, after all, did run Major League Baseball's Texas Rangers, an irony that's difficult to miss.)

The Border Patrol was formed in 1924 in an attempt to grant some legitimacy and regularity to the policing of the border, yet its connections to the Rangers were clear: The "anointed 'grandfather of the Border Patrol . . . was Jefferson Davis Milton, one of the original Texas Rangers."[7] Many of the administrators and district directors were former military men; the rank-and-file recruits were often young men who wanted to "engage in macho exploits, many were too fast on the trigger, could often be found in corner bars, or even milked their neighborhood contacts to set up smuggling rings."[8] There were numerous attempts to make the Border Patrol more respectable and representative of the nation at a time when, after World War I, Congress was enacting legislation to make it harder for Mexicans to enter the country and easier for them to be deported. One sees some of these same players today at the Minuteman gatherings: the Daniel Boone character, the skinheads, and former law enforcement officials. One of the speakers at the Las Cruces meeting was Richard Humphreys, who worked for twelve years in law enforcement and testifies to how the Border Patrol supports the Minutemen.

It is not just Mexicans who historically have provided the rationale for heightened policing. The "last frontier" also has been invoked to create fears about "leftist terrorists" farther south. In 1986, President Ronald Reagan warned that the Sandinistas in Managua were just "two days' driving time" from Harlingen, Texas. During the same time period, United States–funded right-wing forces in Guatemala and El Salvador forced many people, from leftist guerrillas to nonpartisan campesinos, to flee for their lives and cross the border into the United States. From the turmoil he created, Reagan identified a pool of terrorists to justify heightened border patrol. One military analyst in the Reagan administration "predicted the rise of extremist groups that would 'feed on the anger and frustration of recent Central and South American immigrants who will not realize their own version of the American dream.'"[9] To further establish the threat of terrorism from the south (and thus eventually from within), in 1986 Reagan announced that drug trafficking was a threat to national security and declared the War on Drugs. Combined with the threat from leftists in Central America, the Reagan administration justified declaring its own state of exception, legitimating the collusion of the Border Patrol and the military. The Department of Defense became involved in a wide range of antidrug activities. The Border Patrol became responsible for drug enforcement, which allowed it access to high-powered military-issue rifles such as semiautomatic M-14s and M-16s.[10] It was a period of low-intensity conflict, of expanded use of helicopters, night-vision equipment, electronic ground-sensor systems, television surveillance equipment, and airborne infrared radar.[11] The buildup continued under George Bush Sr. and under Bill Clinton. Although Clinton was initially more interested in free trade than in immigration issues, he joined in the rhetoric about the border and terrorists after the World Trade Center was bombed in 1993, saying, "The simple fact is that we must not and will not surrender our borders to those who wish to exploit our history of compassion and justice. We cannot tolerate those who traffic in human cargo, nor can we allow our people to be endangered by those who would enter the country to terrorize Americans."[12]

When the current Bush administration invokes the border as the last frontier, it performs a delicate balancing act between maintaining the idea of a frontier that justifies states of exception while simultaneously promoting the success of the United States in transforming the frontier into a manageable border that protects the nation even as it facilitates trade. Today's state of exception must be normalized in order to convince the public that both conditions obtain. Here's where the Minutemen prove useful to the administration.

The Communitarian Ethos

As exemplary neoliberal subjects, the Minutemen have been warmly received in Washington. They met in May 2005 with members of the Congressional Immigration Reform Caucus at the invitation of its chair, Tom Tancredo, who said, "I would like to thank the Minutemen on behalf of the millions of Americans who can't be here with you today. You are good citizens who ask that our laws be enforced. When did that become a radical idea?"[13] In the summer of 2005, Attorney General Alberto Gonzales was asked about the Minutemen and said he wished they "would let federal law officers handle border security but did not begrudge them their right to watch for border crossers as long as they don't break the law." He added: "My own view is that it's a free country."[14] Asked for his opinion about the Minutemen, Jarrod Agen, an agency spokesman for the Department of Homeland Security, said, "Homeland security is a shared responsibility, and the department believes the American public plays a critical role in helping to defend the homeland."[15] Robert Bonner, commissioner of Customs and Border Protection, which encompasses the Border Patrol, even said that the agency might create "something akin to a Border Patrol auxiliary."[16] The consideration, he said, was a direct result of observing the Minutemen groups: "It is actually as a result of seeing that there is the possibility in local border communities, and maybe even beyond, of having citizens that would be willing to volunteer to help federal agents catch illegal immigrants." He told the Associated Press that the agency was exploring ways to "organize a citizen effort," but the next day the Department of Homeland Security refuted him, saying the department had no plans to develop a civilian volunteer force.[17]

Bonner, however, was merely following the urgings of his commander in chief. During the same speech, in November 2001, in which he urged Americans to be vigilant, President Bush urged them to become volunteers. He announced a new program: "Communities of Character, designed to spark a rebirth of citizenship and service." In his list of possible volunteer duties, he included "new defense services similar to local volunteer fire departments, to respond to local emergencies when the government is stretched thin."[18] By everyone's admission, the Border Patrol *is* stretched very thin—as currently staffed, it cannot sufficiently monitor the 2,000-mile-long border, especially outside the major ports of entry (twin cities such as Ciudad Juárez–El Paso). Here's where the Minutemen step in as enterprising citizens, answering the government's call to do what might be considered the government's job. The Minutemen are quick to assert their desire to work with the Border Patrol; said Chris Simcox at the Las Cruces meeting, Border Patrol agents are "great Americans and support us 100 percent. They respond almost every time we call them." The Minutemen become visible proof that the American public not only welcomes but also participates in the nation's defense, making other acts of homeland security, such as the USA Patriot Act, seem more consensual. At about the same time the Minutemen were getting considerable media attention, in the summer of 2005, the USA Patriot Act was renewed with little fanfare.

Volunteers operate in the territory between the state and the free and amoral exchange of the market, supplying the "compassion" in conservatism. Although many of the Minutemen (such as ranchers) are concerned about their private property, this is not the frontier ethos of "each man for himself" but rather the reinvigorated and "caring" citizen acting responsibly within his community. "It's our civic duty to help law enforcement," says Simcox. As Nikolas Rose describes the communitarian ethos, "Politics is to be returned to society itself, but no longer in a social form: in the form of individual morality, organizational responsibility and ethical community."[19] The good vigilante is the organizer of the neighborhood watch group—or the border watch group. The Minutemen are eager to assert their code of ethics. Wright says they have a strict "standard operating procedure" (SOP) that prohibits contact with any undocumented person. This SOP is breached only when immigrants need water or medical assistance, which the group is quick to assert it provides; Simcox says he has helped save 160 lives.

The group also subscribes publicly to the inclusive definition of the nation that flourished after 9/11, vehemently disclaiming protesters' charges that they are racist: "There is not any racism. We are not an anti-immigration group," says Wright. To provide visual proof of this claim, one of the speakers at the Las Cruces meeting is Al Garza, a veteran of the U.S. Marines, a self-described "fifth-generation American of Spanish, Italian, and Yaqui descent," who relates the stories of his many relatives who have died fighting for the United States: "America is a country where freedom has been purchased at a heavy price." Garza says that as a "Hispanic," he was skeptical about the Minutemen when he first heard of them, but then accompanied Simcox on his rounds one day and decided that "this isn't a white supremacist group, this is a border watch group. I said, 'Where can I sign up?'"

In a neoliberal state, argues David Harvey, the "institutional arrangements considered essential to guarantee individual freedoms are strong individual property rights, the rule of law, and the institutions of freely functioning markets and free trade."[20] The state's role is to secure and protect these rights—hence the contradiction of intervention in the name of freedom. Unlike the Texas Rangers, who were indiscriminate in their racism, the Minutemen are willing to concede that some undocumented people are not terrorists but, rather, desperate for work. As Simcox put it, "These are innocent victims of their governments who aren't guaranteeing them jobs." The Minutemen support the creation of a guest worker program; says Bob Wright, "All we ask is that immigrants come through the gate and sign the guestbook."

A guest worker program temporarily resolves the tensions inherent in the need, on the one hand, for a mobile labor force and, on the other hand, for secure borders. It answers the question of how the very people one defines as threats to national security and purity can also be given some kind of provisional legal status given their critical status to the economy—to the homes and gardens of middle-class Americans, to the hotels and restaurants of every city, to the meatpacking plants of Iowa and Nebraska, to the vineyards and orchards of California. Both Presidents Fox and Bush have called for a guest worker program, although they disagree on the form it would take, and one rationale is that such a program would help distinguish between legitimate workers and potential security threats. As Magdalena Carral, commissioner of the Mexican National Migration Institute, has argued, "The regularization of undocumented Mexicans in the United States would allow for the identification of a large segment of people already settled in the country that do not represent a security threat. The contribution of these Mexicans to the U.S. economy has been recognized by the U.S. private sector."[21] The market sets the terms for "the rule of law"—"aliens" can become temporarily legal and thus gain some rights if they prove their worth to the nation as productive workers and potential consumers. This is just a temporary state of belonging, however, for Bush's guest worker program requires that workers eventually return to their home countries.[22] The border must remain open to the *regulated* flow of workers back and forth as well as to the flow of goods back and forth across the border—produced in the maquiladoras by cheap Mexican labor and consumed in the United States, a process expanded by the passage of the North American Free Trade Agreement in 1994.

In this neoliberal environment, it comes as no surprise that one of the examples of human rights abuses cited by Minuteman opponents is linked to consumerism. In their patrols along the Arizona border in April 2005, several members of the Minutemen detained a Mexican man and forced him to pose for a picture holding a T-shirt with the man, Bryan Barton, who had spotted him. The shirt said, "Bryan Barton caught an illegal alien and all I got was this lousy T-shirt."[23] One wonders if the T-shirt was made just across the border.

"Ordinary People"

The work of the good citizen/volunteer provides the legitimation for more insidious and violent forms of vigilantism and state-sponsored militarism that come to seem necessary, even normalized, given the current security crisis. If Homeland Security and the volunteer force are doing all they can to seal the borders, doesn't that then suggest there is a need for more militaristic solutions? "You are ordinary people, but these are extraordinary times," Wright told the potential volunteers in Las Cruces.

Adherence to the law today becomes the rationale for future violations of the law. Some Minutemen chapters have said they will carry weapons. In California, a Minuteman group led by Jim Chase urged volunteers to bring baseball bats, Mace, pepper spray, and machetes, until the Border Patrol learned about it and raised concerns. Chase said that instead they would carry guns: "The guns are for one reason—to keep my people alive," he said.[24] The Minutemen are attracting neo-Nazis even if they are not recruiting them. According to Amanda Susskind and Joanna Mendelson, researchers for the Anti-Defamation League, the first weekend of Minutemen events was endorsed by Shawn Walker, spokesman for the neo-Nazi National Alliance, a group that describes illegal immigration as an "invasion" that will cause white people to be a "minority within the next 50 years."[25]

Internet Web sites for different border vigilante groups show the overlap of the right-wing extremists, the Minutemen, and the military. For example, at Ranchrescue.com, one is greeted with the words: "Private property first, foremost, and always." The featured image in October 2005 is of a Border Patrol van flanked by two U.S. Army Stryker armored vehicles on the New Mexican border, and the headline reads: "US Army Deploys Stryker armored vehicles to NM border, apparently in support of Minuteman Project." Beneath this image is a photo of two armed men wearing black ski masks and camouflage clothing, holding a U.S. flag. It's an ad for Border Rescue Arizona's Operation Eagle, which seems to be the group's name for its current mission to "reclaim" the border from "drug-running terrorists."

The vigilante in neoliberal times functions not as a complete renegade but rather in conjunction with, or at least alongside, the government, both entities acting outside the law, in the name of the law, in order to enforce the law. The Border Patrol responds to the Minutemen, and vice versa; after Simcox organized the Minutemen in Arizona, the Border Patrol announced that it would dispatch five hundred new Border Patrol agents to that state.[26] Government officials, as cited above, support the vigilantes. A climate is created in which the suspension of civil rights seems legitimate. The USA Patriot Act, for example, expands the definition of "terrorist activity," then gives the government considerable power to detain people linked to any such activity, if the attorney general or his deputy "has reasonable grounds to believe" the person has any links to terrorism. If the person held is charged with any violation at all, such as a minor infraction of immigration law, he or she can be held indefinitely.[27] The judicial system has assisted in creating camplike conditions of extended detention where detainees have virtually no rights. Agamben argues that the passage of the Patriot Act reveals the extent to which the state of exception has become permanent, for under it individuals have no legal status, thus "producing a legally unnamable and unclassifiable being" subject to a "detention that is indefinite not only in the temporal sense but in its very nature as well, since it is entirely removed from the law and from judicial oversight,"[28] a situation made visible at sites such as Guantánamo Bay. Along the border there are growing numbers of detention centers; many of them are contracted out to private entities and are becoming the mainstays of local economies.

Security and Economy

At the intersections of security and economy lies the truth of neoliberalism's defense of the powerful. Any attempt to prevent "terrorists" from entering the United States must not infringe on corporate profits. When he was head of Homeland Security, Tom Ridge declared: "Mexico is one of our largest trading partners and it is absolutely critical that we prevent terrorists from infiltrating the commercial chain to launch an attack."[29] This statement is a slightly balder version of the concerns expressed by the House of Representatives' Subcommittee on Infrastructure and Border Security, which held hearings on this matter in 2003 and summarized their goal: to figure out "how to balance security enhancements with the flow of people and commerce across our borders. The global trading system is increasingly reliant on the swift delivery of goods produced overseas. America's economic stability requires that goods and people cross our borders in and out of the country regularly without long delays. Our security also requires that we know who and what is entering."[30] The United States needs Mexico's cooperation in negotiating commerce and security; the two countries reached a "smart border" agreement, for example, which included measures such as the Secure Electronic Network for Traveler's Rapid Inspections, a system that allows the Bureau of Customs and Border Protection to accelerate the inspections of low-risk pre-enrolled crossers (see Payan's article for a critique of this system).

Given its reliance on the maquiladora industry, Mexico has had little choice but to work with the United States on border control as well as launching its own Operativo Sentinela, sending 18,000 soldiers as well as its navy to protect air and sea ports, borders, and key infrastructure and tourist spots. All this could have been averted, from Mexico's point of view.

As one of the rotating members of the United Nations Security Council, Mexico staunchly opposed the U.S. invasion of Iraq—along with China, France, Germany, and Russia. Gustavo Carvajal Moreno, president of the Mexican congressional foreign affairs committee, "pointed out that U.S. vulnerability to external attacks should have counseled against any uni-lateral action against Iraq. . . . Because of our shared border, such action and possible retaliation against the U.S. made us vulnerable too."[31] The Secu-rity Council passed a resolution saying that Iraq was in "material breach" of previous resolutions, authorizing a new inspection, and reiterating a warn-ing of "serious consequences" if Iraq would not comply with disarmament requirements. Military action should be a last resort. The United States insisted that inspections would not work and pressed ahead. Mexico's for-eign minister, Luis Ernesto Derbez, presciently called into question U.S. claims linking Hussein and al-Qaeda.[32] All of these entreaties, obviously, went unheard by a U.S. government determined to invade Iraq.

Security is in fact an economic issue, but not just in terms of U.S. wealth. This was the case made by Mexican ambassador Ruiz Cabanas at a 2003 forum of the Organization of American States in Barbados. He argued for "emphasizing the geographical and thematic diffusion of security threats born out of political, economic, public health, and environment conditions in the hemisphere" and "reminded his audience that 'human security' had become an essential element of hemispheric security."[33] As long as there is poverty throughout Latin America, produced in no small part through the policies of neoliberalism, people will not be secure: Their lives are in a con-stant state of insecurity and uncertainty about their next meal, their next doctor visit, and the safety of their drinking water. These issues cannot be addressed purely through military means, warns Carmen Moreno, former Mexican ambassador to the OAS, given the devastating history of military intervention: "This is not a good idea, especially if we consider the strength of the armed forces in relation to the fragility of democracy in some OAS countries."[34]

When the U.S.-Mexico border becomes a normalized state of exception, the U.S. government finds it easier to expand the very contours of the bor-der, again in the name of national security. The House of Representatives subcommittee report quoted above said that one component of the U.S. strategy to build "smarter borders" is through "pushing our borders out, pushing our zone of security out beyond our physical borders so America's borders are not the last line of defense, nor the first line of defense, against terrorism."[35] Mexico becomes the permeable barrier between the United States and the rest of Latin America, a purported breeding ground for terrorists; history repeats itself with the variation that Middle East terrorists (Osama bin Laden, al-Qaeda) replace the "communist threat" of the Sandinistas, the FMLN in El Salvador, and other leftist movements—or, rather, that they all join together. There is already considerable evidence to show that the United States is using 9/11 as a rationale for weakening what Moreno calls the fragile democracies that are recovering after decades of brutal military rule in many Latin American countries. In El Salvador in 2004, for example, the campaign of former FMLN guerrilla and presidential candidate Shafik Handal was weakened when the State Department suggested that he had ties to international terrorism and that if he won, the United States would consider El Salvador to be supporting international terrorism, "thereby blocking all financial remittances made by Salvadorans working in the U.S."[36] Handal was subsequently defeated by the conservative ARENA Party—which was responsible for many of the death-squad killings in the 1980s. U.S. conservatives have also tried to link Hugo Chávez in Venezuela and Lula da Silva in Brazil to "international terrorism." The Bush administration has adopted an "Effective Strategy Doctrine" that says "vast 'ungoverned spaces' in Latin American nations provide fertile ground for terrorists to take root," and it has used this notion of ungoverned spaces to legitimate a 52 percent jump in the number of Latin American police and soldiers trained by the U.S. military between 2002 and 2003.[37] With all of that "ungoverned space" to bring under control, the U.S. government is warranted, it appears to the wider public, in turning to the Minutemen and other vigilante groups who will help maintain the U.S.-Mexico border as a governed space, the "last frontier" in what Agamben calls a "global civil war."[38]

Resistance arises from within the discourses and material conditions of neoliberalism, as many of the articles here describe. The Ni Una Mas movement based in Ciudad Juárez protests the murders of hundreds of women, many of them maquiladora workers, as Melissa Wright describes in her analysis of the restraints of operating within the world of nongovernmental organizations. Transnational communities represent the possibilities carved out of global flows, as migrants persist in the face of xenophobia and economic hardships, Laura Lewis shows. Numerous poets and artists along the border have articulated the everyday lives of border residents as alternative narratives to the discourse of neoliberalism; these narratives are analyzed here in the essays by Sadowski-Smith, Camacho Schmidt, and Manzanas Calvo. Finally, this issue offers original cultural production that represents the variegated life of the border in the autobiographical essay by Santiago Vaquera-Vásquez, the poetry of Arturo Dávila, and the photography of Alejandro Lugo. While resistance cannot escape the terms of neoliberalism, then, rearticulation is possible and indeed necessary for the imagining of a new—more just and life-sustaining—configuration of the U.S.-Mexico border.

Notes

1 Olga R. Rodriguez, "Terror—Latin America," Associated Press, August 21, 2004, www .newslibrary.com (accessed July 10, 2005).

2 Quoted in Amanda Susskind and Joanna Mendelson, "Extremists at Border: Minuteman Project about More Than Enforcing Policy," *L.A. Daily News*, May 15, 2005, www .dailynews.com (accessed July 4, 2005).

3 Giorgio Agamben, *Means without End: Notes on Politics*, trans. Vicenzo Binetti and Cesare Casarino (Minneapolis: University of Minnesota Press, 2000), 39.

4 Giorgio Agamben, *State of Exception*, trans. Kevin Attell (Chicago: University of Chicago Press, 2005), 2.

5 Quoted in Jim Malone, "U.S. Continues to Tighten Immigration Following 9/11 Attacks," VOA News, May 3, 2005, www.voanews.com (accessed July 4, 2005).

6 Most recently, Harvard professor Samuel Huntington expressed this fear of the brown Other. In an article in *Foreign Policy*, he warned of "the intense and continuing immigration from Latin America, especially from Mexico," that is threatening the linguistic and religious foundations of the United States. He asks, "Will the United States remain a country with a single national language and a core of Anglo-Protestant culture?" Or, ominously from his point of view, are we witnessing the "transformation [of the United States] into two peoples with two cultures and two languages?" Huntington, "The Hispanic Challenge," *Foreign Policy* (March/April 2004), www.foreignpolicy.com (accessed July 10, 2005).

7 Alexandra Minna Stern, "Tracking the Border Patrol: Gender, Race, and Boundary Maintenance," in *Continental Crossroads: Remapping U.S.-Mexico Borderlands History*, ed. Samuel Truett and Elliott Young (Durham, NC: Duke University Press, 2004), quote on 312.

8 Ibid., 307.

9 Quoted in Timothy Dunn, *The Militarization of the U.S.-Mexican Border, 1978–1992* (Austin: University of Texas Press, 1996), 26.

10 Dunn, *The Militarization of the U.S.-Mexican Border*, 53.

11 Ibid., 58.

12 Quoted in Joseph Nevins, *Operation Gatekeeper: The Rise of the "Illegal Alien" and the Making of the U.S.-Mexico Boundary* (New York: Routledge, 2002), 89.

13 Jim Gilchrist, "Minuteman Going National, Will Start in New Mexico," June 11, 2005, www.libertypost.org (accessed July 10, 2005).

14 Leslie Linthicum, "AG Won't Discuss High Court Chances; Gonzales in Town for Border Talks," *Albuquerque Journal*, July 7, 2005.

15 Duncan Mansfield, "'Minuteman' Groups Grow,'" *Albuquerque Journal*, July 18, 2005.

16 "Border Patrol Considering Use of Volunteers, Official Says," *New York Times*, July 21, 2005.

17 Jeremiah Marquez, "No Plans for Border Patrol 'Auxiliary,'" *Albuquerque Journal*, July 22, 2005.

18 "President Discusses War on Terrorism," Address to the Nation, November 8, 2005, archives.www.cnn.com/2001 (accessed July 6, 2005).

19 Nikolas Rose, *Powers of Freedom: Reframing Political Thought* (Cambridge, England: Cambridge University Press, 1999), 174–75.

20 David Harvey, *A Brief History of Neoliberalism* (Oxford: Oxford University Press, 2005), 64.

21 Magdalena Carral, "Migration and Security Policy Post-9/11: Mexico and the United States," paper presented at the Second North American Meeting of the Trilateral Commission, New York, November 14–16, 2003.

22 As this issue went to press, Congress was debating different versions of a guest worker program, and Bush's position on whether he would support sending the workers home after a certain number of years or allow them to apply for citizenship was not clearly stated.

23 "Border Volunteers Cleared of Wrongdoing," April 8, 2005, cnn.usnews.com.printthis.clickability.com (accessed April 20, 2005).

24 Quoted in Mansfield, *Albuquerque Journal*.

25 Susskind and Mendelson, "Extremists at Border."

26 "Sources: 500 New Agents to Patrol Arizona Border," March 29, 2005, cnn.usnews.com.printthis.clickability.com (accessed April 20, 2005).

27 John Greenya, "Immigration Law in Post-9/11 America," *DC Bar*, August 2003, www.dcbar.org/forlawyers/washington_lawyer/august_2003 (accessed July 4, 2005).

28 Agamben, *State of Exception*, 3–4.

29 Quoted in Loretta Bondi, *Beyond the Border and Across the Atlantic: Mexico's Foreign and Security Policy Post-September 11* (Washington, DC: Center for Transatlantic Relations, 2004), 90. Bondi, a former Italian journalist, is a member of the resource group advising the United Nations High Level Panel on Threats, Challenges, and Change. Between May 2003 and March 2004, she interviewed dozens of Mexican and U.S. policy makers for this book.

30 "Balancing Security and Commerce," Hearing before the Subcommittee on Infrastructure and Border Security of the Select Committee on Homeland Security, House of Representatives (Washington, DC: U.S. Government Printing Office, 2005), 1–2.

31 Bondi, *Beyond the Border*, 12.

32 Ibid., 14.

33 Ibid., 54.

34 Ibid., 58.

35 "Balancing Security and Commerce," 8.

36 Nico Armstrong, "Crying Wolf: International Terror and the New Shadow upon U.S.-Latin American Relations," *International Studies Review* 2 (2005): 3–14, quote on 5.

37 Ibid., 8.

38 Agamben, *State of Exception*, 2.

Melissa W. Wright

Public Women, Profit, and
Femicide in Northern Mexico

Since 2002, a social justice movement called
Ni Una Mas has brought international attention
to the violence that, over the last decade, has
claimed hundreds of women's lives in the northern Mexican cities of Chihuahua and Ciudad
Juárez. Many of the victims have been tortured,
mutilated, and dumped, like garbage, around the
city. After twelve years of documented violence,
only one person has been convicted for one murder, and at this writing, these "most intolerable
crimes," as Amnesty International has described
them, continue along with the lack of convic-
tions.[1] Activists and scholars have called this
violence *femenicidio*, or "femicide," in reference
not only to the crimes but to the impunity that
surrounds them.[2]

Ni Una Mas, which means "not one more,"
consists of diverse domestic and international organizations and individuals, and their
demands are plain: one, that the state imple-
ment strategies for preventing further deaths
and kidnappings; and two, that the state conduct
competent investigations into the crimes already
committed. Far from being simple, however,
these demands have provoked a high-stakes con-

South Atlantic Quarterly 105:4, Fall 2006
DOI 10.1215/00382876-2006-003   © 2006 Duke University Press

troversy over the meaning of women's economic, political, and human rights in a neoliberal and democratizing Mexico.

The controversy stems from the declarations of political and corporate elites that the victims are not legitimate victims and that the Ni Una Mas participants are not legitimate activists, due to their allegedly illicit activities as "public women." The "public woman" referred to here is the woman who is found on the street, in the office, at political events, and any other place construed as "nondomestic." According to the dominant discourse of "public woman" still pervasive in Mexico (among other places), the public woman has her most famous representative in the figure of "the prostitute," the consummately public woman who makes her living by selling her body on the street. This discourse also draws a link between public women–prostitutes and social decay: The former are said to lead to and reflect the latter.[3]

In calling them "public women" who, as the discourse of the "prostitute" would have it, taint the social movement known for them, the governing elites deploy a powerful set of discursive tools that threaten not only the women of this movement but any woman who dares to venture into Mexico's public sphere. The sexism within the language of this public woman discourse is blatant, particularly when contrasted to the concept of "public man" (*hombre público*), which is one way of saying "citizen" or "politician." Yet the Ni Una Mas participants have no choice but to engage with it because the discourse draws upon old beliefs that strike a chord with many. The power of this discursive practice, as with others, lies in the familiarity borne of its repetition.[4] It draws upon an idea familiar around the world: that women who occupy public space should be regarded with suspicion.[5] It draws upon several other familiar ideas: that women who engage in the public economy are somehow contaminated; that female sexuality is dangerous and that women who sell sex are threats to society;[6] and that profit is another form of opportunism and exploitation. All of these ideas are so well-rehearsed through discourses common around the world that they seem normal and sensible. They are, therefore, quite powerful.

When Ni Una Mas was initially formed, its participants confronted the discursive strategy of political elites to use the prostitute-as-contaminant connection as a way to blame the victims for the violence they had suffered. As this familiar tactic goes, any woman who is a prostitute or who resembles one does not represent a legitimate victim of violence because she, through her immoral activities, caused her own problems. In other words, she has no right to justice because she is not a justifiable (i.e., "innocent") victim. Political and corporate leaders alike have repeatedly deployed this blame-the-victim account as a means of both discounting the crimes and claiming that the victims are not worthy of all this attention.[7]

Yet over years of dedicated events and organization, the Ni Una Mas activists have been successful in exposing such claims for what they are: a smokescreen for distracting attention from the political and economic policies that contribute to the violence and the impunity enjoyed by its perpetrators. In effect, the activists have turned a regional civil rights dispute into an international human rights campaign. Amnesty International has adopted this dispute as one of its prominent campaigns and in 2003 issued a blistering critique of regional political and economic leaders for their responsibility in relation to the crimes.[8] The United Nations has also criticized regional and federal officials and called for immediate action. Political leaders, activists, artists, academics, and journalists from around the world have brought attention to the unsolved murders and to the socioeconomic factors that contribute to them.

In the face of Ni Una Mas's success in internationalizing the movement, regional elites have been on the defensive in both international and national circles. They have had to respond to questions regarding the region's economic and social stability from potential investors who note how the violence reveals problems associated with the maquiladora development model and inadequate urban infrastructure.[9] Regional political elites have also had to address the issue of violence against women within American political campaigns, as different political parties claim that "the other party" has done nothing to make the border more secure.[10] Essentially, regardless of political party and because of Ni Una Mas, regional political elites have had to address the significance of the violence against women for their own political programs and for the region's economic future as a manufacturing base for foreign investors.

In response, again across party lines, they have sharpened their strategies for applying the discourse of the contaminated whore, via the euphemism of "public women," by focusing on the economic activities of the nonprofit organizations that participate in Ni Una Mas and the women who work in them. In this application of the "whore" discourse, the elites claim that Ni Una Mas participants are "selling family pain" (particularly that of victims' mothers) to an international market (of journalists, activists, academics, artists, and the like) always looking for juicy stories about the border that can generate sales for their own goods (newspapers, organizations, publications, performances, and so on). Even though within this discursive scenario, Ni Una Mas activists are not selling sex, they are, as it goes, "like prostitutes," contaminating the integrity of their communities, their families, and their nation with their sleazy activities.[11] Political elites have been particularly critical of Ni Una Mas participants for selling family pain as a way to tarnish the region's economic image at a time when competition from China is seriously threatening the industrial base.[12] They charge, in effect, that the activists are tainting the region's international reputation by selling tawdry stories of sex, rape, and murder to a lascivious global public.

In this essay, I combine a Marxian critique of value with a Foucauldian analysis of discursive production to expose how the elites' deployment of the public woman discourse is dangerous for women, as citizens and as human beings, in contemporary Mexico. I use Marx's insight that all profit under capitalism (as a form of surplus value) derives from the exploitation of underpaid labor to illustrate how the elites' accusation of profiteering public women targets the Achilles tendon of the Ni Una Mas movement. Its leaders and the nonprofit organizations that constitute it are unable to deny that many of them do, in some sense, "profit" from the publicity generated by their movement. Many do indeed fund their projects by writing grants (i.e., selling their causes) to an international public (including other NGOs) that provides donations via tax write-offs; some NGOs receive grants for their activities, while others do not; some activists receive salaries, while others do not.[13] In short, the need to compete and survive within a capitalist economy means that NGOs and their employees must compete against each other for the economic resources that allow them to survive. This competition leads to divisions among them as well as to an exacerbation of existing class and other tensions that afflict the movement.

By subsuming this accusation of exploitation within the discourse of the public woman (as troublesome whore), regional elites create an even more poisonous attack on the movement by claiming that Ni Una Mas leaders are prostituting family pain and thereby exploiting unpaid victims' families who work in the protest. In this sense, the discourse functions as *techne*, as defined by Foucault: a tactic for rendering a set of beliefs into practical and effective strategies for governing via exclusions of particular subjects.[14] The *techne* behind the public woman discourse is to dismiss Ni Una Mas as an illegitimate movement via the discursive production of its participants as illegitimate women-citizens who contaminate community and country by profiting from the prostitution of family pain on the international market. Ni Una Mas activists have little option but to take on this *techne* as they fight not only for the rights of women to participate in Mexico's public sphere but also for the rights of women to exist in public space without endangering their very lives.

The Public Woman

For most of the twentieth century, Ciudad Juárez has been known as a city bursting with public women. During the Prohibition era in the United States, women could find work on Ciudad Juárez streets by selling sex or companionship to men who were looking for the entertainment and alcohol prohibited in their own country. The internal migration of Mexican men who sought work across the border as part of the Bracero Program (which ended in 1965) also contributed to the growth of Ciudad Juárez as a place providing unregulated sexual services. With such changes, Ciudad Juárez became famous within and beyond Mexico as a city full of "public women." Furthermore, Ciudad Juárez is one of the few places in Mexico where prostitution is legal throughout the city.

This city's reputation for "public women" grew even more with the inauguration of the maquiladora industry in the mid-1960s and its famous "feminization of the international division of labor," which was accompanied by an even further feminization of Ciudad Juárez streets as thousands of women poured in from the Mexican interior to find jobs in the manufacturing sector. Images of the city, teeming with young women, unaccompanied by their families, who worked long shifts and then shopped and danced at all hours, further fueled claims that Ciudad Juárez was a den of public women and their many iniquities.[15] When the murders and kidnappings first became known in Ciudad Juárez in 1995, with early reports of some fifty victims, political and business elites found themselves having to answer hard questions about how their economic and political programs have contributed to the city's growing violence problems. For instance, between the passage of NAFTA in 1994 and the year 2001, the homicide rate for men increased by 300 percent, while for women it increased by 600 percent.[16] An early example of how regional elites deployed the discourse of the "public women" to dispel such questions is found in a 1999 interview with the then-spokesperson for the Ciudad Juárez Maquiladora Association (AMAC) that was aired on ABC's *20–20*. When asked why the violence was occurring, the spokesperson responded: "Where were these young ladies when they were last seen?" he queried. "Were they drinking? Were they partying? Were they on a dark street?"[17] Similar responses have rolled off the tongues of two Chihuahua state governors, of city mayors, of business leaders, and others who represent political incumbents and corporate interests in the region.[18] In blaming the victims for provoking the violence that they have suffered and, thereby, for not being "innocent" victims, these leaders reproduce the subject of the public woman as the source of the problem; for this reason, they suggest, no one should be surprised when a prostitute is raped, beaten, or murdered.[19] Indeed, this discourse normalizes such violence by producing the prostitute as the site of normalized rape, torture, and murder.[20] She is guilty of her own crime. She, not the perpetrator, is in fact the criminal.

This discourse threatens to dominate public conceptions of the activists, functioning as a *techne* that participants of Ni Una Mas have had to confront at every step of their campaign. Victims' families and the activists working with them have had to make the case that their private pain about the loss of a loved one represents a public injustice and not merely a "family" or "personal" problem. For instance, family after family confronting public officials and the state police has encountered the attitude that the brutal murders and kidnappings represent problems internal to the families and are not public crimes requiring state intervention. Upon reporting a murder or disappearance, families have had to field the following question: "Did she [the woman/girl in question] lead a 'double life'?" A woman who leads a "double life," within this formulation, is a woman who has a public persona in addition to the private one defined by her familial relationships. As such, this question, which has been asked of victims' families since the crimes began, hinges on the binary of the public and private woman. The former is the woman who via her own activities on the street invites the violence she suffers; she is not an innocent victim of a public crime. Instead, her suffering indicates a moral breakdown of the family from which she emerged. The problem therefore resides within the family and does not represent a matter of state. If the victim did not lead a "double life"—that is, if she were undeniably private—then perhaps a crime has been committed. But as the pervasiveness of the question indicates, the Chihuahua state police insist on first making a determination of the victim's status: Was she a public woman?

The Ni Una Mas activists have made this "double life" question the focus of their activities, arguing, in effect, that the victims, no matter their public or private lives, are innocent women who deserve public justice. Via street protests, marches, occupations of public buildings, press conferences, and public confrontations with elected officials, they have presented this argument in the public arena so that the international and domestic media will gain awareness of their cause and circulate the story as evidence of a social injustice. For this reason, Ni Una Mas participants have employed dramatic gestures designed to attract media attention. Many of them wear black garments with pink hats to symbolize the figure of a "mother in mourning." Others have worn grisly masks to represent the "silent screams" of the victims. They have erected crosses adorned with mangled mannequin figures and nails to bring attention to the suffering of the victims, many of whom were sexually tortured, burned, and dismembered before their deaths. They carry posters of victims' faces and paint pink crosses on telephone polls. They have held funerary processions at international conferences attended by public officials and have draped public offices with funeral wreaths and veils. They hold public events during which family members dispute portrayals of their lost loved ones as "whores who deserved what they got." And they repeatedly talk of their loss, pain, and anger.

At one such event in August 2003, when Ni Una Mas activists met with members of a United Nations special delegation, some mothers and fathers of the victims spoke about their suffering and frustration. The audience was shaken by the emotionally wrenching stories of their experiences, of realizing that a loved one was missing and then discovering the horrible details of the death or of not receiving any police assistance to locate the family member. Several people cried with the parents who exposed their emotions in the hopes that they would have some impact. Local media covered the event; stories circulated internationally; the UN special delegation promised to write a report and make it available to other NGOs; and several academics, including me, took notes with the idea of writing articles. As one Ni Una Mas participant told me at a Ciudad Juárez march in February 2004, "Our only hope for justice is for public outrage and support. We need media attention. We need donations to pay for the events." With these words, this activist was explaining how through this publicity, Ni Una Mas enters the circuits of resource production and consumption that connect NGOs to international media and to their donor base.

In the most basic sense, Ni Una Mas activists use family stories of their loss and suffering and of the victims' good characters to attract the interest of journalists, academics, artists, and women's rights and human rights organizations, who in turn use these stories to generate their revenues, through the selling of newspapers or the raising of donations. These activities generate profits that are distributed to shareholders, owners, and self-employed individuals through the complicated networks of nonprofit organizations that continually recycle and distribute "profits" as part of their self-sustaining operations. As a result of such activities, Ni Una Mas participants have had to respond to the accusations that they, as a spokesperson for the Mexican Department of Commerce recently put it, "have profited too much from the pain that we all feel."[21]

The Commodity of Family Pain

On February 23, 2003, I interviewed Alma Gomez, a participant in one of the civil associations, Las Barzonistas, that had been active since the inception of the Ni Una Mas movement. Like many of the other NGOs in Ni Una Mas, Las Barzonistas (a woman-run legal aid association in Chihuahua City) had joined the campaign out of a sense of civic duty, and its members participated in marches and protests along with other groups, such as Mujeres por México, La Comisión de Solidaridad y Defensa de los Derechos Humanos, El Grupo 8 de Marzo, La Red Nacional de Abogadas Femenistas, among others. On the morning of my scheduled interview with Alma in Chihuahua City, the city's daily, *El Heraldo de Chihuahua*, ran the headline "NGOs Profit with Deaths" ("Lucran ONGS con las Muertas"). The corresponding article explained that this accusation stemmed from the then–State's Attorney General, Jesús Solís Silva, that the NGOs within Ni Una Mas were profiting, politically and economically, by effectively "selling [*vender*]" the pain of victims' families, and of their mothers in particular, to an international market, eager for stories that would sell newspapers and other sorts of media.[22] When I asked Alma about this accusation, she replied: "The question that we should be asking ourselves is: What do we mean by 'profit' [*lucrar*]?"

This same question arose in an analysis made more than a century before by Karl Marx as he sought to explain the fundamental principles of capitalism. Rather than accept profit as a fair reward for good investments,[23] he urged his readers to explore the origins of profit so that they would see the injustice, misery, and exploitation at its core. Profit, according to Marx, is nothing more and nothing less than unremunerated labor, such that the people who profit are, in his analysis, stealing resources from workers.[24] Even though Alma was not thinking about Marx when she inquired into the meaning of profit, a Marxian analysis can help explain how the accusation that she and others are "profiting by selling family pain" has proven so effective in challenging the integrity of the Ni Una Mas movement in contemporary Mexico. To illustrate this point, I will begin, as Marx did, with a brief description of "the commodity" to demonstrate how family pain, under the capitalist conditions in which Ni Una Mas operates, does indeed circulate as a commodity that generates profit and, as Marx would have it, perpetuates injustice.

A commodity, says Marx, is something that produces value (abstract labor) as it flows through the capitalist circuits of production and consumption. Abstract labor consists in the vision, energy, creativity, patience, and all of the other qualities that go into a human being's ability to transform material life through work. The worker, as Marx shows, receives wages in exchange not for the "abstract labor" (or the stuff of value) but instead for "labor power," the potential to work during a determined period of time, and the wages represent the magnitude of time (what Marx calls the "socially necessary labor time") required to socially and physically reproduce the worker's ability to work at a certain level of skill. In other words, the value consumed by the laborer to reproduce herself is not the same magnitude of value produced by the laborer during the labor process. If all things go as planned and as they must in order for a capitalist enterprise to flourish, the amount of value consumed by labor must be less than the amount of value produced by labor, such that the laborer receives less value than the value that she provides to the enterprise.[25] Only then does profit emerge. For this reason, Marx argues that profit is nothing but unpaid labor that reveals the injustice in capitalism's foundation.

This Marxian exegesis about profit and the accusation of profit used to attack Ni Una Mas are connected in that the activists face the task of producing social justice out of the private pain of the victims and their families. The movement can be likened to a productive system that requires labor (social activism) to turn its raw materials (family pain, in this case) into a product that is packaged and presented—or in short, transformed—as a form of injustice. The movement's goals are thus to transform private pain into a public injustice, a process that requires labor at all stages. Part of this labor involves publicizing the injustices surrounding the murders so the international market of media consumers will want to read or hear about the events (and purchase newspapers or attend films) and also so that international organizations see the relevance of these crimes for their own causes, such as human rights, women's rights, and civil rights. To make this publicity, people have to work. They have to organize events, attend them, speak at them, and so forth. They have to raise money, pay expenses, make posters, stand in the street, and yell at officials. This is labor — energy, vision, dedication, patience — as various organizations and individuals collaborate on the project of attracting public attention so that justice can be had. The victims' families were the first to engage in this project in the 1990s, and out of their frustration, as well as evidence of their success in gaining some public attention, they formed family organizations or sought the help of existing NGOs who could help them by providing some of the labor required for their project of making these crimes known around the world. By and large, the victims' families have few economic resources, and they have struggled to meet the inevitable expenses, such as travel costs or lost wages, of participating in the movement. Most of their labor remains unpaid. Many NGOs also have had a hard time finding the resources to participate. However, others within the movement, such as those from middle-class backgrounds or those who work with well-financed NGOs, have clearly had more resources, via fund-raising, or have even been remunerated for their activities within Ni Una Mas. Undoubtedly, the movement has indeed succeeded in selling the story of injustice, as international newspapers, televisions news shows, filmmakers, novelists, artists, and academics have generated revenues and profits through its circulation.

In this sense, while Ni Una Mas is not reducible to a capitalist labor process, it does contribute to the generation of profits from the circulation of a commodity formed during the labor process for publicizing injustice. In this sense, "publicized injustice" takes the form of a commodity: something that is exchanged and generates profits. As such, this commodity operates according to the capitalist laws that Marx identified: This commodity of public injustice must produce more value than is returned to those people whose labor generates it out of the raw material of private pain. It is to this kind of social justice–as-commodity that political and business elites turn their attention to argue, in much the same way as Marx, that the profit generated via its circulation accrues to some at the expense of others. Many people feel the pain; many contribute to its circulation as evidence of injustice; but not all profit from this circulation. Again, as the spokesperson for the Mexican Department of Commerce said: Ni Una Mas activists "have profited too much from the pain that we all feel."

So the next question is: Who profits at whose expense?

The Profit of the Nonprofits

In today's world, even though nonprofit organizations are not organized around the aim of making profit, it does not follow that they are organized *against profit*.[26] The most successful nonprofit NGOs often have fund-raisers whose job is to figure out ways to tap into the profits of companies, individuals, and other NGOs that are distributed around the world and that yield tax breaks for the donors. Under such a system, philanthropy does not require benevolence as much as it requires good business sense and some familiarity with the relevant tax code, and NGOs have proliferated over the last two decades as the Internet and other communication technologies have facilitated their ability to connect with an international donor base.

In Mexico, these changes have had enormous impact on the country's civil sector. Unlike, say, those in the United States, NGOs in Mexico have not been able to rely upon a domestic donor pool that provides funds through mail solicitations or other anonymous fund-raising strategies. Instead, donations are obtained through personal networks, which are much more limited in scope than an anonymous donor base. Since the early 1990s, therefore, Mexican NGOs have increasingly sought support for their activities from international donors, including large transnational NGOs such as the Ford and Kellogg Foundations, and from individuals, particularly in the United States, where there is a growing base of support for human and civil rights movements in Mexico.[27]

Over this same period of time, NGOs have proliferated in Mexico in response to two interrelated events that have transformed Mexico's political economy. One has been the embrace since the early 1980s by Mexican political and economic elites of neoliberal reforms that have focused on privatization, particularly of utilities, and on the cutback of subsidies for housing and food. These policies accelerated under the Carlos Salinas administration (1988–94), which combined privatization schemes with an opening of the Mexican economy to foreign investors, a process culminating in the 1994 implementation of the North American Free Trade Agreement (NAFTA). With privatization and subsidy reductions, combined with a devastating currency devaluation in 1995, community organizations emerged around the country to help fill the gaps and provide social and economic support at the local level. Ciudad Juárez, for example, saw a sizable increase in the number of its NGOs in the mid-1990s as more people created organizations oriented toward community education, youth programming, violence prevention, family health, and economic development. Access to the

Internet and to international NGO Web sites and grant programs helped many of these local groups get off the ground. When news broke in the mid-1990s about the violence against women in Ciudad Juárez, some pre-existing NGOs, particularly anti-privatization, community development, and women's rights organizations located in Ciudad Juárez and in Chihuahua City, added this issue to their programming. They were later joined by family-support groups, such as Voces Sin Eco and Nuestras Hijas de Regreso a Casa, which were organized specifically in response to the violence.

A second event that has directly influenced the trajectory of Mexico's NGOs and of those participating in Ni Una Mas has been the political transition of the country's governance from a corporatist to a multiparty electoral system. Since the early 1980s, the state of Chihuahua had taken a lead as a state with strong political opposition to the PRI Party, which had governed the country autocratically since 1929. Women in Ciudad Juárez and Chihuahua City were especially active in the democratization movement, monitoring polls and calling for an international media presence during elections through the 1980s and 1990s.[28] Through such efforts, northern Mexico became a base for the opposition PAN Party, which in 2000 successfully dethroned the PRI in the country's first multiparty federal election and assumed the presidency under the leadership of Vicente Fox. This political transition was a watershed moment for NGOs; it opened space for organizations that were not allied with the PRI to assume a greater presence in the country's political landscape. Again, many of the NGOs participating in Ni Una Mas emerged as part of this democratization, and several of their leaders were prominent protagonists in the efforts to diversify the country's electoral system. Ni Una Mas, therefore, represents a convergence of diverse organizations that have formed around numerous issues, ranging from political and economic reform to women's rights to family support groups. Their international support base has grown with them over the years, such that people around the world have heard about the crimes in northern Mexico as a result of the networks that link local NGOs to media and to NGOs in other countries.

With such international support, the Ni Una Mas NGOs have been able to fortify their presence at the local level, and their leaders have increasingly emerged as spokespeople with access to and notoriety on the international stage. That most of these spokespeople are women (*voceras*) should not come as a surprise, given the traditional preponderance of women in non-profit and philanthropic organizations.[29] In Mexico, particularly, middle-class women who are able to volunteer their time represent what is at least perceived to be the principal social segment that shoulders the work of community and philanthropic groups.[30] Within Ni Una Mas, as international interest in the violence against women has grown, and as international resources have supported the local campaign, more of the participating NGOs have been able to access international donations to cover equipment costs and events. A few of the Ni Una Mas NGOs have been able to raise funds for paying salaries and increasing staff size, so that formerly unpaid volunteers have been able to earn salaries for their work. This confluence of events, with more women gaining international standing as *voceras* who are sometimes paid, has added fuel to the claims that they are "public women"—that is, women who earn a living in the public sphere and are therefore not motivated by their commitment to family and other domestic concerns.

Certainly, since 2001, when the many organizations of Ni Una Mas coordinated several highly publicized events, political elites have responded to the increased international pressure for an end to the violence by attacking the *voceras* as "public women" who, by seeking to "profit" economically and politically, directly contribute to the violence. For example, this strategy for disqualifying the activists as "public women" has been used to great effect by the former governor, Patricio Martinez, and his state's attorney general, who accused the activists of causing "social disintegration" by "selling the pain of families" to the international media.[31] With these words, the governor's office and its supporters essentially accused the activists of seeking to fill their own pockets and satisfy their own political ambitions by exposing families, weakened by their painful ordeals, to a rapacious international media that makes money from selling sensationalist stories of sex and violence along the border. This accusation proliferated through numerous public accusations that the "public women" of Ni Una Mas were provoking a "denigration" of the family, of the nation, and of the border economy and were also inciting youth to engage in socially destructive events, such as graffiti and vandalism.[32]

The NGOs have not been able to dispel the accusation of profit because they are indeed competing in a global market for resources that derive from profit. As Alma Gomez defiantly said to me, "If they say we are profiting because we write grants and pay our workers with them, well, then, we are profiting. That is how we survive."[33] While the strategy for criticizing Ni Una Mas for producing profits does exacerbate existing class tensions within the movement by exposing the reality that all profits derive from unpaid labor, the accusation is further strengthened by linking these profits to "public women" and the social problems linked to them. The force of this accusation as part of a governing *techne* for discrediting Ni Una Mas was made clear when Alma told a newspaper reporter that the government had "declared civil war" against the movement.[34]

The corrosive effects of this discourse are evident within the movement itself, as some organizations within the network have picked up this line in order to distinguish themselves from the "profiteering" public women. For instance, Astrid González of Lucha Contra Violencia announced in an article that appeared in the *Heraldo de Chihuahua* on February 25, 2003 (two days after the initial "profit" accusation by the state's attorney general), that — in an echo of the governor's words — the "social decomposition of Ciudad Juárez" had penetrated the nongovernmental organizations. She said, "There are pseudo-organizations and pseudo-leaders who profit [*lucran*] not only politically, but also with the donations that they receive in bank accounts in the name of women assassinated in Ciudad Juárez."[35] She continued, "The time has come to identify a difference, in order to clean up the image of the NGOs." Again, this call to "clean up" the movement by distinguishing the "public women" from the ones with "purer" or "nonpublic" intentions rests upon that old story of the dirty whore who sullies all that she touches. Within such logic, to "clean up" the movement is to get rid of such women.

However, while the Ni Una Mas movement has been weakened by the "profiting public woman" accusation, some of the NGOs are fighting back and finding that the contradictions raised by this discourse open some new opportunities for their movement and for women's political and economic participation more generally. By way of a conclusion, I turn my attention to some of these recent strategies.

The Politics of Public Women

In February 2004, more than a dozen NGOs from Ciudad Juárez, Chihuahua City, and El Paso, Texas, along with individuals from other areas, organized an antiviolence march in Ciudad Juárez. Several hundred people gathered at midday on the Mexican side of the international bridge that connects downtown Ciudad Juárez to downtown El Paso. Dozens of activists had walked across the bridge from El Paso to join the group. Most activists wore black and held signs, either in English or Spanish, to protest the violence against women and the lack of adequate response. The event was a collaborative event of Ni Una Mas and the V-Day social movement, which was started initially by *Vagina Monologues* author Eve Ensler to raise awareness and funds and provide support for organizations that fight violence against women around the world. Through her V-Day Foundation, Ensler helped fund the Ciudad Juárez march; she had previously given grants primarily to a sexual assault center in Ciudad Juárez. Among several other prominent women artists, politicians, and actresses, Ensler spoke at the Ciudad Juárez event. "We needed them for the publicity," one of the organizers told me.

Actually the event had already received much publicity, but not, however, of the sort desired by its organizers. A couple of days before the march, one of the Ni Una Mas NGOs, a prominent family organization, announced that it would not participate in the V-Day march but would instead organize an alternative protest on the same day in Ciudad Juárez. The group wrote a letter to Ensler, which was translated into English and posted on the Internet,[36] claiming that "American activists" were changing the nature of the Ni Una Mas struggle by focusing on domestic violence and feminist issues at the expense of keeping attention on the murders and the impunity. This letter followed on the heels of accusations by the splintering organization that the Mexican organizations participating in the V-Day event were, again, "profiting" by effectively selling out to these American activists.

The other family organizations did not support this faction, nor the accusations of "profit" and misguided feminism in its complaint, and they, along with hundreds of others, marched in the V-Day event through downtown Ciudad Juárez and held a rally at the city's central plaza. Perhaps in response to the factionalism that was on the minds of many that day,[37] the marchers seemed to find a consolidated voice in their response to the accusations that they were "prostituting" the movement. As groups lined up behind their banners calling for justice, for peace, for an end to impunity and violence, and as people held up their signs with victims' faces, a new chant grew across the crowd. "Justicia para todas, para obreras, estudiantes, prostitutas, madres, hijas . . ." (Justice for all women, for workers, students, prostitutes, mothers, daughters). "We have to fight the idea that any woman, a prostitute, a worker, anyone does not deserve justice," said one activist. "And we have to fight the idea that we, as women, do not have the right to demand justice. This is our struggle now." "Am I a public woman?" replied one marcher, who was dressed in a black tunic and carrying a sign with a victim's face on it, in response to my question. "Yes. I am a public woman. And I am proud of it."

In the wake of the V-Day event, several Ni Una Mas NGOs have renewed their vow to continue the campaign by countering the discourse of "the public woman."[38] Said another activist during the V-Day march, "They say that we can't be on the street. Well, that's where we are now. This is a democracy. And we are in the street because we are citizens. We have rights." "This is my country," said another, "and I won't let them shut me up."

In their refusal to shut up or to stop marching, the Ni Una Mas activists are demonstrating the significance of the governing strategy, the *techne*, for silencing them. They show how this discourse takes direct aim at women's worth as citizens, as community members, as human beings. Every time someone claims that prostitutes and any women resembling them are social contagions, this person is participating in the devaluation of women across the spectrum. Ni Una Mas participants have no choice but to confront this practice head-on as they seek the international resources they need to bring attention and pressure to regional elites, who are responsible for public safety, and as they seek the social and economic resources to do their work. In their activism, they are rearticulating the *techne*, defining new modes of governance that incorporate the public woman.

Since the 2004 V-Day march, dozens more women and girls have been murdered in northern Mexico. Ni Una Mas activists have held more press conferences, marches, and public confrontations with elected officials. They continue, in other words, to step out as "public women" despite the attacks against them. As they do so, they expose the despotism behind the discourse that degrades women for participating in the public sphere, whether to sell their bodies or to sell a cause. As they venture out into the streets, into public office buildings, and into the media, these women are engaged in the radical project of rearticulating the discourse of the public woman that has long disqualified women's political and economic activism around the world. Understanding the complicity binding the discourse of the contaminated-contaminating woman to the impunity surrounding the violence against women and girls in northern Mexico is essential to understanding what these activists face as they try to produce justice. Only then can we appreciate what it means to be a "public woman" in northern Mexico.

Notes

My thinking in this article reflects many conversations with Guadalupe de Anda, Arminé Arjona, Sarah Hill, Rosalba Robles, Soccorro Tabuenca, Julia Monárrez, and Clara Rojas. I would like to thank them for their insights and comments regarding my argument.

1 Amnesty International, *Muertes Intolerables — México: 10 años de desapariciones y asesinatos de mujeres en Ciudad Juárez y Chihuahua* (London: Amnesty International, 2003).

2 Juliana Monárrez Fragoso, "Feminicidio Sexual Serial en Ciudad Juárez: 1993–2001," *Debate Feminista* 25 (2001): 279–308.

3 D. Castillo, M. Rangel Gómez, and B. Delgado, "Border Lives: Prostitute Women in Tijuana," *Signs* 24.2 (1999): 387–422. Women who work in the sex industry have long encountered this discourse around the world, and many have organized against it and its logical implications. For instance, Ciudad Juárez sex workers have had to organize against a police effort to "clean up" the city by removing them from the downtown; see Melissa Wright, "From Protests to Politics: Sex Work, Women's Worth, and Ciudad Juárez Modernity," *Annals of the Association of American Geographers* 94 (2004): 369–86. Nevertheless, the discourse that the public woman qua prostitute represents social contamination (and its many problems) remains alive and well around the world. When I refer to the "public woman," I refer to this discourse and not to the actual experiences of women who define themselves as public women within and outside the sex industry.

4 Judith Butler, *Bodies That Matter: On the Discursive Limits of Sex* (New York: Routledge, 1993).

5 J. Landes, ed., *Feminism, the Public, and the Private* (New York: Oxford University Press, 1998).

6 Gail Hershatter, *Dangerous Pleasures: Prostitution and Modernity in Twentieth-Century Shanghai* (Berkeley: University of California Press, 1999).

7 M. W. Wright, "The Dialectics of Still Life: Murder, Women, and the Maquiladoras," *Public Culture* 29 (1999): 453–73.

8 Amnesty International, *Muertes Intolerables*.

9 C. Cruz Sáenz, "Negro Panorama Para Maquiladoras," *El Diario de Ciudad Juárez*, April 6, 2003.

10 Heriberto Barrientos Marquez, "En 10 años la PGR No Ha Detenido Ni Un Homicida: Patricio," *El Heraldo de Chihuahua*, March 13, 2003.

11 Benjamin Martínez Coronado, "Desintegración sociofamiliar, germen de crímenes: Patricio," *El Heraldo de Chihuahua*, February 20, 2003.

12 Cecilia Guerrero and Gabriela Minjáres, "Hacen Mito y Lucro de Los Feminicidios," *El Diario de Ciudad Juárez*, July 22, 2004.

13 Mexico has a legal distinction between "civil" and "social" associations. The former are "nonprofit" organizations; the latter are not. In this essay, I follow the common usage in Mexico, using NGO (*organización no gubernamental*) as a reference for "civil" associations. Although the term could cover "social associations," NGO usually refers to nonprofit organizations, particularly within the Ni Una Mas disputes.

14 M. Foucault, "Governmentality," in *The Foucault Effect*, ed. G. Burchell, C. Gordon, and P. Miller (Chicago: University of Chicago Press, 1991), 87–104; A. Barry, T. Osborne, and N. Rose, introduction to Barry, Osborne, and Rose, eds., *Foucault and Political Reason* (Chicago: University of Chicago Press, 1996).

15 Debbie Nathan, "The Missing Elements," *Texas Observer*, August 30, 2002, available at www.womenontheborder.org/articles_resources.htm.

16 Adam Jones, "The Murdered Men of Juárez," April 2004, available at http://adamjones.freeservers.com/juarez.htm (accessed May 8, 2006).

17   John Quiñones interview with Robert Urrea, *20/20*, January 20, 1999.

18   Socorro Tabuenca Córdoba, "Día-V permanente en Ciudad Juárez," *El Diario de Ciudad Júarez*, March 2, 2003.

19   The theorization behind my logic here derives from my use of Judith Butler's theory that discursive repetition produces material reality, such that repetitions of the discourse of the whore-as-contaminant is, in fact, a practice aimed at producing this subject out of the bodies of real, living women. See her argument in *Bodies That Matter*.

20   Wright, "From Protests to Politics."

21   M. Orquiz, M. Cruz, and A. Mena, "Basta de denigar a Juárez: Sectores," *El Diario de Ciudad Júarez*, April 22, 2004.

22   David Piñon Balderrama, "Lucran ONGs con Muertas," *El Heraldo de Chihuahua*, February 23, 2003.

23   In the *Grundrisse*, Marx explains that profit is simply one form of surplus value, which is the actual topic of his analysis. I refer to "profit," rather than "surplus value," for the sake of simplicity. See Marx, *Grundrisse* (1857–58; reprint, London: Penguin, 1993).

24   Ibid., 376–86.

25   Again, here I use a Marxist analysis: in *Capital*, vol. 1 (1867; reprint, London: Penguin, 1990), Marx demonstrates how all inputs represent versions of labor, or what he calls living and dead labor.

26   Miranda Joseph, *Against the Romance of Community* (Minneapolis: University of Minnesota Press, 2002).

27   This information comes from interviews I conducted with NGOs in Mexico City, Ciudad Juárez, Chihuahua, and Morelia, from 2000 to 2004.

28   Elsa Patricia Hernández Hernández, "La participación política de las mujeres en el gobierno local: El caso de las regidoras de Juárez, 1980–2001," master's thesis, La Universidad Autónoma de Ciudad Juárez.

29   Joseph, *Against the Romance of Community*.

30   Interviews by author, February–April 2003, in Ciudad Juárez, Chihuahua City, and Mexico City.

31   Edgar Prado Calahorra, "Reiniciarán campaña Mujeres de Negro," *El Norte de Ciudad Juárez*, July 9, 2003.

32   Orquiz, Cruz, and Mena, "Basta de denigar a Juárez"; Edgar Prado Calahorra, "Protestan Mujeres Ante Procurador," *El Norte de Ciudad Juárez*, August 14, 2003; Martínez Coronado, "Desintegración sociofamiliar."

33   Interview by author, February 23, 2003, in Chihuahua City.

34   Enrique Perea Quintanilla, "Declaró PGJE la Guerra Sociedad Civil," *El Heraldo de Chihuahua*, February 25, 2003.

35   Froilan Meza Rivera, "Sí Reciben Donativos las ONGs," *El Heraldo de Chihuahua*, February 25, 2003.

36   "The Mothers of Juarez's Letter to Eve Ensler," available at http://amsterdam.nettime.org/Lists-Archives/nettime-l-0401/msg00055.html, accessed April 18, 2006.

37   Clara E. Rojas Blanco, "The V Day March in Mexico: Appropriation and (Mis)Use of Local Women's Activism," *National Women's Studies Association Journal* 17.2 (2005): 217–27.

38   Interviews by author, February–April 2004.

Santiago Vaquera-Vásquez

Notes from an Unrepentant Border Crosser

> Estoy haciendo fila, haciendo fila, estoy haciendo fila
> para salir del país. Es algo natural, cosa de todos los
> días. A mi izquierda, una familia en una vagoneta
> Nissan; a mi derecha, un gringo de lentes oscuros en
> un Mitsubishi deportivo. Por el retrovisor veo a una
> muchacha en un Volkswagen. Adelante, un Toyota.
> Vamos a salir del país y es algo natural, cosa de todos
> los días.
>
> [I'm in line, in line, in line to leave the country. It's
> natural, an everyday occurrence. To my left, a family
> in a Nissan station wagon; to my right, a gringo with
> dark sunglasses in a sporty Mitsubishi. In my rear-
> view mirror I see a girl in a Volkswagen. In front of
> me, a Toyota. We're leaving the country, and it's OK.
> It's natural, an everyday occurrence.]
> —Luis Humberto Crosthwaite, "La fila"

Telling Stories, Making Place

The beginning of the story "La fila" ("The
line") by the *tijuanense* writer Luis Humberto
Crosthwaite serves as an apt epigraph for this
discussion of borders, borderlands, and border
crossings.[1] The narrator is waiting to drive his
car across the border into the United States. The
story is one of wandering and of waiting, for

South Atlantic Quarterly 105:4, Fall 2006
DOI 10.1215/00382876-2006-004   © 2006 Duke University Press

on the endless journey to the border gate there are innumerable stops and starts. Even when it begins to look as if they might finally move, "la fila no avanza" (the line does not move). Yet the people continue toward the border, for crossing the border, as the narrator states, "es algo natural, cosa de todos los días" (is something natural, an everyday occurrence).[2] Some do it in cars, some do it by swimming, some by running. But to cross the border, any border, is a natural thing, an everyday occurrence.

At the same time, the narrator is telling himself a story, one about waiting in line at the border. Patricia Price, in her book *Dry Place*, argues that "place . . . is a processual, polyvocal, always-becoming entity."[3] In telling a story, the narrator is making a place in a space that is of movement (and, in the case of the waiting line to cross, nonmovement): the border.

This is a story of borders, borderlands, and border wanderers. This is a story about living in/on/across borderlines. But today, this is just a story: a story of movement, a story of wandering, a story of stories about the U.S.-Mexico border, and a story about rethinking the borderlands.

In These Borderlands There Is Movement

My identity is as rooted in place and space as it is enforced by movement. As a child of Mexican immigrant parents, I was born and raised in northern California, with frequent excursions to visit relatives in the northern Mexican border city of Mexicali. Though the drive took between twelve and fourteen hours, it was nothing for my young parents, who considered gas inexpensive and found the pull of family stronger than the burden of driving twelve hours down the center of the state. In those frequent migrations from north to south and back again, we became a part of what Breyten Breytenbach has called the Middle World: a world between nations and populated by migrants. Its citizens—"uncitizens," as he calls them—in constant migration.[4]

As a teen I would often walk to the border from my grandmother's house. Sometimes I would stand at the fence separating Mexicali from Calexico, my fingers reaching through, illegally touching the other side. Though it did not feel any different, I would try to imagine that it somehow was. At times there would be others with me, staring through the chain link at the other side. Once when my family and I were waiting in our car to pass, I saw a couple of teenagers at the top of the fence sitting defiantly in the space between nations. Breytenbach's Middle World refers to a world between the first and the third, a liminal space where "truths no longer fit snugly and certainties do not overlap." He emphasizes that though the Middle World is everywhere, "belonging and not belonging," it is not "of the Center . . . since it is by definition and vocation peripheral; it is *other*, living in the margins, the live edges."[5] The physical border between the United States and Mexico can be read as a material manifestation of this Middle World: the seam—or, to use Gloria Anzaldúa's famous formulation, the *herida abierta*—that exposes the uneven relations between the two nations.[6]

When I was fourteen, my family was living in Imperial Beach, in San Diego County. Our apartment was on the edge of Border Field State Park, a large, undeveloped wetlands area from where we could look out and see Tijuana built up to the border fence. I remember the nightly flyovers by the border patrol, the searchlights piercing through the windows of our apartments. One night my mother found two brothers trying to hide from the *migra* on our back patio. Without thinking twice she offered them a place to stay inside the apartment. They were trying to make their way to Stockton, in northern California. The older brother had a wife and family waiting there; he was bringing his brother across for the first time. They had chosen to throw themselves into the uncertainty of the Middle World. While the searchlights of the INS helicopters crisscrossed our apartment complex, my mother offered the brothers a place to stay. She also volunteered to drive them north. And she did, with all of us kids in tow. She used the trip as an excuse to visit my *tios* in northern California.

In the mid-1990s I often went to the border to visit a friend who lived in Playas de Tijuana. On one trip we headed down to the beach to the fence, a solid wooden wall that continued into the ocean. On the wall large white pieces of plywood had been erected. On them, in stark black paint, were painted the names, ages, and places of origin of those who had died crossing the border since the institution of Operation Gatekeeper in the early 1990s.

North America, I am your scar, the border might say at times.

Rethinking la(s) Borderlands: The Border Is . . .

While the term *borderlands* has come to be associated—at least in the United States—with the southwestern United States and, in particular, as a Chicano/a space, the geographic borderlands is much larger. Extending from the Pacific to the Gulf of Mexico, the U.S.-Mexico borderlands is a vast geographic region that encompasses not just the southwestern United States but also northern Mexico. Since the 1980s, the geographic borderlands have often been rendered in cultural studies in metaphorical terms—hybrid space, liminal space, gateway, no-man's-land—and in many cases some of these metaphors have come to represent the totality of the geographic borderlands. As James Clifford rightly notes, "A specific place of hybridity and struggle, policing and transgression, the U.S.-Mexico frontier, has recently attained 'theoretical' status. . . .The border experience is made to produce powerful political visions: the subversion of all binarisms, the projection of a 'multicultural public sphere (versus hegemonic pluralism).'"[7]

In a review of U.S.-Mexico border studies, it has been noted that there are generally two ways of talking about the border. According to Kathleen Staudt and David Spener, "Version 1 is old-style border studies, grounded in history and the empiricism of the social sciences. Version 2 is new-style literary studies."[8] That is, while version 1 gives primacy to the physical border and the geographic borderlands, version 2 constructs a metaphorical borderlands that can reduce the complexity of the geographic region, often through elevation of a few border artists/writers/theorists as "the" border representatives. Pablo Vila, in his work *Crossing Borders, Reinforcing Borders*, writes, "I arrived in El Paso with the 'mission' of validating with an ethnographic work the ideas of García Canclini, Anzaldúa, and Rosaldo . . . ideas that were developed within a literary criticism framework, not an ethnographic one. Yet as soon as I launched my fieldwork, I discovered that these ideas were only partially addressing the much more complex process of identity construction in the area."[9]

Staudt and Spener argue, quite correctly, for mixing these two types of border studies, and more recent works reflect this hybrid type of analysis.[10] While in complete agreement that a strictly metaphorical reading of the border is questionable, I would like, however, to examine some of these metaphors—or, more precisely, narratives—that do conform to a particular type of border experience. Here I examine these stories told about the border and the ways in which these serve to create particular "imaginative geographies" for the region. I will focus primarily on Tijuana.

The diverse landscape of northern Mexico engenders distinct cultural productions that in turn both reflect and constitute their cultural context. In viewing the borderlands as a heterogeneous field crossed by multiple geographies, my focus is on itinerant "identities that are constantly subject to mutation. Always in transit, the promise of a homecoming—completing the story, domesticating the detour—becomes an impossibility."[11]

If we take the position of the borderlands as a complex field made up of a variety of imaginative geographies, we could then read the borderlands as a dynamic region that is constantly under construction. In viewing the borderlands as presenting multiple—alternative—histories, the mapping of this space should be accomplished through the illumination of the diverse cultures in the border region.

The Border Is: Danger

Some friends and I are in a cheesy piano bar of some tourist hotel in Ciudad Juárez. A man is telling us about the dangers of Juárez, about how it is far more dangerous than Tijuana. He asks one friend of mine, a *tijuanense*, how many killings there have been in the past year. My friend does not know, but he ventures a guess. The man snorts and states that since the beginning of the year in Juárez there have been twice that many murders. He talks about having to ride in an armored car, how he has a bodyguard, how he has to be extra careful in a city like Juárez. He never mentions the *femicidios*, the murdered women, in that city. We just listen to this man talk and later end up in a diner trying to make sense of it all.

Norma Klahn has written of a "South of the Borderism" trope in U.S.-Mexico relations, referring to the ways in which the United States culturally constructs its southern neighbor: often the Mexican becomes "everything the Anglo was not."[12] A similar process has taken place in Mexico, in what Socorro Tabuenca has called a "North of the Borderism."[13] In each case, this cultural "othering" becomes self-serving, as it affirms national identities. For the United States, South of the Borderism justifies the myth of manifest destiny and the continued militarization of the border; for Mexico, North of the Borderism vindicates cultural nationalist projects to combat the spread of American culture.[14] These two tropes—stating what "the border is"—also shape the most common negative stereotypes about the border as a zone of danger or vice.[15]

To read the border as danger, as is most often the case in the media, is to both reinforce notions of cultural identity and justify the increasing militarization of the border. Tijuana stands out within the imaginary of the United States as a particularly dangerous site. In a column for the Mexico City daily, *Milenio*, Luis Humberto Crosthwaite writes: "Me he dado cuenta de que una buena manera de hacer amigos fuera de Tijuana es diciendo que eres de Tijuana. Esto deposita sobre ti un aire místico, como de gangster, como de cowboy. Y, claro, para esos momentos, uno siempre trae consigo una buena historia para contarle al primero que se deje."[16]

He goes on to write about the image of Tijuana as a violent city, especially since Arturo, his editor at *Milenio*, only likes to hear these types of stories:

> Entonces yo tengo que elaborar cuidadosamente mi testimonio, para no poner en entredicho la imagen que él y muchos otros tienen de esta ciudad fronteriza.
>
> "N'ombre, pos ta reduro. El otro día ya ni se podía cruzar la calle frente a mi casa por la cantidad de cadáveres."
>
> "N'ombre . . . allá en Tijuana puedes comprar coca hasta en el seminario."
>
> "N'ombre . . . mi papá me dio mi primer pistola a los cinco años."
>
> "N'ombre . . . el otro día quise cruzar a San Diego, nos salió la migra y nos metió una corretiza."
>
> "N'ombre . . . yo perdí mi virginidad a los diez años, y mis compañeros de primaria se burlaron de mí por retrasado."
>
> Los ojos de Arturo brillan, se llenan de lágrimas, mientras toma notas en una libreta y suspira.[17]

Crosthwaite goes on to say that he used to feel insulted that his city was imagined in the worst possible light, "alejada de todo lo que es mexicano y engullida por todo lo que es gringo,"[18] until he said to himself that *tijuanenses* are as Mexican as Kellogg's Frosted Flakes and all the talk about the violence was pure myth. Once he came to that realization, he decided that he could tell any story he wanted. He chooses to propagate the myth of Tijuana as a den of violence purely for narrative effect. For the rest of the column he proceeds to talk about the most recent act of violence that he had witnessed, an argument at his house that escalates to guns being drawn against the neighbors. The situation is diffused by the arrival of Tere, Crosthwaite's wife, who had gone over to San Diego to shop at a Kmart pillow sale. She proceeds to beat all those present—neighbors, friends of Crosthwaite, and Crosthwaite himself—with the new pillows. Arturo is impressed with the tale, which Crosthwaite finishes, "Dude, the only thing more dangerous than Tijuanenses are their wives."

The story subverts both North/South of the Borderism with Crosthwaite's characteristic humor. His references to the violent image of the city are undercut by the constant play of references to the binational location of Tijuana and the transnational mixings that take place there. In the process of parodying the narrative of violence about the border, he is also reveling in the local culture.

The Border Is: Vice

I am eighteen and awkward. Uncomfortable in my own skin. Mexicali. Christmas break. A very large family reunion. Some of my American uncles decide to hit the town with a couple of my Mexican *tíos*. They take me along, though I am battling a cold that adds another surreal layer to the night. We travel through the Mexicali strip clubs, consuming mass quantities of alcohol. In the clubs we see all sorts of women, young, old, stepping out to bad disco music. This is Mexico, one of my uncles states. My *tíos* no longer listen. We are traveling in another zone. The night becomes a blur to me.

Related to the image of the border as danger zone, this rendering configures the *leyenda negra* of the border: a zone of illicit activity, of transgression, of prostitution. The border strip club comes to represent the border cities. The northern Mexican writers Rosina Conde, from Tijuana, and Rosario Sanmiguel, from Ciudad Juárez, have written of these spaces as a means of subverting the South of the Borderism implicit within the *leyenda negra* that surrounds the border cities.

In drawing on the theme of the Tijuana nightclubs in her story "Viñetas revolucionarias," Conde appears to reinforce the *leyenda negra*.[19] But this is not the case. In focusing on this "masculine" theme—the city as a space of prostitution, or as spectacle—Conde reconfigures this negative stereotype by focusing on the women who work in the clubs and by using a direct language that does not pretend to overdramatize or romanticize her characters. In this way, Conde demystifies one conception of Tijuana by subverting the male gaze in the club. By shifting the focus to the women, she puts the men on display. The women who star in the vignettes demonstrate their power over the male public. But the story is not an idealization of the stripper lifestyle. More generally, in recurring to the figure of the stripper, Conde questions the role of woman in the city. She demonstrates how these women in the city, by living in a second city—the world of the nightclubs— survive and flourish in this space. When the men enter the club, they are not entering a male-dominated space; they are the ones on display, not vice versa.

The club space here is a nonplace, a space of transit. The people who frequent the clubs, like the women who work them, are homeless. There is no sense of a male colonizing gaze; there is only the opening of this liminal space that opens outward, connecting other places into a larger night city. While shifting the gaze away from the masculine, Conde also does not offer a vision of redemption in these "revolutionary vignettes": There is no salvation for those who have found themselves in this nonplace. And in this way the tropes of North/South of the Borderism are themselves displaced. These vignettes, in their deliberate forcefulness—in the narrator's direct, unwavering, feminist gaze—do not moralize or romanticize the space of the strip club. Rather, as Castillo and Tabuenca point out, the vignettes "serve as a performative act by which the theme of the border as brothel takes shape."[20] By acting out this theme, the story destabilizes the forces of North/South of the Borderism—the forces that would attempt to inscribe the border into a particular, static conception.[21]

The Border Is: Global Corridor

Here is an old photo. A pregnant young woman holds a two-year-old child in front of her. They are both seated on a donkey pulling a cart. The donkey is painted as a zebra. This is, after all, the border. The young woman and the child on the burro both wear sombreros; his says "Cisco Kid," hers, "Tijuana." The *carreta* is painted with bright colors (I imagine, given that the photo is in black and white). In the center is an image of a woman who appears to be doing laundry by the side of a river in a tropical jungle setting. She is looking (smiling?) up at a man dressed in full *charro* regalia and seated on a horse. It is an image that represents *México*, that of Mexico's golden age of film—its *cine de oro*, as captured by the likes of Gabriel Figueroa—that of the national tourist agency, that of the national myth. "México, rrrrrrrrrooooommmmmaaaaanntiiiiccc México," as the border *brujo* Guillermo Gómez Peña would sing.

In *Passport Photos*, Amitava Kumar asks why readers of newspapers so readily accept photographs as truthful representations: "Why do we so drastically reduce the immense complexity of reality, its wide heterogeneity and scope of dissent, by what we so quickly accept as the singular truth represented in the shallow frame of an image?"[22] In this old photo we only see tourism in Tijuana. Yet the imaginative geography that constructs this Mexican postcard is complex. This is Mexico, romantic Mexico. Smiling tourists, tropical jungles, content women washing by the side of the river, men on horseback looking as if they should be backed by a full complement of mariachis. The painted image on the donkey cart contrasts with the region where the photo was taken: Baja California, northern Mexico, a region that is largely arid. In Tijuana, the only tropical forests are the ones painted on the donkey carts.

I was almost two when the photo was taken, my mom and me, at the end of spring, spending time with my grandparents on the border. Beneath the bucolic image painted on the donkey cart was painted the words, "Tijuana 1968 México."

Tijuana, viewed as a mirror of Mexico, is an outpost in the Middle World that is created in its practice, in the itineraries of the people who use it. In Mexico, the naming of streets after important Mexican historical events, heroes, and places serves to unite a national narrative literally at street level. This naming functions within a project of national unification; all urban areas partake in the nation of Mexico, but these meanings often become lost as new significations are ascribed to the streets by those who walk them.[23] In Tijuana, Avenida Revolución is the main touristic drag and, as such, serves for many as an introduction to "Mexico."

Avenida Revolución, "la Revu," is a site of contact, of meeting, where, in a sense, all roads lead. Its urban architecture is a mishmash of styles. Juan Villoro notes that its landscape "cambia como si respondiera al *zapping* de la televisión."[24] Anchored—if it can be called that—on one end by the Frontón Jai Alai, a large structure with a vague Moorish air, it ends—if it can be called that—at a small triangular plaza where the mariachis meet, across from the *zona norte*, Tijuana's red-light district. In between these two zones are megadiscos; open markets—with the air of a bazaar—that sell a dizzying number of items (sign over one: "Cheap Liquor. Public Bathroom. Welcome to Mexico. Want to buy a blanket?"); liquor stores; restaurants (Cesar's, a large, vaguely Art Deco palace and the birthplace of the Caesar salad); donkey carts. There is a sense of placelessness, as there seems to be no architectural unity. While there are markers that evoke Mexico—a plaza where mariachis meet, the signs that welcome you to Mexico, the images on the donkey carts—at the same time the visitor is placed in a zone that evokes Mexico and a lot of other places. As Lawrence Herzog states, "Revolution is carnival—buildings decorated like zebras or Moorish castles, flags and colorful blimps floating overhead."[25] Reminding us, too, that in Tijuana, Revolution is an avenue.

The many donkeys-painted-as-zebras—what Heriberto Yépez has termed the "zonkey"—posed for photographs on Avenida Revolución lead carts that

are usually adorned with the imagery of "traditional" Mexico: images of vol-
canoes, pre-Columbian cultures, and the national symbol of the serpent and
eagle on the cactus—imagery that has very little do with the reality of Baja
California.[26]

The result is a city covered by the texts of a Mexico that never existed
in that region, an atopical Mexico superimposed in a city crossed by itiner-
ants. Covering the city with these hybrid cultural texts effects not only the
invention of a history for the tourists but also the inscription of the city,
and the Mexican border region, into a national narrative. Tijuana becomes,
then, a mirror that reflects the whole country, marking out the differences
between this and that side of the border.[27] Avenida Revolución, as a fragment of the mirror, creates an idealized Mexico: "a fantasy land that is a cari-
cature of what Americans might think Mexico is (land of bullfights, sombreros, burros, and mission-style churches), insulated from the real Mexico,
but with just a touch of a veiled sense of mystery and foreign intrigue."[28]

At the same time, if Avenida Revolución constructs a fictional Mexico,
it does so through an appropriation of styles from all over the world. In a
fragmented text that reads less like an essay and more like a collection of
one-liners (or a quick surf through the TV channels), in keeping with the
fragmented nature of the border, Yépez writes, "*Space Invaders* could easily
define Tijuana. It is a city of 'anarchitecture,' a city of self-destruction. . . . Its
official architecture is pure simulacrum, pure kitsch. Tijuana existed long
before Baudrillard."[29] Despite Gómez Peña's celebrated phrase about all
cities beginning to look like Tijuana on a Saturday night, we could not argue
that Tijuana is a global city. At least not as proposed by Saskia Sassen, where
she defines these types of cities as "centers for the servicing and financing of
international trade, investment, and headquarter operations."[30] Tijuana is
a peripheral city, situated by its history on the margins. However, given this
peripheral standing, Tijuana, Mexico's northern frontier in general, is a participant in a global economy and forms a part of a global corridor, bridging
the global cities of Los Angeles and Mexico City.

Do Not Attempt to Adjust Your Television

Spending a lot of time on the border has meant being able to watch channels
from both sides, even before the advent of satellite cable service. During
my summers in Mexicali, we often watched broadcasts from Yuma, Arizona. The television waves traveled across the border and were caught by

the antenna installed by my uncles on the roof of the house. We watched broadcasts from both sides, traveling across language and geography, passing through the Middle World. Sometimes the channels from this and that side came in snowy, the television seemingly under control from the outer limits. The waves were lost somewhere in the desert, I imagined, spiraling around in whirlpools of wind that raced through the mountains. In a sense, too, we were somewhere out there, on the edge of two nation-states that attempted to place controls on their borders.

Watching television in the age of cable means cleaner reception and a wider variety of broadcasts. A couple of years ago the Tijuana border crossing briefly became a fixture on cable. We dubbed it the Border Channel, or BTV. An odd channel, it had no station ID coming up every few minutes, and there were no commercial breaks. It was simply a video camera, more than likely a consumer model, trained on the Mexican side of the border. There was a soundtrack, of sorts—usually classical music, though one night I tuned in and heard *rock en español*.

There is this too: BTV had no production whatsoever. There was no fancy editing, save for the times when the video camera, in demo mode, began to show off its built-in transition effects. BTV felt like pirate television, as if somebody had jacked into the wired network of broadcasting. And this too seemed fitting. The first time I tuned in, I thought it was something shown at the end of a broadcast day. But the next day BTV was still there.

And my friends and I watched. We watched because of the channel's oddity, because we wondered how long it would stay on before a "proper" television station replaced it. We watched because BTV was reality television taken to the outer limits. Mainly, though, we watched because of the sheer mesmerizing sense of viewing a surveillance camera trained on a monstrous thing, a massive border machine. We joked about looking for people we knew in the process of crossing, but the camera was too far away to make anybody out. Those times when we saw a short wait we were filled with a desire to cross the border. Secretly we hoped to see something happen: a rush of people through the borderline, racing out onto the freeway; a drug bust, with trained dogs passing between the cars; a fight between drivers angered over the long wait. By being transfixed by BTV, we too were caught in the border machine. Mostly, though, we saw only what it was: a time of delay, a time when patience is strained. Sometimes the border is this: tedium.

It appears that before the revolution, the border will be televised.

The Border Is: Language

I was born a Mexican in the United States; my parents crossed the border
a few months before I was born. Spanish was my first language. I began
preschool at an early age and became a part of the English-speaking world.
I became, then, a Mexican American, doubled, speaking with a forked
tongue: Spanish at home with family, and English at school. In my university years I became politicized and took on the Chicano identity, but I
continued to speak with my forked tongue, often mixing the two languages
into Spanglish. Leaping, as I tell my classes, *de una lengua a otra* in a single
bound, *como* Superman. A few months ago one of my colleagues in linguis-
tics asked me to participate in a language study and the result was that I
scored very high as a bilingual: that is, both my languages were *más o menos*
on equal footing. What does it mean to speak with a forked tongue? To maintain dual languages on equal footing? What does it mean to be a one that is
more than one? A one that is, at times, two or even more?

Until I was around thirteen, there was a special word my siblings and I
used for crossing the border. We learned it from our mother, who wasn't
allowed to invoke it: She was born in Mexico. She had a card that she flashed.
But for us, her children born on the other side, we had a word. *Mercacirce.*
As I grew older I continued to work on this term, trying to approximate
my mother's pronunciation: *Mercacirize. Murica cdc.* I didn't know what it
meant. It was a word that we had to say whenever we crossed the border.
It made no sense, like the border made no sense. My grandmother and my
tios lived in Mexicali, and to go shopping we would cross over to Calexico.
Sometimes we would walk alongside the chain-link fence dividing the two.
I couldn't comprehend why there was a fence. There were cars and streets
and shops on this side, and the other side had them too. We spoke Spanish in
Mexicali, and we spoke Spanish in Calexico. Back then there were no mega-
flags proclaiming sovereignty over the respective sides. To speak nonsense
like *mercacirce* made sense. It was almost a magic term, like "Abracadabra,"
that would allow us (some of us) to cross through the Middle World of the
border region and its state controls.

It was finally one of my U.S.-born aunts who cleared the matter up for me.
"American citizen."
Then I understood.
We had learned the word from our Mexican mother, who had a differ-
ent way of saying things. I had never before questioned her accent, as I had

not previously stated a national citizenship. I knew that I was not Mexican, having been born in California, but I did not feel secure in calling myself American, as I had Mexican parents. I was a mix of the two, and a word like *mercacirce* fit this combination. Once I understood what the word meant, the border lost all its mystery. It was simply a long wait in a line of people or in cars.

Mercacirce is also a word best spoken by those with forked tongues, those from Breytenbach's Middle World who "have broken away from the parochial, to have left 'home' for good (or for worse) whilst carrying all of it with you, and to have arrived on foreign shores (at the onset you thought of it as 'destination', but not for long), feeling at ease there without ever being 'at home.'"[31] The Middle World posits a counternarrative to the flows of power that would attempt to control, to delimit. Language may be one such marker of a Middle World identity.

Even now, when I am about to cross the border over to this side, I consider pulling up to the border agent and saying, "Mercacirce." Yes, proudly. *Mercacirce.*

The Border Is: Sound

Tijuana, again. Sitting in a darkened bar with a couple of students from the university. We are drinking beer and listening to *norteño* music coming from the jukebox. There is a small dance floor, and a couple goes out onto it. They are the only two dancing a slow waltz under a blue light. Outside is the Plaza de Santa Cecilia, a square where the mariachis converge. It is on the border of the *zona norte*, the red-light district. Avenida Revolución, Tijuana's tourist strip, feeds right into it. We leave the bar and walk up Revolution Avenue, among the underage college students trying to get into the megadiscos and bars, oblivious to the cantinas where the locals go. We are heading to La Estrella, a *norteño* honky-tonk and, I am convinced, one of the incubators for the Nortec sound. La Estrella is a dance club where the musical landscape stretches from Sinaloa, a twenty-hour drive south from Tijuana to the border. No techno. Just *banda*, just *norteños*, just Tex-mex. It figures prominently in the narrative of Luis Humberto Crosthwaite, native *tijuanense* and one of the most important new narrators coming out of Mexico. La Estrella was also taken up by academics from the university as a site of contact and for its drink special, fifty Coronitas for fifty pesos. The beers come in metal buckets of ice. We go to dance, drink, hang out.

Contemporary rock criticism champions the musical hybridity of performers like Beck. But if one were to turn to rock coming from northern Mexico, this would be found inscribed into the musical DNA. Bands like Plastilina Mosh, El Gran Silencio, and the electronica collective known as Nortec map out musical geographies that unite disparate places. *Aquamosh*, the first record by the Monterrey duo Plastilina Mosh, could serve as the perfect soundtrack for the multimediated generation—what Juan Villoro calls the "Generación Molotov"—nurtured on Nintendo and Sega. The album moves from lounge to hip-hop to hardcore industrial, from Spanish to English to Japanese. The Nortec collective, from Tijuana, unite diverse places in a similar way. By mixing tape loops of northern Mexican *banda* with European techno, the collective constructs a soundtrack for another type of migrant passing through the Middle World: the migrant who follows the global flows of electronic music. El Gran Silencio, also from Monterrey, constructs a hybrid sound through a band setup that recalls more traditional *norteño* groupings; an accordion, acoustic and electric guitars, drums, keyboards. But instead of playing "traditional" northern Mexican music, their sound slips and slides between *cumbia*, *norteño*, Colombian *vallenato*, hiphop, punk, ska, and reggae. Uniting Latin American rhythms with American rock, they lay bare the connections across borders and align themselves with histories of migration, both northern and southern. What bands such as these do is not just cut up the musical DNA but scramble and reconfigure it to show off the borderlands' aural landscape. They remind us that the border is sound.

Josh Kun has written of this other way of sensing the border.[32] It is in the sounds of the cars waiting to cross; in the crowds; in the mix of sounds from the mega dance clubs and the honky-tonks steps away from each other in the border cities. Cruising Revolution Avenue in Tijuana on a Saturday is a trip across a varied aural landscape. The urban sounds connect distinct places. By disrupting notions of national homogeneity (if such a thing ever existed), the mixed sounds and languages coming from the megadiscos, the nightclubs, and the stereos of passing cars negate the physical material border instituted by nations trying to impose border controls.

If at Times You Can't Read This It's Because Estoy en el Otro Lado

During the construction of the borderlands there will be many maps drawn, some more closely tied to the region than others. The geographies traced here are just some of the possibilities of a complex and heterogeneous region that offers up a diversity of itineraries. Borderlands metaphors aid in the dearticulation of the hegemonic images that the centers of power attempt to impose on the region and offer up a representation of a diverse region: rearticulating a map that is theirs. In telling stories, those who live on the border are making place. In analyzing the borderlands, it is necessary to remember that the border is not just a single unit; rather, it represents a different face for different people. As Vila writes, "I think that on the U.S.-Mexico frontier we have several borders, each of them the possible anchor of a particular process of identity construction." [33]

While living and teaching in Texas, I began to design a course on the U.S.-Mexico border and on the borderlands region as geography and as field of study. The class, called "Borderlands," was a natural offshoot on my research inquiries into contemporary border culture. A component of the course was to introduce the students to border studies from the Mexican side, a perspective that is so often displaced in contemporary criticism that focuses on the borderlands as a Chicano space. One of the first readings included in the course packet was a text by Guillermo Gómez Peña, "The Border Is." [34] It seemed an apt way to get the students into thinking about the border. What I came to realize was that though most class members are "borderers" themselves—the majority were students from south Texas—their own border experiences were distinct from the border manifesto by Gómez Peña. His position within the border arts movement was distinct and largely filtered through an aestheticized/fetishized/romanticized Tijuana and San Diego dancing to a *banda* beat. My students knew that the border contained some of what the border *brujo* was proclaiming but that it was also more.

As a juncture in the Middle World, the border is where identities can be reinscribed, re-formed, revalued. It asks us to step right up, to partake in its multiple representations, and examine our own histories and identities in relation to the border. As a line that is, as Alfred Arteaga writes, "half-metal, half water," the border is not *un* border *puro*. [35] At times a wall, it is also a door, a bridge, and a path.

Standing on the beach of Tijuana in the summer of 2005, I crossed out the border. A few days earlier I had watched as workmen dismantled the border in preparation for building a larger wall. The old border fence of wood and tin was rusted and rotting. As a temporary barrier, the workmen set up an orange plastic fence. It lasted only one day before being washed away by the high tide. On that summer morning, I stood on the border, one leg on each side. I wasn't the only one—others, too, were freely crossing back and forth. There were no guards telling us to stay on the other side. And so we crossed—unrepentant border crossers—crossing out the border in a process that is, as Crosthwaite reminds us, "algo natural, cosa de todos los días."

Notes

1   Luis Humberto Crosthwaite, "La fila," in *Instrucciones para cruzar la frontera* (Mexico City: Joaquín Mortiz, 2002), 13–21.
2   Ibid., 15.
3   Patricia Price, *Dry Place: Landscapes of Belonging and Exclusion* (Minneapolis: University of Minnesota Press, 2004), 1.
4   Breyten Breytenbach, "Notes from the Middle World," *Timothy McSweeney's Quarterly Attempt* 6 (2001): 13–23.
5   Ibid., 13, 14.
6   Gloria Anzaldúa, *Borderlands/La Frontera* (San Francisco: Spinsters/Aunt Lute, 1987).
7   James Clifford, "Traveling Cultures," in *Cultural Studies*, ed. Lawrence Grossberg, Cary Nelson, Paula A. Treichler, et al., 96–116 (New York: Routledge, 1992), 109.
8   David Spener and Kathleen Staudt, eds., *The US-Mexico Border: Transcending Divisions, Contesting Identities* (Boulder: Lynne Rienner, 1998), 14.
9   Pablo Vila, *Crossing Borders, Reinforcing Borders: Social Categories, Metaphors, and Narrative Identities on the U.S.-Mexico Frontier* (Austin: University of Texas Press, 2000), 6.
10 See Claire F. Fox, *The Fence and the River: Culture and Politics at the U.S.-Mexico Border*, Cultural Studies of the Americas 1 (Minneapolis: University of Minnesota Press, 1999); Alejandro Lugo, "Reflections on Border Theory, Culture, and the Nation," in *Border Theory: The Limits of Cultural Production*, ed. Scott Michaelsen and David E. Johnson (Minneapolis: University of Minnesota Press, 1997); Santiago Vaquera, "Wandering in the Borderlands: Mapping an Imaginative Geography of the Border," *Latin American Issues* 14 (1998): 107–32; and three works by María Socorro Tabuenca: "Colonizaje intelectual en las literaturas de las fronteras," paper presented at SCMLA Convention, San Antonio, November 1, 1996; "Viewing the Border: Perspectives from 'the Open Wound,'" *Discourse* 18 (1995–96): 146–68; and "Reflexiones sobre la literatura de la frontera," *puentelibre* 4 (1995): 8–12.
11 Iain Chambers, *Migrancy, Culture, Identity* (London: Routledge, 1994), 5.
12 Norma Klahn, "Writing the Border: The Languages and Limits of Representation," in *Common Border, Uncommon Paths: Race, Culture, and National Identity in U.S.-Mexican Relations*, ed. O. J. Rodriguez and K. Vincent, 123–41 (Wilmington: SR Books, 1997), 123.
13 María Socorro Tabuenca Córdoba, "La frontera textual y geográfica en dos narradoras de la frontera norte mexicana: Rosina Conde y Rosario Sanmiguel," Ph.D. diss., SUNY Stony Brook, 1997.
14 North of the Borderism also maintains—if a bit tenuously—the dominance of the capital in the cultural life of the nation, through a curious project of "official" decentralization in the aim to incorporate the Mexican *agringado* north into the bosom of the nation.

15 For an extended discussion on these tropes, see works by María Socorro Tabuenca, including "Colonizaje intelectual en las literaturas de las fronteras," "Viewing the Border," and "Reflexiones sobre la literatura de la frontera." See also Jennifer Insley, "Redefining Sodom: A Latter-Day Vision of Tijuana," *Mexican Studies/Estudios Mexicanos* 20.1 (Winter 1994): 99–121; and Vaquera, "Wandering in the Borderlands."

16 "I have come to realize that a good way to make friends outside of Tijuana is to say that you are from Tijuana. This places in you a mystical air, something like a gangster, something like a cowboy. And, of course, for these moments one always has to carry with them a good story to tell." "Entre cowboys y gangsters," *Milenio Diario* (June 2003).

17 "And then I have to elaborate carefully my testimony so that I do not contradict the image that he and many others have of this border city: Dude, it is so difficult. The other day, I could barely cross the street because of the number of bodies strewn about. Dude, over there in Tijuana you can even buy cocaine in the seminary. Dude, my father gave me my first gun at the age of five. Dude, the other day I tried to cross over to San Diego, the border patrol saw us and gave us a mighty chase. Due, I lost my virginity at the age of ten and my elementary school friends teased me for coming late to the party. Arturo's eyes shine, and fill with tears while he takes notes and breathes deeply." Ibid.

18 "Separated from all that is Mexican and bloated with all that is gringo."

19 Rosina Conde, "Viñetas revolucionarias," in *El agente secreto* (Mexicali: UA Baja California, 1990).

20 Debra Castillo and María Socorro Tabuenca, *Border Women: Writing from La Frontera*, Cultural Studies of the Americas, 9 (Minneapolis: University of Minnesota Press, 2002), 136.

21 Castillo and Tabuenca, in their discussion of another story by Conde, note how the female narrator uses femininity for material gain and "creating an unfamiliar, dislocated space for a feminist intervention in the unlikely staging of a helpless femininity. . . . Awareness of the undercurrents of language and of the shifting ideological frames allow the women . . . to use men's strategies and expectations against them" (ibid., 142). I would argue that "Viñetas revolucionarias" operates in a similar way.

22 Amitava Kumar, *Passport Photos* (Berkeley and Los Angeles: University of California Press, 2000), 45.

23 Michel de Certeau points out that as the original signification of the name of a street is worn away and inscribed with another signification, "they [the streets] become liberated spaces that can be occupied. A rich indetermination gives them, by means of a semantic rarefaction, the function of articulating a second, poetic geography on top of the geography of the literal, forbidden or permitted meaning" (*The Practice of Everyday Life* [Berkeley and Los Angeles: University of California Press, 1988], 105).

24 Juan Villoro, "Nada que declarar. Welcome to Tijuana," *Letras libres* 17 (2000): 16–20; quote on 16.

25 Lawrence Herzog, *From Aztec to High Tech: Architecture and Landscape across the Mexico–United States Border* (Baltimore: Johns Hopkins University Press, 1999), 208.

26 Heriberto Yépez, *Tijuana: Processes of a Science Fiction City without a Future* (Mexico: CNCA, SRE; Madrid: Comunidad de Madrid, UNAM, 2005).

27 But it is a poor likeness since—as Jean Baudrillard states of a simulacrum—"it bears no relation to any reality whatever" (*Simulations*, trans. Paul Foss, Paul Batton, and Philip

Beitchman [New York: Semiotext(e), 1983], 11). Tijuana subverts, then, both national nar-rativization and the border. In political discourse, not only from Mexico City but also from Washington, D.C., Tijuana, as also the rest of the border, is a danger zone. On the U.S. side of the fence there exists a type of border machine that attempts to set limits to the border. Border Patrol operations such as Operation Wetback or Gatekeeper not only mili-tarize the border but also function as strategies to maintain the line, protect the nation from its southern Other. On the Mexican side, federal practices to inscribe the north into a national narrative—through the creation of writers' programs, for example—function in a similar way, to maintain the homogeneity of the nation, to keep the Other back, to protect the border.

28 Herzog, *From Aztec to High Tech*, 210.
29 Yépez, *Tijuana*, 46–49.
30 Saskia Sassen, *The Global City: New York, London, Tokyo* (Princeton, NJ: Princeton University Press, 2001), xxiii.
31 Breytenbach, "Notes from the Middle World," 17.
32 Josh Kun, "The Aural Border," *Theatre Journal* 52.1 (2000): 1–21.
33 Vila, *Crossing Borders, Reinforcing Borders*, 6.
34 Guillermo Gómez Peña, "The Border Is," in *Warrior for Gringostroika: Essays, Performance Texts, and Poetry* (St. Paul: Graywolf, 1993).
35 Alfred Arteaga, *Chicano Poetics: Heterotexts and Hybridities*, Cambridge Studies in American Literature and Culture (Cambridge: Cambridge University Press, 1997).

Claudia Sadowski-Smith

Twenty-First-Century Chicana/o Border Writing

Since the 1990s, binational agreements like the 1994 North American Free Trade Agreement (NAFTA) have accelerated the industrialization of Mexican border towns with largely U.S.-owned maquiladora factories, which have created conditions for heightened environmental pollution and increased labor migration from Mexico's interior. Neither development stops at the border. While the U.S. government has been slow to respond to environmental degradation, it has quickly reacted to increased immigration by taking border enforcement to historically unprecedented levels.

Three recent Chicana/o short story collections—Ito Romo's *El Puente = The Bridge*, Richard Yañez's *El Paso del Norte: Stories on the Border*, and Lucretia Guerrero's *Chasing Shadows: Stories*—fictionalize the effects of border militarization and, in Romo Ito's case, environmental degradation on U.S. communities of Mexican descent along the Texas–Nuevo León, Texas-Chihuahua, and Arizona-Sonora portions of the international boundary.[1] The work of Romo, Yañez, and Guerrero further suggests that the reinforcement of divisions between Mexican and Mexican American populations embodied in bor-

South Atlantic Quarterly 105:4, Fall 2006
DOI 10.1215/00382876-2006-009   © 2006 Duke University Press

der militarization is mirrored in spatialized gendered, class, and political differences *within* U.S. Mexican communities. Ongoing migration from Mexico tends to exacerbate these differences as it continually (re-)creates economic, cultural, and political distinctions among newcomers and better-established Mexican Americans. Aside from emphasizing the spatiality of the Mexico-U.S. border, the collections by Romo, Yañez, and Guerrero thus stress hitherto largely underexamined internal distinctions within Mexican American communities.

In their focus on the complexity of Mexican border developments and their effects on U.S. residents, *El Puente, El Paso del Norte,* and *Chasing Shadows* provide a much-needed corrective to current, extremely limited public discussions in the United States about the porosity of U.S. borders to undocumented immigrants and terrorists.[2] The three collections of fiction also speak to a long-standing yet somewhat underexplored current in Chicana/o writing that uses the border as setting, theme, and narrative structure. Exemplified in the work of Gloria Anzaldúa, Aristeo Brito, Norma Elia Cantú, Oscar Casares, Dagoberto Gilb, Rolando Hinojosa, Arturo Islas, Miguel Méndez, John Rechy, Alberto Ríos, Sergio Troncoso, and Helena María Viramontes, among others, this literature cannot be easily moved to another place without distortion or loss of significance.[3] While it places questions of Chicana/o identity and community in the literal territory of the border, this work also acknowledges or contributes to this area's long-standing symbolic value for articulations of Mexican American identity and culture.

The association of the border with questions of Chicana/o identity dates back to the creation of Mexican Americans after the redrawing of the international boundary in the aftermath of the 1848 Mexico-U.S. War. Post–World War II–era political struggles for inclusion into full U.S. citizenship rights further reinforced the connection between Chicana/os and the territory ceded by Mexico to the United States.[4] Cultural nationalism of the 1960s and 1970s, a stage in the movement, articulated radical land claims to the Southwest, which were embodied in the idea of the Chicana/o homeland Aztlán. Popularized by poet Alurista, Aztlán drew on the Nahuatl myth of an envisioned return to the place from which the Mesoamerican Aztecs migrated to today's Mexico. As it declared Chicanas/os to be the genetic heirs of the Aztecs, Aztlán became the foundational notion of Chicana/o studies at the time of their institutionalization in the U.S. academy. Alongside other work, Gloria Anzaldúa's *Borderlands/La Frontera* (1987) refigured the Southwest and its designation as Aztlán in the more explicitly transnational notion of the "borderlands," which became the new guiding metaphor of Chicana/o studies.[5]

The short story collections by Romo, Yañez, and Guerrero continue many of the formal and thematic concerns of Chicana/o border literature like Anzaldúa's, but they also highlight some of the more problematic underpinnings of the problematic underpinnings of her work. Anzaldúa's attempts to forge a mestiza border consciousness overshadowed her less centrally articulated spatialized concerns with border developments. It is true that she addressed changes along the Mexico-U.S. boundary at the time of her writing, including intensified U.S. border militarization, the growth of maquila industries in Mexican border cities, violence against undocumented border crossers, and the transformation of U.S. ranching into large-scale agribusiness with negative effects on the environment.[6] But Anzaldúa's focus on revising Aztlán also perpetuated the metaphorical use of the border as a signifier of Chicana/o border crossings, migration, and hybrid identity formation.[7]

The texts by Romo, Yañez, and Guerrero move beyond this symbolic focus on the border as a terrain of Chicana/o identity formation (and largely beyond imagery associated with Aztlán) to locate Chicana/o border communities within debates about globalization in Mexican border towns. I propose to employ the spatialized understanding of border literature that has dominated approaches from south of la frontera to this newly emerging Chicana/o fiction about the Mexico-U.S. border by calling it "U.S. fronteriza fiction." While border writing in the United States is associated with Chicana/o cultural productions, definitions of Mexican border literature encompass both *literatura de la frontera*, that is, literature produced from the northern borderlands, and *literatura fronteriza*, a more general category of writing *about* the border that also includes representations from Mexico City.[8] As they situate their fiction in the U.S. towns of Laredo, El Paso, and Nogales, the three collections of fiction by Romo, Yañez, and Guerrero highlight locations with majority Mexican-descended populations and their relationships to the increasingly larger and more populous Mexican twin cities as a result of maquiladorization. In their emphasis on places that have undergone radical transformations, the three works highlight underexplored connections between humanities-based issues of Chicana/o identity formation and the effects of globalization on local places like U.S. border areas that appear to have been the purview of the social sciences. Romo, Yañez, and Guerrero work toward criticism of the United States' role in contemporary processes of globalization by identifying the impact that changes in Mexican border towns have on U.S. communities of Mexican descent. As U.S. fronteriza writing focuses on growing urbanized spaces that are moving from the margins of individual nations to the center, this literature combines an attention to borderlands and urban areas as two locations that, according to Saskia Sassen, have emerged as new scales of importance beyond the nation-state.[9] Here the strategic, precise, and focused nature of the conditions under which neoliberal globalization is emerging has become most clearly visible.

The texts by Romo, Yañez, and Guerrero also demonstrate that, as Doreen Massey puts it, space is integral to the formation of latent political subjectivities that highlight the openness of the future.[10] The authors depict U.S. border cities as spaces where Chicana/o civil rights struggles may reemerge in the form of individual and collective activism for border-crossing rights and environmental justice. Because of its spatial focus, this literature also opens itself up to comparative connections with cultural productions about the Mexico-U.S. boundary that represent the perspectives of other ethnic and national border communities on local manifestations of globalization.

The Spatiality of Chicana/o Border Writing

Chicana/o literature is often characterized in terms of its connections to two interrelated factors: its interest in formal innovation and its ties to the U.S. Southwest. As Monika Kaup writes, Chicana/o literature has employed the border both as a theme and as an aesthetic form.[11] Or, as Margot Kelley puts it, Chicana/o writing exhibits "a deliberate and increasing incorporation of orality into literature, an attention to border places and border subjectivities, and a concerted revision of the short story and the novel to transform the *Bildungsroman* genre."[12] Héctor Calderón and José David Saldívar have described Chicana/o cultural production as "an expression of a social group that has given *the* distinctive cultural feature to the American West and Southwest."[13] The two scholars date the beginning of Mexican American artistic forms to the Texas-Mexican War (1836) and the U.S.–Mexican War (1846–49), which resulted in the imperialist absorption of half of Mexico's territory into the United States and in the creation of Mexican Americans. While early cultural production from or about the absorbed territory by authors like Jovita Gonzáles, María Ampara Ruiz de Burton, and Américo

Paredes does exist, Chicana/o art began to flourish primarily in the context of 1950s–1970s activist and cultural nationalist struggles, which further consolidated the territorial link between Chicanas/os and the Southwest.[14]

Activist struggles for labor, education, and land rights largely took place in the border states of California, Texas, Arizona, and New Mexico. The cultural nationalist version of Chicanismo, a stage within the movement, was also firmly grounded in the U.S. Southwest. In the founding document of Chicanismo, "El Plan Espiritual," the poet Alurista established a poetics of resistant territorialism, specifying the border area as the lost Chicano homeland Aztlán. He supported these territorial claims by declaring Chicanas/os to be the descendants of the Aztecs, the aboriginal inhabitants of (parts of) the Southwest before they migrated to today's Mexico. "El Plan" defined Chicanas/os as constituents of a "mestizo nation," whose members were displaced to the U.S. Southwest from the Mexican motherland as a result of the 1848 Treaty of Guadalupe Hidalgo.[15] While the Chicano movement was never homogeneous, the myth of Aztlán gained ascendance in activist struggles and in cultural nationalist efforts to institutionalize Chicana/o studies. According to José Aranda, long after its demise as an effective organizing tool for political activism, Aztlán surfaced as an operating metaphor in many Chicana/o literary projects.[16] Influenced by this cultural nationalist approach, much Chicana/o literature began, as John R. Chávez shows, to represent the Southwest as a territory to be reclaimed rather than (merely) as a geography where a majority of Mexican Americans live.[17]

At the time of its publication in 1987, Gloria Anzaldúa's *Borderlands/La Frontera* captured the ongoing displacement of Aztlán from the center of Chicana/o studies. Though other Chicana/o writers were involved in similar projects, Anzaldúa's work has had the largest cultural impact.[18] Her text made the border the new foundational metaphor of Chicana/o studies, even though it maintained several of Aztlán's nationalist tenets, including its emphasis on Mexican Americans' displacement from Mexico and their genetic affinity with indigenous peoples. But Anzaldúa's book also drew attention to the transnational character of the Southwest as a borderland. She employed a highly experimental form of aesthetics to portray the Mexico-U.S. border both as a geography dividing two nation-states and as a place of hybrid, Chicana identity formation. This part of the border, where pre-1849 settlements were divided so that their residents became citizens of two different countries, also served as the model for narratives of Aztlán.[19] But Anzaldúa connected the same territory to differently articulated questions of identity. She linked the Texas-Chihuahua borderlands, the place where she grew up, to her own divided identity as a Chicana, describing the border fence as "running down the length of my body, / staking rods in my flesh, / splits me splits me / *me raja me raja* / This is my home / this thin edge of barbwire."[20] To theorize a space in which these divisions can be overcome, Anzaldúa forged the notion of a *mestiza* borderland consciousness that comprises white, Mexican, and Indian elements. She replaced Chicanismo's use of male Aztec mythology by elevating *female* Mesoamerican myths to models of empowered femininity in order to make room for Chicanas in the largely male-centered Chicano movement.

Anzaldúa's conflation of the border with issues of Mexican American identity formation has been highly influential in Chicana/o studies, which is dominated by literary criticism and theory.[21] Katherine Payant (1999), for example, has drawn on Anzaldúa's work to discuss borderland themes in Sandra Cisneros's *Woman Hollering Creek* (1991).[22] This text is largely set in San Antonio, Texas, a town removed from the border yet located in a border state.[23] Payant identifies several tropes that make Cisneros's work a border text. These include an emphasis on Chicanas'/os' origins in Mexico and their continuing linkage to Mexico in terms of immigration, a focus on shared pre-Columbian or *mestizo* myths and legends, and a depiction of Chicano/as as straddling "two or three cultures, requir[ing] them to combine several ways of thinking and being, a stressful situation that also has great potential for empowerment."[24] As Payant puts this last point by borrowing language from Anzaldúa, Cisneros's characters, many of whom struggle to transcend culturally dictated gender roles, live "on the border"; they constantly cross several linguistic and cultural barriers.

The border tropes Payant identifies in Cisneros's work could theoretically be found in most if not all Chicana/o literary texts, independently of their actual spatial or local focus. Or to put this idea in terms of a distinction established by Monika Kaup, in this reading, the notion of the border encompasses both a spatial emphasis and a more symbolic focus on Chicana/o mobility and changes in ethnic identity.[25] Some critics have taken the association of the border geography with issues of identity to the point of arguing that the "image of the border has become fully meaningful not only when we consider it as a physical line, but when we decenter it and liberate it from the notion of space to encompass notions of sex, class, gender, ethnicity, identity, and community."[26] But one of the more troubling aspects of "liberating" the border from its spatial referent to denote Chicana/o concerns with homeland, migration, identity, and aesthetics is that it mutes the views of other border communities, especially the perspectives of residents of the Mexican borderlands. In fact, Chicana/o fiction and scholarship rarely ventures on to the Mexican side of the border.[27] Juan Bruce-Novoa has shown that even when Chicana/o cultural productions pay attention to Mexico, they do so primarily to address questions of U.S. identity. Bruce-Novoa argues that Chicana/o representations throughout the 1980s have produced largely idealized and monolithic notions of Mexico, in which the country becomes a source of nostalgia for a lost paradise or a place of disillusioned encounters between Chicana/o or Mexican American protagonists and the Mexican "homeland."[28]

While U.S. border writing is associated with symbolic questions of ethnic identity, Mexico border literature is identified with the geographical space of border region, given a larger national context where region serves as one major way to anchor identity.[29] Mexican writing about the border thus encompasses both *literatura de la frontera* — that is, literature produced from the northern borderlands — and *literatura fronteriza*, a more general category that also includes representations from Mexico City.[30] In the United States, in contrast, border areas have generally not been approached as independent regional units. While literary regionalism has addressed other traditionally marginalized areas, such as nonurban locations, the South, and the (South)West, it has neglected U.S. urban border areas, the fastest-growing portions of the country. I do not propose, however, to resuscitate regionalist paradigms for the analysis of Chicana/o border literature. Regionalism has historically limited discussions of marginalized geographies to the context of the nation-state, often to contain the distinctiveness and autonomy of a specific territory within discourses about the nation. Instead of regionalist frameworks, I am interested in examining the spatial orientation of U.S. fronteriza writing, the ways in which this work places questions of Chicana/o community formation in the context of regional manifestations of global developments and thus opens itself up to connections with other work about the border. U.S. fronteriza writing draws attention to the fact that as "products to be used" and as "means of production,"[31] specific geographies, such as U.S. borders, embody and are transformed by social, political, economic, and topographic conditions that enable, shape, and sustain certain forms of social organization as well as cultural production.[32]

The Urban Spaces of Chicana/o Border Fiction

Recent texts by Ito Romo, Richard Yañez, and Lucretia Guerrero, first publications for each author, focus on the majority populations of contemporary U.S. border towns and their connection to Mexican twin cities. Romo specifies the setting of *El Puente* as a "little city by the river" (85), "the largest inland port of the United States" (29), which points to the author's hometown of Laredo.[33] Laredo's proximity to Nuevo Laredo and the two cities' connection by a bridge is described thus: "Looking toward the bridge, Convent [street] ran right onto the bridge, and the bridge ran right onto Guerrero. Guerrero became Convent. Convent became Guerrero. Two different streets. Two different countries. Two different worlds. Hot black pavement separating them. That's all" (48–49). Romo here refers to the division of Laredo by the 1848 Treaty of Guadalupe-Hidalgo, which set the two towns on separate yet interlinked paths of development. As Laredo officially became part of Texas, Mexicans who wanted to retain their Mexican citizenship moved across the river; still, today three-quarters of Laredo's residents are of Mexican descent. The area previously settled as part of Laredo was named Nuevo Laredo. Since the 1990s, Nuevo Laredo has developed into a strong industrial center, and the maquiladora industry has become the city's second largest economic sector. By 2000, Nuevo Laredo's population had grown almost three times as large as that of its U.S. counterpart.[34] While Romo's focus on the international bridge draws on its long-standing usage in U.S. border fiction and U.S. and Mexican memoir, it also underscores the arbitrary nature of a national border drawn along a water boundary. The author has said that he chose the bridge as his setting because he wanted to "let people see that it really was a passage, plain and simple, from one country to another."[35]

El Puente fictionalizes connections among various border populations in individual narrative fragments that are more clearly interrelated into a coherent text than the separate pieces that make up the other two short story collections. Romo's book explores the lives of fourteen women of diverse national, class, and ethnic origin from both sides of the border during the span of a few days. Each woman is given a short vignette that is individually complete yet linked to the other stories in the collection through a web of relationships that unfold at the international bridge. Its experimental use of narrative sets *El Puente* in the tradition of the short story cycle or composite novel, whose individual shorter texts are held together by common settings, protagonists, themes, or principles of storytelling.[36] As it has gained popularity in modernist fiction, the genre has surged in the work of U.S. ethnic writers such as Sandra Cisneros.[37]

Each of the short vignettes in *El Puente* is devoted to individual protagonists who become part of a crowd that gathers at the bridge to watch the international river's color change. This event is represented in the aesthetics of magical realism. As Romo describes it, "The waters of the Rio Grande had begun to turn a dark, dark red, like the Nile turning into blood in Cecil B. DeMille's *The Ten Commandments*, like magic" (130). Explanations for the river's change range from religious miracle or industrial waste poisoning to government conspiracy. As in much magical realism, however, the river's transformation can also be explained in realistic terms. *El Puente* begins with the lament of Tomasita, a housewife from the Mexican border city of Nuevo Laredo, who just lost her husband to cancer. He worked as an industrial waste disposal superintendent for a U.S.-owned maquiladora assembly plant, which also releases waste into the stream behind their house. Over the span of a month, Tomasita collects and grinds up dried mulberries and the shards of her favorite cooking pot into a very fine powder capable of being absorbed by the Rio Grande/Rio Bravo. She then "empt[ies] her washtub and the sorrows of her soul" (3) into the stream where the maquila's "big-mouthed pipe com[ing] out of the factory wall . . . emptied into the river" (130). When the Río Grande/Río Bravo turns bright red, its change attracts the attention of border residents, whose individual stories come to intersect at the international bridge. Tomasita's form of protest against the environmental pollution of her home does not represent a spontaneous act of outrage and grief; rather, it is the outgrowth of a long, deliberate process of mourning and introspection. Romo writes, "The night she ground the last chard of clay and the last handful of berries, she had filled the tub almost to the top. Now bathed in perspiration, she looked up into the stars and suddenly was lost; the space inside of her was the same space she was staring into. She was nowhere and everywhere at the same time. She knew exactly what do" (128–29).

As she spreads the powder into the stream that feeds into the Río Grande, from the pipe heading from the maquila to the mouth of the river, Tomasita's action underscores one of the most disastrous side effects of border industrialization. Binational agreements that culminated in NAFTA have enabled corporations to systematically take advantage of lower labor and operating costs, tariff and value-added tax differentials, and the limited enforcement of already weak environmental and labor regulations in Mexico. The creation of maquila assembly factories and the subsequent population growth in Mexican border towns in the absence of adequate public infrastructures has worsened existing environmental problems, such as the pollution of air, water, and land and the overconsumption of water and other natural resources.[38] In the context of lax environmental laws, waste produced by maquilas, especially industrial solvents suspected of having links to growing rates of cancer in the border region, is improperly treated or simply dumped on land and in the water.

The environments where poor residents live or work are disproportionately affected by degradation, which has drastic consequences for their health. After her husband José's death, Tomasita's health also fails; she goes deaf and loses her sense of smell. Asked to leave the company rental house, Tomasita moves into a two-room shack in a *colonia*. Lacking paved roads and sanitary-water and sewer systems, this low-income housing development exemplifies the unplanned and unregulated nature of growth in Mexican border cities. Tomasita's *colonia* is located by the international river, which functions simultaneously as her backyard, toilet, and bathroom. She is exposed to water that is polluted by untreated sewage, agricultural chemicals, and pesticide runoff as well as by extensive dumping of industrial by-products like heavy metals and toxic chemicals.[39] In addition to José's cancer, *El Puente* also fictionalizes other effects of environmental pollution that are related to contaminated water. A child is born with a spinal deformity, which is traced to the mother having drunk tap water, and a dentist in Juárez recommends purified rather than public water to avoid the risk of infection after dental work.

As the novel's central plot, the river's color change articulates a symbolic critique of U.S.-style globalization that draws on the originary political impetus of Latin American "boom" writing. Coined originally in reference to 1920s German expressionist painting, magical realism (alternatively called "realismo magico" and "lo real maravillos") expressed the emergence of a new political consciousness that was shaped in part by some more militant forms of anti-American nationalism and that represented attempts to conceptualize localized knowledge as an alternative to the onset of U.S.-style globalization.[40] In the context of intensified globalization since the 1990s, magical realism has become "perhaps [the] most important contemporary trend in international fiction."[41] Much of this contemporary work seems to have moved beyond the political commitments central to 1960s magical realism, flattening distinct local traditions and presenting pre-modern realities and communities in ways that minimize the burden of this past.[42]

El Puente does not seem to follow this pattern. The book employs magical realism to represent Tomasita's individualized protest against maquila pollution, whose public manifestation in the river's change also spark collective responses. *El Puente*'s protagonists visit the international bridge at roughly the same moment: when an eighteen-wheeler honks; when Soledad from Nuevo Laredo gives birth; when Pura, a retired Laredo resident, dies of a heart attack; and when Rosa, a fifteen-year-old Mexican American, attempts suicide by jumping off the bridge. Some protagonists fail to realize the full import of the river's transformation and its effect on events at the bridge. Romo fictionalizes, for example, an upper-class Mexican American who maintains her class difference from the Mexican undocumented workers she hires by speaking only English, just as she remains an uninvolved observer to events on the bridge. The book's only Anglo character, the truck-stop waitress Cindy, and Christina, the self-declared militant Chicana, also completely miss the dramatic developments on the bridge. Cindy is blinded by her search for the media spotlight, and Christina is preoccupied with investigating the cause of the river's redness, which she suspects to be a government conspiracy against Chicanas/os. But some of the collection's other characters recognize that the interlinked events of death and childbirth at the bridge also signal connections among them. During her search for her husband (who we find out probably died crossing the river), Sofia helps Soledad deliver her child. She raises "the child to the heavens, blood dripping from the baby onto her face, onto the sidewalk, into the red, red water of the river" (118). Out of death emerges a life that is also deeply affected by the politics inscribed in the geography of the international bridge, a location that grants the child the much-coveted U.S. citizenship.

Tomasita also realizes her connections to some of the other protagonists. On her way across the bridge to Laredo, Tomasita miraculously regains her sense of hearing and is thus able to witness the newborn's cry. Tomasita places her hands on the child's head, leaving a red stain in the center. She performs the same gesture of benediction when a Mexican guard posted at her house does not follow his orders to shoot her. As she tries to cross the bridge back to Nuevo Laredo a few days later, though, an American soldier recognizes Tomasita from wanted flyers and shoots to kill her. Having left red stains on the Mexican soldier and Soledad's newborn child, Tomasita dies with a bullet hole in the middle of her forehead. The circumstances of Tomasita's Christlike death on the bridge articulate a strong critique of border militarization that David Harvey has identified as one expression of the neoconservative reconsolidation of U.S. nation-state powers since the 1990s.[43] The tightening of enforcement at popular border crossings in Texas, Arizona, and California with fences, walls, new technologies of control, and additional Border Patrol personnel over the last decade has, by all accounts, failed to deter growing numbers of immigrants.[44] They have instead been detoured to other, more dangerous stretches of the border, where many more immigrants have died. The prevalence of military might and violence at the border has created an environment in which border deaths have become commonplace. An increasing number of immigrants die trying to cross, and they are routinely mistreated by smugglers, thugs, and the Border Patrol, at the same time that Border Patrol agents themselves are under attack.[45] While Tomasita is just another of these border casualties, she also becomes their most visible representative, dying in the spotlight the U.S. media has cast onto the bridge.

Her association with Christlike martyrdom and her death's proximity to water also suggest the possibility of redemption and rebirth. This possibility is prefigured by the actions of the other women protagonists. Many of them give or take something important to the river in an act that changes their lives. For example, Estella, another housewife from Nuevo Laredo, drops into the river a dish of poisoned mole that was supposed to kill her cheating husband, and Lourdes discards a ring she took from a body she found by the international river. One may surmise that the dead man is Sofia's husband who did not return to Laredo from his work in the Mexican city. He may have been a victim of thugs and growing border crime, or he may have drowned in his attempt to swim across the river. At Tomasita's burial, her bullet wound is covered by an enormous sparkling emerald donated by "a wealthy Mexican housewife" (148) who also volunteered to take care of Tomasita's body. In one of his many cameo appearances throughout the novel, CBS anchorman Tom Brokaw tells the audience that Tomasita's death sparked grief within this otherwise "typically quiet border community" (148–49). *El Puente* leaves us with the hopeful image of rebirth in the figure of another Mexican housewife taking care of Tomasita's remains (and perhaps continuing her mission). The book also gestures toward the possibility that the border community's grief may transform into other forms of protest against manifestations of neoliberal politics at the border that have contributed to Tomasita's violent death.

In contrast to *El Puente*'s attention to the international bridge, Richard Yañez's *El Paso del Norte* focuses on the geography of El Paso and its connection to Ciudad Juárez. The title of the collection points to the sixteenth-century collective designation of the two border cities as El Paso del Norte. As a result of the 1848 Treaty of Guadalupe-Hidalgo, the area that today encompasses El Paso became U.S. territory, and in 1888, the city of El Paso del Río del Norte changed its name to Ciudad Juárez in honor of Benito Juárez, hero of the revolution against France. Today the two towns are interconnected yet separate. El Paso was the first U.S. border city with urban concentrations of Mexicans,[46] and currently two-thirds of its residents are of Mexican descent. El Paso's economy manifests neoliberal growth without prosperity, which is characterized by the prevalence of labor-intensive, low-value-added jobs.[47] The Mexican twin's economy is dominated by maquila production with similar features; the population of Ciudad Juárez is at least three times as large as El Paso's.[48]

While each of the short stories in *El Puente* can stand on its own, some also contain interrelated characters and themes that focus on connecting Chicana/o communities to change at the border. Most of the stories are set in Ysleta. They take place on a residential street, pretentiously called Nottingham Drive, and in several convenience stores in Ysleta, a working-class El Paso neighborhood that is located less than a mile from the Zaragoza International Bridge.

In Yañez's book, Ysleta marks internal differences among the Mexican majority population of El Paso. These economic, gendered, and political divisions become spatialized in residential segregation or, as Raymond A. Rocco (1998) has conceptualized this phenomenon, in the multiplication of Latina/o-Chicana/o communities.[49] In his study of Latina/o communities in Los Angeles, Rocco argues that their diversification somewhat supersedes developments that have historically segregated Mexican Americans into a relatively cohesive group, separated from other communities. Yañez's opening story, "Desert Vista," focuses on Raul Luis, a junior high school student whose family moved to Nottingham Drive a year ago. Here Raul Luis has to renegotiate the boundaries between his family's tenuous middle-class status and his new working-class neighborhood whose schools are marked with graffiti and whose common language, Spanish, Raul Luis does not really speak. The neighborhood is internally divided along even more complex class lines, spatialized in a barrier of wooden posts and metal rails with a No Passing sign (5). The barrier marks off the poorer parts of the street, whose houses had "no basketball courts. No birdbaths. No mulberry trees" (16). The house of a classmate Raul Luis tries to befriend is described thus: "One side of the roof was missing shingles and appeared ready to cave in. The front door was more rust than any color of paint. [One] couldn't tell where the cement driveway ended and the grassless yard began. Trash and tumbleweeds clenched the chainlink fence" (17). Boys from the other side of the barrier often express their disapproval of this division by draping Raul Luis's house in toilet paper and peppering it with balls of mud.

Another story in the collection suggests that Raul Luis's family will eventually move away from Ysleta. In "Amoroza Tires," Tony Amoroza, the owner of a tire shop in Ysleta, daydreams about moving to Nottingham Drive, which he considers a better neighborhood because of its newer schools and its park, because it has fewer gangs, police sirens, and gunshots at night. Tony resides in a house that, like most others in the neighborhood, is too small for the families that live in them, often holding several generations. The gang graffiti throughout his neighborhood and the gunshots also worry Tony, as they seem to suggest that "soon enough we'll crawl inside and take the little that your family has left" (42). Throughout his working life, Tony is overwhelmed with the responsibilities of running a business and providing for his family. He eases his anxieties by reading and collecting outrageous tabloid articles, whose headlines provide him with hope for the future. His wife's sudden death leaves him with too many unpaid bills to fulfill his dream of moving to a better neighborhood. After Tony experiences his own kind of tabloid story—a glimpse of *el cielo* as he gets accidentally buried in a tire stack—he regains some optimism. The end of the story suggests that the Amoroza family may be gluing itself back together after the death of his wife, even if they will have to stay in their neighborhood. Tony declares an end to the customary time of mourning—Luto—and celebrates his daughter's birthday, which had been put off by his wife's death.

Two of *El Paso del Norte*'s short stories, "Rio Bravo (a Corrida)" and "Rio Grande," are set in El Paso's twin, Ciudad Juárez. "Rio Bravo" highlights divisions among Mexican Americans and Mexicans, particularly the imperialist attitude of Mexican Americans toward Juárez, where they engage in underage drinking and the solicitation of prostitutes. Chuco, a former gang member from El Paso, crosses "over into the rest of the night" (72) to a bar called Rio Bravo. Drunk, he leers at a heavily made-up young woman in a suede miniskirt and halter top and consequently gets beaten up by her older female companion who defends her "honor." Virtually enslaved to the bar, the young woman turns out to be only about thirteen years old, three years younger than his current girlfriend, whom he would never imagine treating like the young Mexican girl.

"Rio Grande," the last and arguably most impressive story in the collection, is set in both cities, El Paso and Ciudad Juárez. The story directly addresses the effects of border militarization on Mexican American residents. Throughout the collection, El Paso has been portrayed as a place where manifestations of border enforcement are ever present. Intoxicated Mexican American teenagers are afraid to be "mistaken for wetback smugglers or drug runners" (85); they are constantly aware of the "helicopters above—the ever-present migra—. . . busy watching for mules or coyotes, drug and wetback smuggling" (23). "Rio Grande" fictionalizes politicized reactions to these developments. The story opens as the teenage narrator José and his Anglo friend Steve drive around in their truck drinking. José's association with Steve and his desire to be called "Joe" indicate his degree of assimilation to white U.S. society. The two adolescents witness how the Border Patrol arrests undocumented immigrants in front of the local Kmart. When a teenage girl slips away, a Chicano agent named Roberto Duran pursues her, threatens her with his gun, and beats her so severely with his baton that his Anglo colleague John Wayne eventually intervenes. A fight ensues, in which a "mass of green uniform rolled around in the oil stains and gravel of Kmart's parking lot. Arms and legs and boots flew into each other's bodies. If their Stetsons hadn't been knocked off, it would have been hard to tell exactly who was who. The Chicano agent had a brown bald spot. The other agent's hair burned gold in the Texas sun. The illegals jailed in the Suburban rocked it back and forth, making all kinds of noise, presumably rooting for the gringo. A first, I'm sure" (82). As both agents are eventually carried away in an ambulance, the girl sets all the other undocumented migrants free.

These events and their complication of distinctions among Anglo and Chicano identities on the border initially do not seem to have an effect on José; there is no clear evidence that he feels solidarity with the Mexican nationals who are mistreated by a Border Patrol agent of Mexican descent. Instead, the two friends cross into Juárez to get drunk in one of the bars that caters to "mostly El Paso high school students and Fort Bills's GI's"

(85). As it juxtaposes the two forms of border crossings, *El Paso del Norte* points to the irony that while undocumented immigrants are prevented from entering the United States in pursuit of work that keeps the U.S. economy afloat, underage U.S. citizens can pursue far worse illegal activities on the other side of the border without any consequences. Upon his return home, José observes a Border Rights Coalition demonstration against proposed projects to replace the chain-link border fence with a steel wall. The forty to fifty protesters pass around petitions against the building of the wall, carrying signs that read "2 Cities = 1 People," "Justicia Para Todos," "No More Fences," and "Free Bridge" (89). José recognizes some of these slogans from headlines of newspapers that he usually skims for the sports section. Border Patrol agents dressed in riot gear use tear gas to break up the demonstration. Even though he tries to remain detached from what he sees as "none of [his] business" (90), José is knocked down, beaten, kicked, and arrested. He then experiences, in attenuated form, the treatment of undocumented border crossers that he observed that morning in front of the Kmart. The INS detention cell he spends the night in "smelled worse than the infested Rio" (91), but he knows that it is much better than the other, collective holding cells where hundreds of undocumented immigrants are held. José's experience spurns a newfound awareness about the effects of border developments on his own life that may translate into activism. After he is released, he recounts that "yesterday's numbness is gone" (92).

Like Yañez's book, the eleven stories in Lucretia Guerrero's *Chasing Shadows* are held together by their geographical focus on a border town named Mesquite. The town is characterized by internal divisions among Mexican American communities and their separation from residents of Mexico. Unlike Yañez, who explicitly names his border setting, and Romo, who gestures toward it, Guerrero creates a fictive location that evokes the twin border city of Nogales, Arizona, where the author grew up. However, in an interview the author has stated that while the setting of the "border . . . was crucial" for her work, "Mesquite is not Nogales. It can be all that is Nogales and more—all that I make it."[50] For a long time, developments in the two cities of Nogales, which emerged out of separate settlements, were interlinked. In the early 1920s, for example, Mexicans of relative means lived on the U.S. side of the boundary, while most working-class Mexicans employed on the U.S. side lived in Mexico. It was difficult to distinguish between the two national territories in a meaningful sense.[51] Since the 1980s, however, Nogales in Sonora has evolved from a small town to a booming industrialized city, its growth fueled by maquiladora factories. The population of Nogales, Sonora has increased to about ten times the number of Nogales, Arizona, whose population has remained relatively stable. Eighty-one percent of its residents are of Mexican descent.[52]

Like Romo, Guerrero emphasizes gender as an important variable in border issues, but hers is the only text that also evokes some of the indigenous Mexican mythology underlying Chicanismo and its feminist transformation by writers like Anzaldúa to depict developments along the border. Not as cohesive as *El Puente*, the individual short stories in *Chasing Shadows* are nevertheless more clearly interrelated than the various narrative pieces in *El Paso del Norte*. Connections among Guerrero's stories unfold chronologically in time. Guerrero has said that publishers encouraged her to interlink the various stories, some of which had already appeared separately.[53] Most of the characters' lives intersect in the impoverished U.S. neighborhood of Frontera Street or in other public spaces in Mesquite, such as its elementary school and its bus depot. Located literally on the border, Frontera Street represents one of two sites where the internal division of the border town is visibly delineated by "a tall chain-link [that] separates Mesquite into two cities" (110), the fifteen-foot fence that replaced less sturdy barriers in 1995.

In "The Curse," inhabitants of the Mexican Mesquite wait by the fence to ask U.S. residents for water. Except for the collection's central protagonist, a young girl named Tonantzin Salazar, no one wants to help because, as one character puts it, "our water level is low, too, so nobody can expect us to share with the Mexicans" (32–33). Tonantzin is named after the Virgin of Guadalupe, and the connection is reinforced by her only valuable belonging, a pendant featuring the Virgin and the Hummingbird. This association highlights her suffering and marginalization; Tonantzin is even poorer than the majority of the residents of Frontera Street's apartment complex, and her father's persistent absence exposes her to threats of male violence and potential pedophilic abuse. On the other hand, Tonantzin's linkage to indigenous mythology also emphasizes her empathy and solidarity with those less fortunate than herself. The novel connects Tonantzin's attempts to help Mexicans from the other side with the Chicana/o myth of a unified Southwest, the "land of [la] raza, now in Arizona, once in Mexico, and before when it simply was" (152–53). In a different way from the other two short story collections by Romo and Yañez, Guerrero here evokes some of the indigenous mythology underlying Aztlán, particularly its feminist transformation by Chicana writers like Gloria Anzaldúa, Cherríe Moraga, Sandra

Cisneros, Denise Chávez, and Lorna Dee Cervantes, who reconceptualized Chicanismo into what Arthur Ramírez (1995) has called a neo-indigenous "Chicana Aztlán."[54]

The theme of female self-empowerment runs through Guerrero's collection. One Frontera Street resident who was physically and emotionally abused by her husband realizes that she needs to become economically independent. The protagonist in "Gloves of Her Own," a pun on Virginia Woolf's famous essay *A Room of One's Own*, finds independence from her much venerated grandfather. After his death, the main character realizes that her grandfather had banned her mother from his house simply because she cut off her long hair without his permission. The last story in the collection, which brings many of the book's characters together in a wedding ceremony, represents hope for a change in gender relations. The happily married newlyweds, who seem to enjoy more equality in their relationship, move into the apartment on Frontera Street that was vacated by a family where the man abused his wife.

Besides gender, *Chasing Shadows* also highlights political differences within Mexican American communities that often intersect with class. More established and often more well-to-do residents in the United States fear the competition of newcomers who are at the bottom of the U.S. socioeconomic ladder. Cookie McDonald, a Mexican immigrant who has lived in the United States for twenty years, exemplifies successful assimilation to U.S. society, despite her initial unlawful entry into the United States. Cookie's undocumented immigration and her subsequent marriage to an Anglo afforded her class mobility from housemaid and peasant in Mexico to homeowner and member of what she believes is the U.S. middle class. In the book's only passage about Mexico, Cookie remembers how her class status in that country was further reinforced by her dark skin. Her story reports on the impossibility of overcoming these class and racial barriers, partially because of the belief in "dañando la sangre"—the possibility that pure aristocratic, European blood traceable to the Spanish colonizers could be damaged by marrying someone of lower class and racial status.

Rather than reject the racially inflected class ideology that oppressed her in Mexico, however, Cookie affirms its U.S. variant. She constantly reminds her daughter of the importance of light skin color and keeps herself apart from the poorer residents of the apartment complex in Frontera Street that she sees from her house on the hill. Cookie even inscribes into space the economic and political divisions between herself and the residents of the apartment building. She asks her husband to put barbed wire around the fence of their own house, "like the taller one at the border," and to plant a hedge so high that she "won't be able to see the street below" (24). As the unnamed narrator of this story asks, "Doesn't she have a right to protect her position?" (19). When approached by a Border Patrol agent, Cookie even agrees to spy on Frontera Street families and to report undocumented border crossings. She is especially interested in Joaquín de la Torre, a cotton field laborer, border rights activist, and poet, who is politically involved with students and migrant workers and helps to bring undocumented people across the desert. His name evokes the figure of Joaquín Murrieta, a colorful early California bandit with Robin Hood charisma who has become a larger-than-life myth. As Guerrero states, this myth "gives people hope and courage."[55] Cookie's diligent reports to the Border Patrol place Joaquín under surveillance. He almost gets arrested on trips across the border, and one night Joaquín does not return home at all.

While his fate remains unclear at the end of the collection, it is intimated that he may have died in the desert at the hands of authorities. His mother has a vision of Joaquín's "death-limp body left on the desert floor, his face so pale it seemed as though his tan were only fading paint, translucent in the glow of the ghostly white moon" (168). While his is another border death conditioned by the intersecting neoliberal and neoconservative forces of border industrialization and militarization, the collection ends on a hopeful note. Flaco Valencia, a longtime friend of Joaquin's, arrives to comfort Joaquín's mother. Throughout the collection, Flaco has shown compassion for members of the community weaker than himself, often at considerable risk. As Flaco comes to speak to Joaquín's mother, "it is as though — for just a moment — all the dreams she passed on to Joaquín return, pulse back into her heart" (175). Perhaps Flaco will continue Joaquin's mission, a form of individualized political activism for border-crossing rights.

The Multiplicities of Border Writing

The texts by Romo, Yañez, and Guerrero move beyond cultural nationalist concerns with questions of Chicana/o identity formation and beyond the more metaphorical use of "borderlands" in works like Anzaldúa's. While *El Puente*, *El Paso del Norte*, and *Chasing Shadows* are not completely free of metaphorical imaginings about the region and continue to favor U.S. towns and their majority populations, they remind us of the spatial nature of borderlands that has become somewhat relegated to the margins of humanities understandings of "borders." *El Puente, El Paso del Norte,* and *Chasing Shadows* experiment with narrative form to explicitly connect Chicana/o communities to changes in Mexican border towns. While Romo emphasizes the environmental consequences of maquiladorization, his work, like that of Yañez and Guerrero, also explores the effects of border militarization on Mexican American communities. These texts fictionalize spatialized divisions among the city's majority populations as mirroring the ongoing military enforcement of la frontera, which draws on and reinforces economic and social differences between residents of Mexico and the United States. The authors depict U.S. border cities as spaces where Chicana/o civil rights struggles may reemerge in the form of individual and collective activism for border-crossing rights and environmental justice that can bridge existing divisions. As twenty-first-century U.S. fronteriza fiction continues the political struggles inherent in cultural nationalist versions of Chicanismo, it moves from a politicized emphasis on identity formation to an interest in the effects of globalization on local places like U.S. border areas.

In its imaginative treatment of the somewhat overlooked connections between Mexican American communities and Mexico-U.S. border developments, the U.S. fronteriza fiction examined in this essay intersects with literature about the national boundary by authors of other ethnic and national backgrounds. Works by Leslie Silko, Karen Tei Yamashita, and Carlos Fuentes, for example, examine neoliberal developments, such as border industrialization, militarization, and immigration, in relationship to Mexican residents, indigenous peoples, Chicanas/os, and Asian Americans.

A focus on the Mexico-U.S. boundary as a distinct geography and site of processes associated with globalization thus also enables the recognition of the border's complex and layered multiethnic character. Some Chicana/o border literature has already paved the way for such connections. For example, Helena María Viramontes's short story "The Cariboo Cafe" (1995) examines the lives of Salvadoran undocumented immigrants in a U.S. border city, Dagoberto Gilb's "Photographs Near a Rolls Royce" (1993) explores the relationships between a Mexican American family and Nicaraguan immigrants in Los Angeles, and Alberto Ríos's *The Curtain of Trees* (1999) references intersections among Mexican contract workers called *enganchados* who worked on railroad lines in the U.S. West alongside Chinese, German, and Irish workers.[56] While Texan and Arizona border towns are in fact dominated by Mexican American communities, other ethnic groups have also inhabited these border spaces: Nogales, for example, was originally called Isaactown after its founder, Jacob Isaacson, a Russian Jew who constructed a small store and warehouse straddling the international boundary. The perspectives articulated in *El Puente, El Paso del Norte,* and *Chasing Shadows* suggest the possibility of more explicitly comparative and transnational approaches that link U.S. boundaries to a wider range of issues and ethnic and national communities than those hitherto imagined in the metaphor of the border.

Notes

I would like to thank Joni Adamson, Claire F. Fox, Elizabeth Horan, and Marta Sánchez for their valuable and insightful comments on this essay.

1 Ito Romo, *El Puente = The Bridge* (Albuquerque: University of New Mexico Press, 2000); Richard Yañez, *El Paso del Norte: Stories on the Border* (Reno: University of Nevada Press, 2003); and Lucretia Guerrero, *Chasing Shadows: Stories* (San Francisco: Chronicle Books, 2000). Subsequent citations are given in parentheses in the text.

2 The conflation of terrorism and undocumented immigration in reference to U.S. borders is manifested in the recent institutional transformation of the Border Patrol. While its primary task had been to police undocumented immigration and drug smuggling at U.S. borders, in March 2003 the Border Patrol became a division of U.S. Customs and Border Protection (CBP). CBP is a unified U.S. border agency within the Department of Homeland Security, whose priority is to prevent terrorists and terrorist weapons from entering the country. See the Border Patrol Web site at www.cbp.gov. For one of many examples of public discourses that conflate Mexican undocumented immigration and Middle Eastern terrorism, see "Who Left the Door Open," *Time,* September 20, 2004, 51–66.

3 Examples of Chicana/o border fiction include Aristeo Brito's *The Devil in Texas = El diablo en Texas,* trans. David William Foster (Tempe: Bilingual Press/Editorial Bilingüe, 1990); Norma Elia Cantú's *Canícula: Snapshots of a Girlhood en la Frontera* (Albuquerque: University of New Mexico Press, 1995); Dagoberto Gilb's *The Magic of Blood* (Albuquerque: University of New Mexico Press, 1993); Rolando Hinojosa's work on Belken County, including *Klail City* (Houston: Arte Público Press, 1987) and *Becky and Her Friends* (Houston: Arte Público Press, 1990); Arturo Islas's novel *Migrant Souls* (New York: Morrow, 1990); Miguel M. Méndez's *Peregrinos de Aztlán/Pilgrims in Aztlán,* trans. David William Foster (Tempe: Bilingual Press/Editorial Bilingüe, 1992); Américo Paredes's *With His Pistol in His Hand* (1958; reprint, Austin: University of Texas Press, 1970); John Rechy's *City of Night* (New York: Grove Press, 1963), Sergio Troncoso's *The Last Tortilla and Other Stories* (Tucson: University of Arizona Press, 1999); and Helene María Viramontes's *Under the Feet of Jesus* (New York: Dutton, 1995) and *The Moths and Other Stories* (Houston: Arte Público Press, 1985). Gilb and Cantú often describe class differences and the political and spatial complexity of Mexican-Chicana/o and Chicana/o–Central American interactions. Gilb's work, for example, addresses in an exploratory sense the impact of border enforce-

ment on Mexican Americans who are stopped by Border Patrol because they "look" suspiciously like an "illegal" and the distrust and economic divisions between Mexican day laborers and Mexican Americans. Cantú, Paredes, Gilb, and Hinojosa have ties to the Texas-Chihuahua border area, while Ríos grew up in Ambos Nogales, along the Arizona-Sonora divide. Viramontes was born and grew up in the extended California–Baja California borderlands of Los Angeles.

4 Mainly active in California, César Chávez's United Farm Workers' Union (UFW) introduced most of the symbols of Chicanismo and the idea of collective land ownership, which it borrowed from the Mexican Revolution. Reies López Tijerina's Alianza Federal de Mercedes (Federal Alliance of Grants) in New Mexico highlighted violations of the 1848 Treaty of Guadalupe Hidalgo, which secured community land grants provided in the seventeenth century to Mexican farmers and villagers. José Angel Gutiérez's Mexican American Youth Organization (MAYO) emphasized community control of institutions and resistance to educational segregation, organizing school boycotts or "blowouts" in California, Colorado, New Mexico, and Texas.

5 Gloria Anzaldúa's *Borderlands/La Frontera: The New Mestiza* (San Francisco: Aunt Lute Books, 1987); Juan Flores, "Latino Studies: New Contexts, New Concepts," in *Critical Latin American and Latino Studies*, ed. Juan Poblete, 191–205 (Minneapolis: University of Minnesota Press, 2003), 198.

6 Joni Adamson stresses that Anzaldúa's *Borderlands/La Frontera* describes the negative effects of the transition from small-scale farming to agribusiness on the physical environment of the border; see Adamson, "Literature-and-Environment Studies and the Influence of the Environmental Justice Movement," in *Blackwell Companion to American Literature and Culture*, ed. Paul Lauter (Oxford: Blackwell, forthcoming). And Terrel Dixon writes that Anzaldúa's work reveals the cultural origin of environmental destruction in the borderlands, which is created to enforce ethnic, economic, and class divisions; see Dixon, "Letter," Contribution to Forum on Literatures of the Environment, *PMLA* 114 (October 1999): 1094.

7 Scott Michaelsen and David E. Johnson were among the first scholars to criticize the Chicana/o narrative of the Southwest as one of property, possession, and genealogy of occupation, where the borderlands are claimed by Chicano culture; see "Border Secrets: An Introduction," in *Border Theory: The Limits of Cultural Politics*, ed. Scott Michaelsen and David E. Johnson, 1–39 (Minneapolis: University of Minnesota Press, 1997), 16.

8 See, e.g., Debra Castillo and Tabuenca Córdoba, *Border Women: Writing from la Frontera* (Minneapolis: University of Minnesota Press, 2002).

9 Saskia Sassen, "Globalization: Developing a Field for Research and Teaching," paper presented at Dartmouth College as part of the conference "Globalization of the Academy," November 15, 2000.

10 See Doreen Massey, *For Space* (London: Sage, 2005), 9–11.

11 Monika Kaup, *Rewriting North American Borders in Chicano and Chicana Narrative* (New York: Peter Lang, 2001), 8.

12 Margot Kelley, "A Minor Revolution: Chicana/o Composite Novels and the Limits of Genre," in *Ethnicity and the American Short Story*, ed. Julie Brown, 63–83 (New York: Garland, 1997), 70.

13 Héctor Calderón and José David Saldívar, eds., *Criticism in the Borderlands: Studies in Chicano Literature, Culture, and Ideology* (Durham, NC: Duke University Press, 1991), 2.

14 The most famous texts located by the Recovering the U.S. Hispanic Literary Heritage project may be the works by María Amparo Ruiz de Burton. Originally published in 1872, *Who Would Have Thought It?* (ed. Rosaura Sánchez and Beatrice Pita [Houston Arte Público Press, 1995]) is now considered the first Mexican American novel written in the English language. Originally published in 1885, *The Squatter and the Don* (ed. Rosaura Sánchez and Beatrice Pita [Houston Arte Público Press, 1992]) is narrated from the perspective of the conquered population of the Southwest and chronicles the subordination and marginalization of that population. See also Jovita Gonzáles, *Dew on the Thorn* (Houston: Arte Público Press, 1997) and Américo Paredes, *George Washington Gómez: A Mexicotexan Novel* (Houston: Arte Público Press, 1990).

15 "*We*, the Chicano inhabitants and civilizers of the northern land of Aztlán from whence came our forefathers, reclaiming the land of their birth and consecrating the determination of our people of the sun, *declare* that the call of our blood is our power, our responsibility, and our inevitable destiny"; see Alurista, "El Plan Espiritual de Aztlán," in *Aztlán: Essays on the Chicano Homeland*, ed. Rudolfo A. Anaya and Francisco A. Lomelí, 1–5 (Albuquerque: Academia/El Norte Publications, 1989), 1.

16 José F. Aranda Jr., *When We Arrive: A New Literary History of Mexican America* (Tucson: University of Arizona Press, 2005), 22.

17 John R. Chávez, "The Image of the Southwest in the Chicano Novel, 1970–1979," *Bilingual Review/La Revista Bilingüe* 14.3 (September–December 1987–88): 41–56.

18 José Aranda, for example, discusses the autobiographies of Richard Rodriguez (*Hunger of Memory*, 1982) and Cherríe Moraga (*Loving in the War Years*, 1983) as precursors to Anzaldúa's critical examination of Chicanismo. He posits that these two works construct a cultural imaginary that confronts the exclusionary practices of the Chicana/o movement even though they identify with many of its aims. See Aranda, *When We Arrive*, 24–33.

19 Kaup, *Rewriting North American Borders*, 12.

20 Anzaldúa, *Borderlands*, 2–3.

21 José Aranda lists several 1990s works of Chicana/o critical theory that have been influenced by Anzaldúa's work, including Héctor Calderón and José David Saldívar's *Criticism in the Borderlands*, Carl Gutiérrez-Jones's *Rethinking the Borderlands: Between Chicano Culture and Legal Discourse* (Berkeley: University of California Press, 1995), José Limón's *Dancing with the Devil: Society and Cultural Poetics in Mexican-American South Texas* (Madison: University of Wisconsin Press, 1994), Rafael Pérez-Torres's *Movements in Chicano Poetry: Against Myths, Against Margins* (Cambridge: Cambridge University Press, 1995), Alvina Quintana's *Home Girls: Chicana Literary Voices* (Philadelphia: Temple University Press, 1996), José David Saldívar's *The Dialectics of Our America* (Durham, NC: Duke University Press, 1991), Ramón Saldívar's *Chicano Narrative: The Dialectics of Difference* (Madison: University of Wisconsin Press, 1990), and Rosaura Sánchez's *Telling Identities: The Californio Testimonios* (Minneapolis: University of Minnesota Press, 1995), 33.

22 Katherine Payant, "Borderland Themes in Sandra Cisneros's *Women Hollering Creek*," in *The Immigrant Experience in North American Literature: Carving Out a Niche*, ed. Kath-

erine B. Payant and Toby Rose, 95–108 (Westport, CT: Greenwood Press, 1999); Sandra Cisneros, *Woman Hollering Creek and Other Stories* (New York: Random House, 1991).

23 Cisneros's most recent novel, *Caramelo or puro cuento* (New York: Knopf, 2002), is also partially set in San Antonio, Texas, where the author now lives.

24 Payant, "Borderland Themes," 95.

25 Kaup, *Rewriting North American Borders*, 11–12.

26 Jesús Benito and Ana María Manzanas, "Borderlands and Border Writing: Introductory Essay," in *Literature and Ethnicity in the Cultural Borderlands*, ed. Benito and Manzanas, 1–21 (Amsterdam: Rodopi, 2002), 3.

27 Pablo Vila has criticized Chicana/o border scholarship for overlooking divisions between Mexican and Mexican American border residents; see Vila, *Crossing Borders, Reinforcing Borders: Social Categories, Metaphors, and Narrative Identities on the U.S.-Mexico Frontier* (Austin: University of Texas Press, 2000), 11. Daniel Cooper-Alarcón and José Aranda have argued that the territorial linkage between Chicanas/os and the Southwest erases the historical record of Native tribes who were harassed, killed, converted to Catholicism, forced into slavery, dispossessed of their tribal lands, and forcibly inducted into European systems of socialization, as well as U.S. Native Americans' nationalist struggles for sovereignty that are based in aboriginal land claims; see Daniel Cooper-Alarcón, *The Aztec Palimpsest: Mexico in the Modern Imagination* (Tucson: University of Arizona Press, 1997), and Aranda, *When We Arrive.* María Socorro Tabuenca Córdoba has posited that the conflation of Chicana/o identity with the Southwest creates "a multicultural space in the United States" (154) that does not recognize the existence of the northern Mexican borderlands; see Tabuenca Córdoba, "Viewing the Border: Perspectives from 'the Open Wound,'" *Discourse* 18.1–2 (Fall/Winter 1995–96): 146–68. Robert McKee Irwin (2001) similarly argues that Chicana/o border scholarship and fiction have given voice to the Chicana/o point of view, while rarely venturing into the Mexican side of the border; see Irwin, "Toward a Border Gnosis of the Borderlands: Joaquín Murrieta and Nineteenth-Century U.S.-Mexico Border Culture," *Nepantla* 2.3 (2001): 509–37.
   Some exceptions do exist. Alberto Ríos's *Pig Cookies*, for example, is set in a northern Mexican border town; see Ríos, *Pig Cookies and Other Stories* (San Francisco: Chronicle Books, 1995).

28 Juan Bruce-Novoa, *RetroSpace: Collected Essays on Chicano Literature, Theory, and History* (Houston: Arte Público Press, 1990).

29 Vila, *Crossing Borders, Reinforcing Borders*, 8.

30 As Castillo and Tabuenca Córdoba have shown (ibid.), centrist Mexican cultural production about the northern borderlands have become more widely read in Mexico and the United States than texts of northern border writers, in part because of the long-standing absence of a literary marketplace in the northern borderlands and the general disinterest in border issues by national institutions, including universities or publishing industries.

31 Henri Lefebvre, *The Production of Space*, trans. Donald Nicholson-Smith (Oxford: Blackwell, 1991), 83.

32 Mary Pat Brady has similarly inserted tenets of cultural geography into discussions of Chicana/o work. She argues in *Extinct Lands, Temporal Geographies: Chicana Literature and the Urgency of Space* (Durham, NC: Duke University Press, 2002), 6, that Chicana/o litera-

ture has from its inception addressed issues of space and of space formation. Brady posits that Chicana/o writing has refused a too-rigid binary between the material and the discursive; it has contested the terms of capitalist spatial formation, especially the use of space to naturalize violent racial, gender, sexual, and class ideologies. While Brady focuses on Chicana/o literature independently of its setting, I am interested in Chicana/o writing that focuses on border spaces and its relationship to theories of cultural geography.

33 *El Puente* has received critical praise from Sandra Cisneros and Helena María Viramontes. In her endorsement on the book jacket Cisneros writes that "the world, according to Romo, is bizarre, troche moche, heartbreaking, rasquache, endlessly romantic, tender and touching. As funny as a fotonovela, triste as a telenovela, and wild as any Fellini." And Viramontes opines that "Romo has created his own bridge between the seeming ordinariness of the women with an extraordinary event, beautifully told. We stand captivated in the presence of full human beings."

34 This demographic information comes from the 2000 census. See laredo.areaconnect .com/statistics.htm (accessed April 18, 2006).

35 Quoted in Angela Becerra, "Bridging the Two Laredos: The Day the River Turned Red," *San Antonio Living*, available at www.woai.com/living/books/story.aspx?content_id=15 AD48F7-7962-4360-B6F7-FB5CBD483796 (accessed August 1, 2005).

36 Maggie Dunn and Ann Morris, *The Composite Novel: The Short Story Cycle in Transition* (New York: Twayne, 1995), 15–16.

37 About the formal experimentation of her first novel, *House on Mango Street*, Cisneros has said that she "wanted to write a series of stories that you could open up at any point. You didn't have to know anything before or after and you would understand each story like a little pearl, or you could look at the whole thing like a necklace" (quoted in Feroza F. Jussawalla and Reed Way Dasenbrock, *Interviews with Writers of the Post-Colonial World* [Jackson: University Press of Mississippi, 1992], 305).

38 Mark Spalding, "Addressing Border Environmental Problems Now and in the Future: Border XXI and Related Efforts," in *The U.S.-Mexican Border Environment: A Road Map to a Sustainable 2020*, ed. Paul Ganster, 105–37 (San Diego: San Diego University Press, 2000), 113.

39 Ibid., 114.

40 Michael Denning, *Culture in the Age of Three Worlds* (London: Verso, 2004), 71; Neil Larsen, "The 'Boom' Novel and the Cold War in Latin America," *Modern Fiction Studies* 38.3 (Autumn 1992): 778.

41 Wendy B. Faris, *Ordinary Enchantments: Magical Realism and the Remystification of Narrative* (Nashville: Vanderbilt University Press, 2004), 1.

42 For examples of recent critical work on magical realism as a global genre, see Wendy B. Faris, ibid., and Frederick Luis Aldama, *Postethnic Narrative Criticism: Magicorealism in Oscar "Zeta" Acosta, Ana Castillo, Julie Dash, Hanif Kureishi, and Salman Rushdie* (Austin: University of Texas Press, 2003). Molly Monet-Viera points to a new wave of "post-boom magical realism" in Latin America, including work by Chilean writer Isabel Allende, Mexican author Laura Esquivel, and Brazilian writer Paulo Coelho, some of which has moved beyond the political commitments central to magical realism; see Monet-Viera, "Post-Boom Magical Realism: Appropriations and Transformations of a Genre," *Revista*

de Estudios Hispanicos 38.1 (January 2004): 95–117. Michael Valdez Moses has argued that because it is written for readers in the first world by cosmopolitan writers, contemporary magical realism allows an imaginary return to a premodern organic virtual community without the danger of having to assume its burdens that are past or passing away; see Valdez Moses, "Magical Realism at World's End," *Literary Imagination* 3.1 (Winter 2001): 106. Michael Denning similarly writes that the new label "world literature" serves as "a marketing device that flattens distinct regional and linguistic traditions into a worldbeat, with magical realism serving as the aesthetic of globalization" (*Culture in the Age of Three Worlds*, 51). I would argue that a discussion of this experimental strategy in relationship to *El Puente* points to significant differences among contemporary cultural productions that utilize this aesthetics. I doubt that all representations employing magical realism can be discussed as expressions of globalization that have moved beyond the political commitments of 1960s "boom" literature.

43 David Harvey, *The New Imperialism* (Oxford: Oxford University Press, 2003).

44 For accounts of border militarization and their effects, see, for example, Peter Andreas, *Border Games: Policing the U.S.-Mexico Divide* (Ithaca, NY: Cornell University Press, 2000); Timothy J. Dunn, *The Militarization of the U.S.-Mexico Border, 1978–1992: Low-Intensity Conflict Doctrine Comes Home* (Austin: CMAS Books, 1996); and Joseph Nevins, *Operation Gatekeeper: The Rise of the "Illegal Alien" and the Making of the U.S.-Mexico Boundary* (New York: Routledge, 2002).

45 The leading cause of death for undocumented immigrants in the mid-1980s was drowning (mostly in the Rio Grande), while in the late 1980s it became homicide and auto-pedestrian accidents; see Karl Eschbach, Jacqueline Hagan, and Nestor Rodriguez, "Deaths during Undocumented Migration: Trends and Policy Implications in the New Era of Homeland Security," *Defense of the Alien* 26 (2003): 11–12, 14. But since urban places like San Diego and El Paso have become nearly sealed, undocumented immigrants have been forced to try to cross the desert terrain of southern Arizona. The Border Patrol, which counts only bodies that it processes, reported a record 172 deaths in fiscal 2004 at the Arizona border, a tenfold increase over the last decade; see, for example, www.maryknollogc.org/ecojustice/hilldrop070505.pdf (accessed April 19, 2006). According to Eschbach, Hagan, and Rodriguez, the INS hoped that by closing of relatively easy terrains to migrants, the difficult terrain of the desert would act as an additional deterrent to migration, discouraging migrants from even attempting the journey because of additional physical difficulty ("Deaths during Undocumented Migration," 5). Incidents where undocumented migrants are shot by the Border Patrol also happen. Juan Patricio Peraza Quijada, a nineteen-year-old immigrant from Mexicali, Baja California, was shot to death in El Paso by Border Patrol agents in 2003. In 1992, the Border Patrol in Nogales mistakenly shot and killed Dario Miranda Valenzuela, a twenty-six-year-old resident of Nogales, Sonora. In 1998, a U.S. Marine in Redford, Texas, accidentally shot eighteen-year-old Esequiel Hernandez, who became the first U.S. civilian killed by a U.S. Marine on U.S. soil. While accidental or targeted deaths of Border Patrol agents also occur, I have been unable to obtain statistics about the extent of these deaths.

46 Mario T. García, *Desert Immigrants: The Mexicans of El Paso, 1880–1920* (New Haven, CT: Yale University Press, 1981), 235.

47 David Simcox, "Growth without Prosperity Plagues the Borderlands," *Forum for Applied Research and Public Policy* 10 (1995): 80–83.

48 This demographic data is from the 2000 census. See www.elpasotexas.gov/demographics .asp and www.dallasfed.org/research/busfront/bus0102.html (accessed April 19, 2006).

49 Raymond A. Rocco, "Latino Los Angeles: Reframing Boundaries/Borders," in *The City: Los Angeles and Urban Theory at the End of the Twentieth Century*, ed. Allen J. Scott and Edward W. Soja, 365–89 (Berkeley: University of California Press, 1998).

50 Wendy Caldwell, "Narrating the Border: An Interview with Lucrecia Guerrero," *South Carolina Modern Language Review* 2.1 (Spring 2004), available at http://alpha1.fmarion .edu/~scmlr/V3/newvoice.htm (accessed October 5, 2005).

51 Nevins, *Operation Gatekeeper*, 45.

52 These are figures from the 2000 Census. See Nogales Arizona Population and Demographics Resources at nogales.areaconnect.com/statistics.htm and en.wikipedia.org/ wiki/Nogales,_Sonora (accessed April 19, 2006).

53 Caldwell, "Narrating the Border."

54 Arthur Ramírez, "Feminist Neo-Indigenism in Chicana Aztlán," *Studies in American Literature* 7.4 (Winter 1995): 71–78.

55 Caldwell, "Narrating the Border."

56 Viramontes, *The Moth and Other Stories* and *Under the Feet of Jesus*; Gilb, *The Magic of Blood*; and Alberto Ríos, *Capirotada: A Nogales Memoir* (Albuquerque: University of New Mexico Press, 1999), *The Curtain of Trees: Stories* (Albuquerque: University of New Mexico Press, 1999), and *Pig Cookies*.

Alejandro Lugo

Photo Essay: *Cruces*

These photographs of the El Paso–Ciudad Juárez borderlands—my own native homeland—were taken between 2000 and 2005. The photographic essay pushes writings on border theory and border crossings in a new direction through the visual analysis of the transnational experiences of working-class Mexican people. The ethnographic photographs, which are part of a larger series, capture both everyday life and everyday death through images of *cruces* (in Spanish, this term means both "crosses," *las cruces*, in its feminine plural form, and "crossings," *los cruces*, in its masculine plural form). These *cruces* bring together such critical social domains as religion and political economy, gender and death, and class inequality and vulnerability, at material sites of intersection—the international border crossing, the streets of Juárez, religious pilgrimages inspected by Border Patrol officials, and the crossroads where Mexican men, women, and children have died and continue to die.

This essay constitutes an attempt to let certain images challenge and speak to the viewer through her or his own assumptions about the U.S.-Mexican border. I produced these photos

South Atlantic Quarterly 105:4, Fall 2006
DOI 10.1215/00382876-2006-005   © 2006 Duke University Press

Puente "libre" ("free" bridge) between Juárez and El Paso

Observers observed: Nobody is illegal

Pilgrimage on Cristo Rey mountain, located in Sunland Park, New Mexico, which borders both El Paso and Juárez.

Mexican roses in Juárez cemetery

Black Crosses on Pink and Mujeres de Negro protesting killings of women

Ni Una Mas protest at El Paso del Norte bridge

Dead paisanos on Paisano Street in El Paso

Juárez is burning: Life and death at the Mercado Cuauhtémoc

through my own personal and academic gaze in order to articulate a call—a call to accept the *cruz*, or *viacrucis*, to actively fight against social injustices wherever they exist. Ultimately, I argue through the photos that in the twenty-first century, the struggle of the Mexican working classes continues on both sides of the border. As long as the social, political, and economic structures of inequality are not fundamentally and democratically transformed, millions of Mexicans will continue *cargando la cruz* (carrying the cross), unfairly and unnecessarily.

I would especially like to thank Jane Juffer for inviting me to participate in this volume. I have presented the complete photo series in three different arenas: At the University of Illinois at Urbana-Champaign, colleagues in the Sociology Transnational Workshop Conference and Mexican parents during the Latino Parents Visit Day provided me with productive suggestions and enthusiastic commentary. At New Mexico State in Las Cruces, the Center for Border and Latin American Studies and the Department of Sociology and Anthropology gave me a space to try my idea of *cruces* on them at a time when the use of crosses as the city's symbol was being legally challenged. More specifically, I would like to thank several individuals for their intellectual support. In Urbana-Champaign: Aide Acosta, Cathy Acevedo, Zsuzsa Gille, Veronica Kann, Winifred Poster, Alicia Rodriguez, Dorothee Schneider, and Angharad Valdivia; in Las Cruces: Elea Aguirre, Cynthia Bejarano, Neil Harvey, Molly Molloy, J. Paul Taylor, Louise Stanford, and Wenda Trevathan.

Arturo Dávila

The Immigrant Song

> Weeping, weeping multitudes
> Droop in a hundred A.B.C.'s
> —T. S. Eliot

I

We took the long road to the city
searching for our men
with children on hunched backs
lonesome eyes and empty beds.
The men were promised a new land
and so they came.
We are still looking for them
in vain.

I remember:
Ivory sand under our feet,
Dusty trees bowing over the silvery riverside,
the vulture's funerary circling in the air.
The air was blue against the moon
so was blue the sadness in our room.

Silent sleepy streams gliding brightly.
In the deep night
        they departed
Grief by grief, sigh by sigh
        They departed . . .

South Atlantic Quarterly 105:4, Fall 2006
DOI 10.1215/00382876-2006-011 © 2006 Duke University Press

Gentle women:
do not sleep too deeply,
keep an eye on the stars
and receive the shadows of their smile.

II

The knife, the throat, the night,
the blues, the boys, the cries,
                    our lives.
The voice, the wall, the void,
the roads, the hoes, the lash,
                    Our death.

III

Walking long alleys in the asphalt valley
Looking for our men
In the mirror of timeless streets
and smoky ceilings full of clouds.
They say we come here to disturb their peace
with dark swarthy clay on our feet
and a nauseous-barbarous smell:
to stain the polished streets
where trimmed ladies walk at ease
with golden jewels and fancy skirts
meeting their men to fornicate
without delay
in lusty hotels.

IV

The dreams in our fields
the dreams in your streets
            are not clear.
The drops inside the rain
the tears inside the walls
            are not clear.

The dreams inside the dream
      are not clear.
and
we took the long road here . . .

Ana Maria Manzanas Calvo

Contested Passages:
Migrants Crossing the Río Grande
and the Mediterranean Sea

Moroccan journalist Rachid Nini claims in
Diario de un ilegal (*An Illegal's Journal*) that the
Mediterranean Sea never loses its temper,[1] but
the calm waters of this narrow strip separating
Spain from the northern coast of Africa are one
of the most deadly international borders; more
so, in fact, than the line separating the United
States from Mexico.

The news makes the headlines almost every
morning: a *patera* has been intercepted in the
Mediterranean Sea or the Atlantic Ocean; some
of the travelers manage to reach the Spanish side,
some are engulfed in the treacherous waters. The
patera, the fragile, half-rotten boat frequently
used for the crossing, is about six meters long
and three meters wide. Made of low-quality
planks and put together at the very last minute
(and often in the desert) to avoid detection, the
patera is the disposable means for reaching the
other side. Usually it is filled up with passengers
to make the trip profitable. Few of its occupants can swim, and none can sail.[2] Between
six hundred and a thousand migrants drown
every year, according to statistics.[3] This strait
varies with tides and clear nights; it becomes
slightly thinner in the summer and widens in

South Atlantic Quarterly 105:4, Fall 2006
DOI 10.1215/00382876-2006-008   © 2006 Duke University Press

the winter. Yet the border becomes wider and wider as new waves of immigrants choose the Canary Islands as their destination in order to avoid the heavily policed beaches of southern Spain. Consequently, the trip has turned more perilous. Gone are the Mediterranean ride and the five-hour crossing. Now immigrants have to negotiate the perilous waters of the Atlantic and about twenty hours of uncertainty.[4]

The strait and Atlantic journeys have become two versions of Spain's Río Grande, the last and most dangerous obstacle between the third and first worlds.[5] There are more parallels as well: The crossing of the U.S.-Mexican border finds a direct counterpart in the night assaults on the recently reinforced double fence separating Ceuta and Melilla, two autonomous Spanish cities in North Africa, from Morocco. Although the barbed-wire boundary has been raised to six meters, night after night the migrants try to break the fence at both its highest and lowest stretches, thus undermining the attempts of Spanish police to contain the hundreds of Africans trying to enter Spanish territory. The different strands of the comparison capture some of the aspects I would like to address in this essay: They identify an unstoppable process whereby waves of migrants are crossing into different versions of the promised land in order to realize the American/European Dream; they also point to migratory flows which, coming from the South, redefine and challenge the contours of the host countries. Interestingly, these migration patterns from the South repeat and revisit previous historical tracks and presences in both the United States and Spain.

As markers of "spatial historicities,"[6] both national borders mark the two nations' spatial and temporal limits, preferably closed and finished, but they also encapsulate and delimit national narrations. For the border is not concerned only with space; it is not only a spatial line but also a temporal boundary that graphically represents and actualizes the flow and the progression of history.[7] History has traditionally established and consolidated geographical, religious, cultural, and economic borders. The resulting boundaries have not only acted as lines differentiating nations and identities but have also established a hierarchy within difference. East has been set up against West; North against South,[8] the present as opposed to the past. Significantly, in the case of the United States and Spain, neither country has perceived any "upgrading" of national identity by claiming proximity to a third-world country to the south.[9] The southern borders in the United States and Spain may actually function as a bastion against a common history and the threat of a "downgrading" of national identity. The need to reinforce the southern boundary also signals to what extent so-called "civilization" needs to defend itself from that history, barbaric and regressive, which threatens to engulf progress.

Contested Passages

Both the U.S.-Mexican border and the Spanish-African strait are supposed to be impenetrable separations between first and third worlds, between the American Dream and what Rubén Martínez calls a "Mexican Manifest Destiny" that expects to be realized on American streets paved with gold.[10] Similarly, the strait separating Spain from Africa is, for contemporary Moroccan writer Mahi Binebine, "the abyss of the world,"[11] the most dangerous obstacle separating a dilapidated continent from a European Dream produced and reproduced by television images. The "abyss" is especially revealing in economic terms, for Spanish salaries are twelve times higher than Moroccan ones, and the difference becomes more acute if we compare Spain with the vast majority of West Africa.[12] Alfred Arteaga's description of the U.S. border as an infinitely thin line that supposedly differentiates the haves from the have-nots, those who are supposedly legitimately rich from those who are (also rightfully) poor of their own accord,[13] seems especially apt for the description of the Spanish-African border. Further, and despite the cultural and historical specificities,[14] it is possible to argue that both lines illustrate a paradoxical double desire on the part of the host countries: The desire for a sealed border that instills confidence in national definition and national identity is simultaneous to the desire for a cheap and submissive workforce, which has boosted agricultural economies in both countries. In both cases, the roots of the desire to migrate, so often questioned by the citizens of the host countries, are no mystery. Mexican migrants express their despair in these terms: "Prefiero morir que seguir con la miseria que tengo allí."[15] Africans voice their predicament in similar words: "Prefiero estar encerrado en una habitación, en una cárcel en Europa, donde una vez al día me traerán comida, que seguir viviendo en África, y sobre todo en Marruecos. Esto es el infierno y Europa sera el paraíso."[16]

Both the U.S.-Mexican border and the line between Spain and North Africa represent specific historical and spatial markers that go beyond the notion of the geographical line, for these southern borders are intrinsically different from other international boundaries. America's 4,000-mile-long border with Canada is basically defended by a couple of fire trucks, and, at

least until 9/11, it was commonly agreed that was sufficient; the southern
border, though half as long, has the equivalent of an army division patrolling
it, and many U.S. citizens think it should be watched and patrolled more
closely.[17] A similar difference can be perceived in the borders that separate
Spain from Portugal and France, on the one hand, and from Africa, on the
other. While the European Union has favored the dismantling of boundaries among its members, it has also reinforced the policing of the thin line
that divides the continent from Africa through the signing of the Schengen
Agreement in 1991. In a way, Spain has become a faulty and porous "Great
Wall of Europe," the boundary that separates countries but also the locus
that defines and secures the integrity of a continent against other mores,
cultures, and economies. Only a closed line with the poorer, alien neighbor
can presumably secure a fixed, stable, and finished identity.

   There are also similarities in what we can call "border dynamics." Both
boundaries are heavily traversed; they have their own coyotes and inter-
mediaries in charge of recruiting new migrants, as well as a series of codes
that have to be carefully observed before initiating the journey. Like a rite
of initiation with no return, the crossing starts in Tangier or Tetuan on the
African coast, or at busy bus stations in Mexico. But the journey as a whole
may start much farther south, in countries such as Mali, Nigeria, or Sene-
gal, or in Honduras, Guatemala, or El Salvador. Africans may walk through
the continent for a couple of years before they reach Morocco and find themselves at the gate of Europe. The money paid for the passage on the African
route varies radically depending on the kind of boat or the shade of one's
skin—racism in misery, as Alí Lmrabet calls it[18]—but it often requires the
passenger's (and his or her family's) life savings; a different sum is charged
for braving military positions on the coast.[19] On the Mexican side, things
are no easier. If you can't pass as *tijuanense*, Luis Alberto Urrea writes, you
are singled out automatically: Salvadorans and Guatemalans are regularly
beaten up, while Indians are insulted and pushed around.[20] Deception is
frequent on both routes. On the Mexican American migration trail, abusive coyotes can use crossers as slaves and can traffic them as indentured
servants.[21] Sub-Saharan Africans may be returned to deserted beaches in
Tangier and told they are now in Spain. An insidious scheme came out into
the open in June 2005: It became clear that coyotes had sent out two *pateras*,
one of which was filled with sub-Saharans as a red herring to attract the
attention of the authorities. When this boat shipwrecked right after departure, some of the passengers managed to swim back to the beach, but most

of the women who were traveling with children had a tragic end. The other *patera*, which was regularly furnished, managed to go undetected in the middle of the tragedy.[22] In 2001 the Red Cross revealed that the mafias operating in the Strait region give crossers vouchers that are valid for a number of attempts.[23] The trip on the *patera* itself harbors unexpected dangers: If a component of the engine gas gets in contact with the salty water deposited in the boat, the deadly chemical reaction may burn the occupants' lungs.[24]

Despite of the dangers, though, 75 percent of Moroccans are ready to leave their country, writes Lmrabet.[25] Every day more than 800,000 people legally cross the border between Mexico and the United States, not to count the 4,600 or so who hop the fence and get caught almost right away.[26] Spanish and especially Andalusian TV stations show the bodies of Africans washed up on Spanish southern shores or on the Canary Islands almost daily. Luckier ones struggle to get ashore, barefoot, disoriented, and cold. Interestingly, there are Good Samaritan figures on each route. Father Luiz Kendzienski, originally from Brazil, runs *la casa el emigrante* in Tijuana, as if to counteract the effect of Operation Gatekeeper.[27] A volunteer group called Humane Borders erects emergency watering stations in the Sonoran Desert to help crossers on their way north. Father Robert Carney, a priest in Douglass, Arizona, holds prayer vigils at border-crossing points and often goes out into the desert to offer migrants toiletry kits and water bottles. Another important figure on this route is Reverend John Fife, an activist in Tucson, who harbors immigrants in his Presbyterian church.[28] These figures have their counterparts on the African route to Spain: The Franciscan Isidoro Macías, better known as "Padre Pateras," has run a sanctuary for African women since five Nigerian women arrived at the refuge in 1999.[29] There are other anonymous Good Samaritans who aid immigrants in southern Spain, where the citizens have organized networks to protect immigrants from police detection. Part of that invisible organization is another priest, Father Andrés Avelino, who gives newcomers sanctuary in his church in the coastal city of Algcciras.[30]

The uncertainties as to the outcome of the voyage itself remain in both crossings, more so with the current process of "widening" the border, as policies are enforced in order to deter migrants. The new waves of migrants prefer the less policed, longer route to the Canary Islands from the western coast of the Sahara Desert; consequently, the trip is becoming costlier and increasingly dangerous. Due to the almost daily assaults on the double fence separating Ceuta and Melilla from Morocco, Spanish authorities have announced the construction of yet another palisade, which will stitch metals bars together around the perimeter of the exterior barbed wire fence.[31] The U.S.-Mexican border has also widened dramatically in the last decade. After the interdiction efforts of Operation Gatekeeper, Operation Safeguard, and Operation Hold the Line, coyotes have chosen more circuitous routes, and the Border Patrol is aware of the increasing risks.[32] Thus, the Border Patrol has achieved its goal of shifting migrating routes away from urban areas by herding crossers into inhospitable areas such as deserts and rivers.[33] The vigilante groups figure prominently as the last addition to a widening boundary. In their reinforcement of the border, these volunteers, many of whom are recruited over the Internet, plan to watch the border and report illegal crossings to federal agents.[34] Some of the members of these groups are armed and have availed themselves of the latest detection devices.[35] As a direct consequence of the increase and implementation of control strategies since 1993, coyotes have raised the cost of illegal entry, and the fees charged have doubled or quadrupled depending on the route and the services offered.[36] One consequence of this "widening" of the border is the increase in the number of migrants who die while trying to gain entry in Spain and the United States (669). Yet the question remains, How thick must the border be to contain "the Other"? Or, to put it another way, how many fences or double or triple palisades are necessary to deter "illegal" migration? What is the next border going to protect and secure? If the physical integrity of the nation is at stake in the act of transgressing its limits, so is its national narration and definition.

Fences protect from physical transgression but also from what is deemed as a forsaken national definition. If the United States has always cultivated the myth of an inviting and boundless Garden of Eden that transforms settlers/immigrants into Americans, Spain has its own history as an exporter rather than an importer of immigrants. About 3.5 million Spaniards left for the Americas between 1850 and 1950. From the 1950s through the 1970s, almost 75 percent of the migrants chose Northern Europe as a destination, a migration facilitated by the guest workers' programs in France, Germany, and Switzerland,[37] yet Spaniards appear amnesic and unaware of the pain of migration. Like the new generations, they feel no shame when, on seeing an African-looking person, they exclaim: "The Moors are back."[38] This phrase captures the paradoxical nature of historical memory. Spaniards cannot remember they provided a stable reservoir of cheap labor to Europe before the Civil War, as well as waves of political exiles when the insurgent General Franco secured the so-called "national" victory. Yet the image of the Moor, defeated and expelled in 1492, remains a (traumatic) part of the national consciousness.

These two migratory flows from the South thus connect the United States and Spain with their respective histories. Mexico and the United States, on one side, and Morocco and Spain, on the other, share a common past in which cultural, linguistic, national, and racial borders are blurred: Mexicans lived in the Southwest of the United States and claim that territory as part of the mythic Aztlán; Africans lived in Spain for eight centuries and secured a stronghold on the southern part of the country, what they called Al-Andalus. Aztlán and Al-Andalus thus provide the imaginaries of Mexicans and North Africans with a historical and mythic referent that constantly conjures the inextricable presence of Mexico in the United States and of Africa in Europe.[39] If Europe mapped out Africa through colonialism, it is possible to argue that "Africa has been in Europe as much as Europe has been in Africa, and still is."[40] Notwithstanding this common past, historical narratives in the United States and in Spain have always revealed a desire for erasing the migration tracks (both narrative and physical) between countries and continents, especially when the past bears witness to incursions into spaces that are now deemed sovereign. This past explains in part why, to some, Mexican immigrants represent the possibility of a "reconquest of the American Southwest."[41]

Similarly, the contemporary crossing of Africans into Spanish soil may bring echoes of a second *reconquista*. As the migrants cross the border, they go through what Mary Pat Brady calls an "abjection machine" that metamorphoses them into something else, into "aliens," "illegals," "wetbacks," or "undocumented," and renders them "unintelligible (and unintelligent), ontologically impossible, outside the real and the human."[42] At the same time, it seems possible to argue that the border makes them historically abject, as it automatically historicizes Mexicans and Africans into the descendants of the "conquering aliens." The image of the conquering Moor is especially present in the Spanish imaginary, as Rachid Nini experiences in his wanderings as an "illegal" worker. In jest, Nini tells one of his coworkers at a pizza restaurant that Africans are coming back. They do not form an army now, have no leader, but are part of a silent invasion. Centuries after the expulsion, Africans are returning only to drown in the sea, as Nini reflects in his journal. According to the images TV disseminates day after day, Morocco appears as a fleet of never-ending *pateras* and desperate youths who would rather die than return to their country. This is the image Spaniards find disquieting. Nini argues, though, that it is a non-stop diaspora. The Jew is not wandering anymore; he has stopped doing so, and now the time of the "wandering Arabs" has started.[43] Immigrants, as Nini explains in an interview and as we can witness every day, will never stop coming. All of them share a goal: to reach Spain. Whatever happens on arrival does not matter; that's open to all kinds of possible imaginings. Potential immigrants know that there are many who return in better condition than when they left.[44] These "wandering Arabs" make up a new class of mobile proletariat who cross new versions of middle passages in search for new opportunities. Like the Mexicans crossing into the United States, Africans will cross as long as there are jobs, their shot at a better future. Just like the Mexican families Rubén Martínez traces in the United States, Africans will keep on coming because for them too, ideas of paradise die hard.[45]

It is this repeating narrative of the past that needs to be neutralized with repeating physical borders. As the outer line of a nation and a national narrative, the border needs be closed not only physically but also ideologically. The border is thus the locus that defines and secures the integrity of a nation. Only a closed border can presumably secure a fixed, stable, and finished national identity. This vision of the closed border/nation bears some resemblance to the concept of the classical body as expressed by Mikhail Bakhtin in *Rabelais and His World*.[46] It is possible to extrapolate Bakhtin's elaboration of the open/closed body to the exploration of the nation and national identity. Bakhtin distinguishes between the classical body/nation, which stands as an image of completeness, and the grotesque body/nation, which is "unfinished, outgrows itself, transgresses its own limits."[47] The grotesque body, we read, "is a body in the act of becoming. It is never finished, never completed" (317). Whereas the classical body is sealed from outer influences, the grotesque is permeable and "stresses elements common to the entire cosmos" (318). Classical univocality thus contrasts with grotesque duality. Bakhtin's descriptions of the classical versus grotesque body have a suggestive applicability to the nation inasmuch as the apertures of the body can be extrapolated to the parts of the nation that are open to the outside world and allow transit. The border can be seen as a sharp line of demarcation that guards and protects an entirely finished and complete nation, but also as a porous line "through which the world enters the body or emerges from it, or through which the body itself goes out to meet the world" (26). As an open wound in the body/nation, to use Anzaldúa's terminology, the border has to be carefully watched because it needs constant care, reinforcing, and mending. This desire for closure or for the finished quality of the classical body/nation is clear in Carlos Fuentes's *La frontera de cristal*.[48] Fuentes describes the U.S.-Mexican border as an artificial line of porous contours always in the process of being both re-created and transgressed. In an illustration of Alfred Arteaga's arguments in *Chicano Poetics*, Fuentes shows how the U.S.-Mexican border instills confidence in national definition and national identity.[49] The United States may dislike illegal immigrants, but it needs them in order to create itself as a nation and to feel good about itself, as a border patroller admits in one of the tales: "Detestaba a los indocumentados. Pero los adoraba y los necesitaba. Sin ellos, maldita sea, no habría presupuesto para helicópteros, radar, poderosas luces infrarrojas nocturnas, bazucas, pistolas. . . . Que vengan. . . . Que sigan viniendo por millones, rogó, para darle sentido a mi vida. Tenemos que seguir siendo víctimas inocentes."[50] Paradoxically, the border requires border-crossers in order to perpetuate itself as a "nontransgressable" zone. The desire for a finished body/nation is therefore rendered impossible, since this image of completion and perfection is contingent and dependent on the arrival of newcomers and border-crossers.

At the border, cutting-edge technology represses the transgressors. Democracies loosen up, and the border becomes the paradigmatic site where the workings of the defensive nation are realized. If, following Eduardo Galeano's argument, we assume that "in the outskirts of the world the system reveals its true face,"[51] it seems possible to maintain that the border is the outskirts of the world, where the systems that fortify the notions of nationality and national identity are truly revealed. In the different versions of the border separating the United States from Mexico, the system reveals its true policed nature; likewise, at the double, three- to six-meter-high fence separating the two Spanish cities in North Africa from the rest of the continent, the European Dream of a solid and prosperous Europe reveals its true values.[52] "El Estrecho," the Strait separating Spain from Africa, was once described by Paul Bowles as "the center of the universe";[53] today it has become a tragic fracture. Yet there are not only external borders; what migrants encounter in the United States and Spain are just myriads of actual lines that have little to do with his or her alleged rebirth into the symbolic figure of contemporary dislocation.

"Mexicans/Africans are taking our jobs"

O Yes? Do they come on horses
with rifles, and say,
                    Ese Gringo, gimmee your job?
And do you gringo, take off your ring,
drop your wallet into a blanket
spread over the ground, and walk away?
— Jimmy Santiago Baca, "So Mexicans Are Taking Jobs from
    Americans"

Baca's poem plays on the stock image of Mexican *banditi* to undermine the solidness of the well-known refrain. "So Mexicans Are Taking Jobs from Americans" presents the vacuity of what seems a universally accepted proposition that transforms Mexicans into an alien, looting force. What Baca offers instead is the result of his search: These Mexican fighters are nowhere to be seen; the only rifles to be heard are those of white farmers "shooting blacks and browns."[54] What he also sees is just the poor "marching for a little work" (139) and "trying to cross poverty to just having something" (139). This crossing frequently translates into the crossing of an elusive border of multiple nuances and inner folds. What the migrants encounter on the other side, then, hardly resembles a mythic homecoming to Aztlán or Al-Andalus. The image of the crosser who encounters a postmodern border cannot be accommodated to the inhabitant of the borderlands as a space of infinite creative potential. Instead of the contact zone, to use Mary Louise Pratt's term,[55] what migrants frequently confront is rather what Walter Mignolo has renamed as a battlefield[56] that calls into question different manifestations of utopian border thinking. Rubén Martínez has explained that Mexicans have always had an uncanny instinct for finding the soft spots of the American labor economy. Like communicating vessels, the Mexican and U.S. economies supplement each other; however, immigration policies collide with necessities. Wherever there are jobs in low-skill, low-wage industries, sooner or later Mexicans will be there. The latest wave of immigration Martínez describes works on meatpacking plants in Wisconsin, tend tomatoes in Missouri, bear the suffocating heat in greenhouse nurseries, or pick tobacco in North Carolina. As Martínez sums it up, "There is no supply of manual labor other than the Mexicans, not only for farming but increasingly for other labor-intensive industries such as meatpacking, textiles, and the bottom rungs of the service sector: hotel and restaurant help."[57] As for the future of this labor force, Martínez offers a lucid analysis:

> The immigrant class serves the white middle class and that is not likely to change anytime soon. It is important that this generation of migrants win dignity and respect, but the real question is what opportunities migrant children . . . will have when [they] enter the workforce. . . . . Mexicans from earlier waves of migration have seen their children mostly remain in the barrio, educated in inferior schools, vulnerable to gangs and drugs, the fate of people who have no future, of families who have no mobility. (300)

The "usefulness" of the migrants is at the core of what we can call "border narratives" such as Helena Viramontes's "The Cariboo Cafe" and *Under the Feet of Jesus*. Viramontes's novel provides a key image for the understanding of the role of so-called "illegals" in contemporary societies. As one of the workers at the camp explains to Estrella, Viramontes's protagonist, "Millions of years ago, the dead animals and plants fell to the bottom of the sea"[58] and made oil. The gradual unpacking of the fuel metaphor constitutes Estrella's realization of her role and her value as a migrant worker, as well as her awareness of the dynamics of economic exploitation on the fields. As Viramontes's young protagonist dissects the metaphor, she realizes that "it was their bones that kept the air conditioning in the cars humming, that kept them moving on the long dotted line on the map. Their bones" (148). The trope is a crucial one in that it introduces what Pat Mora terms "the principle of permutation," that is, the process through which one thing is transformed into another; at the same time, fuel provides an apt metaphor for the situation of migrant workers in an exploitative society.[59]

A similar illustration of the principle of permutation, whereby the toil and the work of the migrants is transformed into the sap that keeps the social and economic fabric moving, is found in the case of North African workers in Spain. In the last two decades, African migrants have consolidated the agricultural economies of southern Spanish provinces such as Almería and the Southeast, as Nini narrates in his journal. Like Mexican workers in the United States, Africans have found two of the soft spots of Spanish economy: construction and agriculture. The province of Almería has been aptly described as a sea of plastic, an uncanny mixture of desert and greenhouses, where the workers endure suffocating heat as well as the side effects of illegal work. To put it simply, as Martínez explained when tracing the Mexican presence in the United States, these Africans are the only available manual laborers. The working conditions are extreme: Workers have no National Health Service coverage, work long hours, and are housed in subhuman conditions in huts or labor camps. Frequently, the employer offers housing but charges a fortune for the services provided. Even if they are needed in the greenhouses (since no Spaniard would accept that kind of job), Africans are not wanted outside the greenhouse.[60] Being outside the greenhouse simply means enjoying benefits and being registered to vote.

A decade of exploitation and de facto segregation exploded in El Ejido, a small town in the province of Almería, on February 6, 2000: A young woman was allegedly killed by a deranged Moroccan worker, and pent-up racial hatred burst out. Locals vandalized or torched stores and businesses run by Africans; cars with African passengers were stopped and overturned; a local organization that aids the migrants was vandalized; reporters were driven out of town; and Africans had to flee and take refuge in the nearby hills. After a week of striking to protest the attacks, Africans returned to the greenhouses. With their strike, Africans protested the passivity and the connivance of both the inhabitants of El Ejido and the police[61] during the outbreak of violence. They also demonstrated how vital their labor was and how the economy of the agricultural business depended on their exploitation. Labor peace is easier to achieve, though, than social integration is. Surprisingly, as an editorial of *El País* argued, Spain, which has for decades supplied Europe and South America with a steady influx of migrants, does not seem culturally ready to accept the migrants who are currently fleeing from hunger and oppression in other parts of the world. Moreover, the structural mechanisms and the policies that should have been implemented have either failed or have not been created. Immigration, concluded the editorial, has been dealt with as if it were more a problem than a reality.[62] The anti-immigrant violence in El Ejido illustrates how a problematic cultural, linguistic, and economic contact zone becomes more of a battlefield.

There are myriads of lines and fences within the battlefield. Without offering instances of violence between the two communities, in his journal Nini further explores and dissects the border of distrust—what he calls "a psychological block"[63]—that separates Spaniards from North Africans. According to the widespread stereotype, the Moor is always suspicious, always dishonest, always a Moor. No matter what their regional or national differences, individuals are going to be reconstructed as the impersonation of the Moor/*el moro*, the Other associated with social problems, hash, crime in its different forms, and, especially since the attacks of September 11, March 11, and July 7, terrorism. One would say that Spaniards construct this "devalued" Other because they do not know the real African. The problem is that interaction hardly changes that static narrative of the Other.[64] Nini provides an excellent example in the way Merche, one of his coworkers at the orange fields, fantasizes about the idea of the African as predator. Merche told the narrator and the other workers that sometimes she fantasized that they killed her, or stole her car, and then made a getaway. "Moors are capable of anything,"[65] she says, laughing. Since reality does not conform to the stereotype, Merche indulges in reverie, in what reality should really be like in order to adapt to the static narrative construction of the Moor. Presented in this oblique way, the stereotype loses all its consistency and becomes a mirror reflecting the speaker, whose thirst for the stereotype is frustrated. The potential for stealing, for performing this "anything," with its overtones of destruction and looting, is precisely what the journal defies: There are no rapes and no sexual abuses; there are no Africans taking jobs from Spaniards, to rephrase Baca's poem. What Merche and the reader find is a group of men trying to work under the most adverse circumstances. Like Viramontes's characters, these workers are part of the "tar pit" which produces the fuel that keeps American and Spanish economies running. They are an essential part of the permutational system that transforms physical toil into the commodities of a consumer society that increasingly relies on cheap, flexible, and so-called "illegal" work. Yet there is no Garden of Eden waiting as payment for all the work; or, to put it another way, there is no green card in exchange for working in the greenhouse.

Permutational Dynamics, Hybrid Nations

When we talk about "crossing borders," then, we need to supplement this process with a simultaneous one: the reinforcing of boundaries, physical, discursive, and historical, that the migrant encounters in the host country.[66] If the space of the borderlands does not necessarily reveal itself as the space of infinite creative potential, the question is, What are the possibilities that the border is a zone of self-fashioning, given the incredible hardships of crossing and working? Or under what circumstances can the border become a "free" zone of self-fashioning at a time of unstoppable mass migrations, migratory flows, and crossing of borders? Arjun Appadurai argues that as a result of the changes produced by these processes, "ethnicity, once a genie contained in the bottle of some sort of locality (however large), has now become a global force, forever slipping in and through the cracks between states and borders."[67] The question is how these unstoppable processes and overflowing of borders will collide with the narratives of the Other and with the alleged downgrading of self and nation as a result of the contact. The latent belief behind this "downgrading" is that the hybrid—the result of genetic, cultural, and linguistic crossing—is a degradation of humanity, of culture, and of everything the West represents. Yet what voices such as Viramontes in the United States and Nini in Spain and Europe represent is the entrance of "denied" knowledges upon the dominant discourse of self and nation. Their texts counter static narratives of the Other as they perform another kind of permutation, a major and fundamental change within the definition of the nation itself. For based on the reasoning that through its multiple and repeating boundaries the system reveals its true face, it is possible to argue that border narratives reveal the discourses undergirding the definition of the nation. From this perspective, border stories immerse us in the grotesque and permeable body of the nation; they place us at a site where definitions do not hold, and where our bearings are constantly challenged, for it is always too hard to remember which side of the fence we are on. Through them we are reminded of the porosity of physical and narrative borders; the politically repressed parts of the world are set side by side with those that are presumed to be liberal, democratic, and civilized; the American and European dreams are hybridized with a vision of repressive practices that make the host countries strikingly similar to those other parts of the world the United States and Spain barricade themselves against. Like the border itself, we learn in border narratives, violence is displaced, spread out, and diasporic. Border narratives thus permute and shuffle definitions of self and Other, past and present, North and South. At the same time, they start the process of questioning the alleged purity of a nation that needs to fortify itself against the alleged downgrading brought about by southern migrants.

Notes

I would like to acknowledge the financial support of the Junta de Castilla y León through my research project on Borders and Mestizaje (ref. SA029/03). Jesús Benito has contributed valuable suggestions to this essay. For his patience and analytical skills I will always be grateful.

1 Rachid Nini, *Diario de un illegal (An Illegal's Journal)*, trans. G. F. Parrilla and M. Embarek (Madrid: Ediciones del Oriente y del Mediterráneo, 2002), 27.

2   Grégorie Deniau, "Yo llegé en patera," *El País semanal*, November 28, 2004, 52, 53.

3   Cornelius quoted in Alfonso Armada, "USA, Final del trayecto," *ABC*, October 24, 2004.

4   Deniau, "Yo llegé en patera," 44.

5   See Jesús Rodríguez, "El Estrecho de Gibraltar. Una alambrada entre dos mundos," *El País semanal*, October 25, 1997.

6   Rosaura Sánchez, "Mapping the Spanish Language along a Multiethnic and Multilingual Border," in *The Latino Studies Reader: Culture, Economy and Society*, ed. Antonia Darder and Rodolfo D. Torres (London: Blackwell, 1998), 107.

7   Alfred Arteaga, *Chicano Poetics: Heterotexts and Hybridities* (Cambridge: Cambridge University Press, 1997), 94.

8   See Jesús Benito and Ana Maria Manzanas, "Border(lands) and Border Writing: Introductory Essay," in *Literature and Ethnicity in the Cultural Borderlands*, ed. Jesús Benito and Ana Maria Manzanas (Amsterdam: Rodopi, 2003), 5.

9   See Pablo Vila, *Crossing Borders, Reinforcing Borders: Social Categories, Meaphors, and Narrative Identities on the US-Mexico Frontier* (Austin: University of Texas Press, 2000), 8.

10 Rubén Martínez, *Crossing Over: A Mexican Family on the Migrant Trail* (New York: Picador, 2001), 17.

11 Mahi Binebine in Ignacio Cambrero, "El estrecho de Gibraltar es un abismo," *El País*, October 31, 1999.

12 Armada, "USA, Final."

13 Arteaga, *Chicano Poetics*, 92.

14 The problems of comparing both borders are clear from the start. As many critics have argued, there are obvious dangers in abstracting and metaphorizing the U.S.-Mexican border—even more than with other international boundaries. See, for example, Debra Castillo and Rosario Tabuenca in *Border Women: Writing from la Frontera* (Minneapolis: University of Minnesota Press, 2002), 3; Claire Fox in *The Fence and the River: Culture and Politics at the U.S.-Mexico Border* (Minneapolis: University of Minnesota Press, 1999), 1; and David E. Johnson and Scott Michaelsen, eds., *Border Theory: The Limits of Cultural Politics* (Minneapolis: University of Minnesota Press, 1997), 3. Yet I am persuaded that it is possible to identify similar border dynamics without endangering the specificity of each locality and historical process.

15 "I'd rather die than put up with the misery I have to live with there" (my translation). Alfonso Armada, "USA, Final."

16 "I'd rather be locked up in a room, in a jail in Europe, where I'll have a meal everyday, than stay in Africa, and above all in Morocco. This is hell, and Europe will be paradise" (my translation). Deniau, "Yo llegé en patera."

17 Nancy Gibbs, "A Whole New World," *Time*, June 11, 2001, 39–40.

18 Alí Lmrabet, "Así crucé el Estrecho," *El País*, October 1, 2000.

19 Benito and Manzanas, "Border(lands)," 6.

20 Luis Alberto Urrea, *Across the Wire* (New York: Anchor Books, 1993), 13.

21 Martínez, *Crossing Over*, 277–78.

22 "La patera en la que murieron 12 subsaharianos fue usada como cebo para 'colar' otra con marroquíes," *El País digital*, June 16, 2005, available at www.elpais.es (accessed July 1, 2005).

23 "Las mafias venden 'bonos' de tres intentos para cruzar el Estrecho," *El País digital*, October 22, 2001, available at www.elpais.es (accessed June 6, 2002).

24 Tomás Bárbulo, "El veneno que viaja en las pateras," *El País digital*, July 17, 2001, available at www.elpais.es (accessed June 1, 2005).

25 Lmrabet, "Así crucé."

26 Gibbs, "A Whole New World," 38.

27 Armada, "USA, final."

28 Terry McCarthy, "The Coyote's Game," *Time*, November 28, 2001, 58–59.

29 Tereixa Constenla, "Un padre blanco con claroscuros," *El País digital*, June 11, 2004, available at www.elpais.es (accessed June 11, 2005).

30 Carmen Morán, "Samaritanos en el Estrecho," *El País digital*, June 12, 1999, available at www.elpais.es (accessed June 15, 2005).

31 "Nuevo intento de asalto masivo de inmigrantes en la valla fronteriza de Melilla," *El País digital*, October 5, 2005, available at www.elpais.es (accessed October 5, 2005).

32 Martínez, *Crossing Over*, 5, 319.

33 Wayne A. Cornelius, "Death at the Border: Efficacy and Unintended Consequences of US Immigration Control Policy," *Population and Development Review* 27.4 (2001): 675–76.

34 "Volunteers to Patrol Arizona," *New York Times*, April 2, 2005, available at www.nytimes.com (accessed April 2, 2005).

35 Martínez, *Crossing Over*, 198–99.

36 Cornelius, "Death at the Border," 668. Subsequent citations are given parenthetically by page number in the text.

37 Omar G. Encarnación, "The Politics of Immigration: Why Spain Is Different," *Mediterranean Quarterly* 15.4 (2004): 175.

38 Nini, *Diario*, 83.

39 Manuel M. Martín-Rodríguez, "Aztlán y Al-Andalus: La idea del retorno en dos literaturas inmigrantes," *La palabra y El Hombre* 120 (2001): 31.

40 José Piedra, "The Black Stud's Spanish Birth," *Callaloo* 16 (1993): 822. Apart from the eight centuries of Muslim domination of the Spanish Peninsula, it is worth recalling that Spain holds two autonomous cities, Ceuta and Melilla, on the northern coast of Africa.

41 María de la Luz Ibarra, "Buscando la Vida: Mexican Immigrant Women's Memories of Home, Yearning, and Border Crossings," *Frontiers: A Journal of Women Studies* 24.2 (2003): 262.

42 Mary Pat Brady, *Extinct Lands, Temporal Geographies: Chicano Literature and the Urgency of Space* (Durham, NC: Duke University Press, 2002), 50.

43 Nini, *Diario*, 145.

44 Nini interviewed by Trinidad de León-Sotelo, *ABC*, June 12, 2002.

45 Martínez, *Crossing Over*, 7.

46 Benito and Manzanas, "Border(lands)," 7–8.

47 Mikhail Bakhtin, *Rabelais and His World* (Bloomington: Indiana University Press, 1984), 26. Subsequent references will appear parenthetically by page number in the text.

48 Benito and Manzanas, "Border(lands)," 8.

49 Arteaga, *Chicano Poetics*, 92.

50 "He detested the undocumented. But he adored and needed them. Without them, damn it, there would be no budget for helicopters, radars, powerful nocturnal infrared lights,

bazookas, guns. . . . Let them come. . . . Let them keep on coming by the millions, the prayed, so that my life can be meaningful. We have to keep on playing the innocent victim" (my translation). Fuentes, *La frontera*, 268.

51 Eduardo Galeano, "In Defense of the Word," in *The Graywolf Annual Five: Multicultural Literacy* (1988): 114.

52 The detention camps in Ceuta and Melilla, the two Spanish cities in north Africa, also represent the underside of the European dream. There thousands of African refugees, often housed in subhuman conditions, keep waiting for a chance to reach Spanish territory. The situation of the sub-Saharans awaiting on the Moroccan side for an opportunity to cross into Spanish territory is even more dramatic. Harassed by Moroccan authorities, they take every opportunity to launch an assault on the Spanish-Moroccan border. Although the border is furnished with the latest technology, the Africans equip themselves with handmade ladders in order to climb over the fence. See Tomás Bárbulo, "La Guardia Civil frena una entrada masiva de inmigrantes en Melilla," *El País digital*, August 27, 2005, available at www.elpais.es (accessed August 28, 2005).

53 In Cambrero, "El Estrecho."

54 Jimmy Santiago Baca, "So Mexicans Are Taking Jobs from Americans," in *Literature, Class, and Culture*, ed. Paul Lauter and Ann Fitzgerald (New York: Longman, 2001), 139. Subsequent citations are given parenthetically by page number in the text.

55 Mary Louise Pratt, *Imperial Eyes: Travel Writing and Transculturation* (London: Routledge, 1992), 16.

56 Walter Mignolo, *Coloniality, Subaltern Knowledges, and Border Thinking: Local Histories, Global Designs* (Princeton, NJ: Princeton University Press, 2002), 12.

57 Martínez, *Crossing Over*, 384. Subsequent citations are given parenthetically by page number in the text.

58 Helena María Viramontes, *Under the Feet of Jesus* (New York: Dutton, 1995), 87. Subsequent citations are given parenthetically by page number in the text.

59 Paula M. C. Moya, *Learning from Experience: Minority Identities, Multicultural Struggles* (Berkeley: University of California Press, 2002), 195.

60 Juan Goytisolo and Sami Naïr, "Contra la razón de la fuerza," *El País digital*, February 2, 2000, available at www.elpais.es (accessed June 6, 2002).

61 Encarnación, "The Politics of Immigration," 173.

62 "Xenofobia y ambigüedad," *El País digital*, February 13, 2000, available at www.elpais.es (accessed June 6, 2002).

63 In Miguel Mora, "Un repaso a la España clandestina," *El País digital*, June 14, 2002, available at www.elpais.es (accessed June 15, 2002).

64 See Vila, *Crossing Borders*, 223.

65 Nini, *Diario*, 15.

66 Vila, *Crossing Borders*, 8.

67 Arjun Appadurai, *Modernity at Large: Cultural Dimensions of Globalization* (Minneapolis: University of Minnesota Press, 1996), 41.

Sarah Hill

Purity and Danger on the U.S-Mexico
Border, 1991–1994

Of this unrest I myself saw nothing. In private I
observed that once in every generation, without fail,
there is an episode of hysteria about the barbarians.
There is no woman living along the frontier who has
not dreamed of a dark barbarian hand coming from
under the bed to grip her ankle, there is no man who
has not frightened himself with visions of the barbarians carousing in his home, breaking the plates,
setting fire to the curtains, raping his daughters. These
dreams are the consequence of too much ease. Show
me a barbarian army and I will believe.
—J. M. Coetzee, *Waiting for the Barbarians*

If you visit American city,
You will find it very pretty.
Just two things of which you must beware:
Don't drink the water and don't breathe the air.
—Tom Lehrer, "Pollution"

In the early 1990s, the U.S.-Mexico border
region acquired an environment—a polluted and
threatening environment.

During this time, there appeared in the media,
in numerous policy and "gray literature" documents, in the parlance of activists, and increasingly in the everyday imaginings of Americans
living both near and far from the boundary
line something commonsensically called "the

South Atlantic Quarterly 105:4, Fall 2006
DOI 10.1215/00382876-2006-010   © 2006 Duke University Press

border environment." This commonsensicality achieved enough recurring believability that "the border environment" took on iconic status and intuitively came to index the predicted dangers inherent in the then-being-debated North American Free Trade Agreement (NAFTA). In fact, "the border environment" became one of the NAFTA critics' most potent weapons for galvanizing popular opposition to the treaty. Although it is impossible to precisely trace the effects of this border discourse on NAFTA's final form, depictions of the border as a polluted zone certainly contributed to the famed side accords on labor and the environment that were intended to temper the deregulatory impact of NAFTA when it was subsequently ratified by the U.S. Congress in November 1993. NAFTA, it has been widely observed, was the world's first trade treaty in which environmental issues played a defining role not only in the actual language of the treaty itself but also in the public perception of what the treaty would do to the conditions in which average citizens lived.[1]

More than a decade later, environmental concerns about the U.S.-Mexico border have receded into the background, while concerns about illegal immigration and global terrorism have taken center stage. Yet all the conditions of the border environment that made their way into the mainstream reporting in the early 1990s can still be found: the shanties, the squatter settlements, the open sewers, the illegal dumping. Indeed, some conditions—such as air quality—are decidedly worse, thanks to increased vehicular traffic in booming border cities. Examining the discursive construction of the border environment in the 1990s, especially through the media's reporting on NAFTA, offers some clues as to why the urgency of thinking about the border environment in the contemporary catalog of American dangers and concerns has diminished considerably. It seems plausible to conclude that environmental concerns have faded at least in part because the environment was never truly the focus of popular opposition; rather, it stood in for, albeit sometimes inadvertently, the belief that the Mexican immigrant was the real source of pollution.

The environment at the center of projections of NAFTA's future was the far-distant environment of the U.S.-Mexico border region. Yet media coverage succeeded in making this threat seem immediate to the lives of Americans all over the nation, so much so that many Americans initially opposed NAFTA, reportedly for environmental reasons. I contend that the environment depicted in NAFTA media coverage was so alarming, even to Americans living far from the border, because this environment mimicked something already inherently antipathetic and threatening to many Americans: Mexican immigration. Indeed, the implicit link drawn in media representations between immigration and the border environment not only enhanced what historians have shown is a traditional American stereotyping of Mexicans as dirty, unhygienic, and self-soiling;[2] it also made the prospects of uncontrolled immigration seem both *naturally* inevitable and consequently more threatening. By linking "dirty" immigrant Mexicans to a "dirty" border environment, the NAFTA-era media coverage of the U.S.-Mexico border not only reinforced existing stereotypes but also provided nativists with another seemingly natural reason to disparage and denigrate Mexicans. Furthermore, it stoked demands for greater immigration control,[3] which in turn further fueled seemingly logical associations between immigration and environmental degradation. This nativist discourse figured—sometimes prominently—in the rhetoric of environmental activist groups that opposed NAFTA, especially those, such as Ralph Nader's, that were based in Washington, D.C. Since anti-Mexican immigration has had a particularly durable persistence in the repertoire of American nativist habits of thought,[4] the "pollution rules" that the environmental opposition to NAFTA inspired were, in fact, rules of Mexican immigrant exclusion.

In her seminal essay on cross-cultural rituals of avoidance, *Purity and Danger* (1966), British social anthropologist Mary Douglas observed that pollution's material composition is always culturally specific; dirt, she noted, lies in the eye of the beholder. Moreover, dirt is never absolute. It is, rather, "matter out of place." By way of illustration, Douglas suggested that shoes on the floor are not dirty, while shoes on the coffee table are.[5] Keeping Douglas's observations in mind, I suggest that what the media presented along the U.S.-Mexico border during 1991–94 was an extreme portrait of "matter out of place" implicitly borne by the movement of people out of place: Mexican immigrants. This is not to say that air, water, and ground contamination did not exist at the border or that border cities had no public health problems. In fact, border cities did face unique public health and pollution situations. But why these very local concerns mattered to people living far from the border in the American heartland can be attributed on the one hand (in part) to the implicit mobility of the border environment itself, as depicted in the media, and on the other hand to the recurring suggestions that Mexicans routinely self-soil so that wherever they travel, their dirt goes with them. The "filthiness" of the border environment appeared in the media as immanently associated with a population that was always on the move and ever threatening to expand beyond its existing territory. In short, the border environment implicitly threatened to expand its elastic boundaries northward and in so doing transport its inherently tainted, degraded conditions deep into mainstream and mainland America.

In this essay, I detail first how reporting in the 1970s characterized the border as porous, vulnerable, and ultimately boundaryless through a mixture of natural and martial imagery. I trace this emerging taken-for-granted character of the border through 1980s coverage of pollution on the border and then turn to the NAFTA period to show how characterizations of the border's degraded environment became a surrogate for immigration-writ-large through depictions of trespassing, soiling, and contaminating matter and bodies that appeared to threaten the integrity, safety, economic security, and hygienic future of the American nation.[6] Finally, I examine in detail the imagery at the heart of the mobile border environment and show how these images contributed to the naturalization of the self-soiling of Mexican immigrants.

The Politics of Representation

The larger question indirectly addressed in this essay concerns the nature of environmental representation and environmental politics.[7] In the enduring age of "virtual reproduction" (to borrow from Walter Benjamin),[8] we experience in mediated form environments that we don't physically come into contact with. That is, we experience them through a medium other than nature itself: the mass media, for example. Thus, we can "know" of "pristine" wilderness environments by viewing images of stately forests, majestic mountains, and dazzling wildlife widely disseminated through television, print journalism and—with growing frequency—the Internet. The endless repetition of such images enables us to believe that environments are *real* even if we've never touched a particular environment.[9] As Bruce Braun demonstrated in his study of the cultural politics of Canada's temperate rainforests, the materiality of any environment is an epistemological problem, one that is both posed and solved (in part) by representation in the media.[10] And as Braun also observed, whether or not humans appear in representations of nature does not fully disguise the fact that such representations implicitly express a human imprint on nature. While it might be hard to see "culture" in pictures of "pristine" nature, Braun argues that images of nature always imply where humans belong (far from nature) and don't belong (in nature), unless the humans depicted are *of* nature (e.g., First Nations). It is, of course, much easier to see the implicit presence of humans in images of degraded nature. We can know that an environment is degraded by iconic images of human things inappropriately mingled with nature: tires clogging a waterway, plastic flotsam and jetsam strewn across a patch of desert, or factory smokestacks staining the sky black with billowing emissions. Each such image not only indexes deteriorated nature, each also implicitly narrates human imprints on nature: *People* litter, *industries* pollute. What is sometimes less clear, however, is what kind of human culture is implied in images of degraded nature, or, in other words, *which* humans are to blame. For this, the images drawn in words as accompanying text become crucial; they guide our reading of pictures and help us see otherwise invisible blame.

While imagery can't tell us everything about environmental politics, it can tell us something important. Representational imagery can reveal what Raymond Williams called the "structure of feelings," the almost inchoate organization of cultural affect around the political economy of nature-society relations. Moreover, as Williams also demonstrated, sociospatial language, metaphor, and representation do not merely reflect views on nature. They both emerge from political history and also effect political and material consequences.[11] The entanglement at the border of environmental imagery with anti-immigration sentiments is one instance of a more complicated late-twentieth-century set of political economic projects that deployed environmentalist rhetoric or goals for otherwise regressive or questionable ends. These kinds of environmentalized projects include "development"[12] and rural resource control and exploitation.[13] In addition, nativist movements elsewhere in the world have found environmental imagery a particularly potent tool in producing anti-immigrant sympathy.[14]

NAFTA's representational trail began in early 1990, shortly after newly elected Mexican president Carlos Salinas de Gortari announced to his U.S. counterpart, George H. W. Bush, that he sought a comprehensive trade pact with the U.S. and Canada. Unions and environmental organizations promptly joined forces to oppose any such treaty.[15] Their mobilization was itself partly fueled by what the media had already revealed about existing trade relations with Mexico, which at that point were largely limited to a narrow "free trade zone" along Mexico's northern frontier, just south of American cities such as El Paso, Brownsville, and San Diego. The steady slide of U.S. manufacturing across the border to a cheaper labor market and the largely unenforced pollution regulation of Mexico suggested to labor unions and environmental organizations that NAFTA would only produce more of the same. They reacted to the news of proposed free trade talks with Mexico swiftly and aggressively. Labor leaders were joined by environmental organizations, both those in the border region and the international environmental "Big Ten," based in Washington, D.C., and New York. In a concerted publicity and lobbying effort, these groups banded together to strike the only vulnerable target of any future trade deals: They sought to prevent congressional renewal of the president's authority to negotiate trade relations on the "fast track," that is, without congressional line-item veto power. Initially, that authority was set to expire in June 1990 (though procedural stopgaps kept the issue open until May 1991).

The monumental scale of NAFTA's proposal—to integrate the economies of nearly half a billion people into a single open market—endowed it with the capacity to generate what anthropologist Phyllis Pease Chock calls a "myth-making" national identity event, a legislative debate that reverberates far beyond congressional hearing rooms with iterations of "canonical versions of national myths and hegemonic ideology" in opposition to immigration.[16] It is perhaps not surprising that NAFTA's prospective equivalency of the Canadian, U.S., and Mexican economies and populations would provoke anti-immigrant and anti-Mexican rhetoric on the part of legislators and that this, in turn, would filter through media representations of areas already affected by trade with Mexico, or areas that would be affected by NAFTA. However, the myth-making that ensued during the fast-track debates drew on, as I shall detail shortly, an existing repertoire of images that showed Mexican immigration to be essentially threatening to the *entire* American nation. In other words, the media provided some of the raw material from which legislators could make their mythical claims, or in the words of a former environmental organization staff member who was closely involved in NAFTA, the media came up with "those shocking visuals" that played particularly well in congressional chambers.[17] In turn, this rhetorical feedback loop between the media and law makers enhanced what Nicholas de Genova terms the larger "border spectacle" that has naturalized the hardening categories of legal and illegal immigration and consequently reified the popular presumption of guilt—for all kinds of alleged crimes—on the part of Mexican immigrants.[18]

Indeed, during the period of the fast-track debates, the media provided ample opportunities for Americans to view the border environment. Sierra

Club's John Audley's Lexis-Nexis research identified that while the majority of the thousands of newspaper articles published during the fast-track debates concerned labor, business and agricultural issues, nonetheless, 15 percent of that coverage presented an environmental focus.[19] Clearly, the media helped link environmental issues to NAFTA for Americans not directly engaged in the lobbying for or against fast-track.

By May 1991, NAFTA had become a central issue for incipient primary campaigning for the 1992 general elections, even though by then the negotiations were well under way. NAFTA's growing popular opposition prompted President Bush to ensure that "labor" and "environment" would be protected through negotiations external to the treaty, conducted on a "parallel track." Despite that gesture, Bush encountered anti-NAFTA challengers from within his own party primary fight in advance of the 1992 presidential elections. Bush found himself fending off anti-NAFTA Republican opponents including Pat Buchanan, whose unvarnished anti-immigrant claims hyperbolically warned that NAFTA would propel millions of Mexicans to cross the border illegally, in the wake of NAFTA's crushing of Mexican economic autonomy. The turning point for the successful Democratic challenger, Bill Clinton, came when he promised to support NAFTA only if the parallel-track negotiations were substantiated.[20] The electorate's growing worries about NAFTA siphoned votes away from Bush and funneled them toward the quixotic billionaire third-party candidate, Ross Perot, who famously promised that NAFTA would result in "a giant sucking sound" of jobs going to Mexico. Despite his defeat, Bush signed NAFTA in December 1992, leaving Clinton to work out the details of his promised side accords in the next nine months before a ratification deadline.

Between January and September 1993, a coalition of seven environmental organizations and several labor unions worked feverishly to draft the side accords. In the meantime, anti-NAFTA labor and environmental organizations continued to lobby against NAFTA's ratification. During this period the press focused intensely on the issues invoked by NAFTA's organized opposition (Audley found a total of 20,000 articles in his Lexis-Nexis search of NAFTA coverage during the entire NAFTA debates, from June 1990 to November 1994). It is important to recognize that most of the feature-length coverage of the border environment appeared after a split between moderate and adversarial environmental groups (in May 1991). While the moderate groups tried to distance themselves from some of the media coverage of the border (at least in how some staffers now recall those days in my discussions with them), the adversarial groups continued to link the border environment to illegal immigration and did not shy away from fanning the flames of fear. The adversarial groups continued to work the press with doomsday environmental scenarios and quite happily joined forces with the nakedly anti-immigrant, anti-Mexican NAFTA opponents Pat Buchanan and Ross Perot. Indeed, Perot's impressive political following suggests he managed to "elevate the symbolic potency of NAFTA's threat to national sovereignty and industrial decline."[21]

In the end, the split in the environmental movement caused many congressional representatives to turn away from the environment as a compelling reason for the treaty's support or objection, meaning that on the day of ratification, environmental issues receded into the background, leaving jobs and prospects for economic growth at the forefront.[22] NAFTA's environmental side agreement essentially boiled down to some commitments to protect the environment of the three signatory nations and a commission to oversee environmental concerns (the Commission for Economic Cooperation) and arguably had little significant impact, in the view of some international legal scholars.[23] Nonetheless, the border environment had by then been created.

Naturalizing Immigration: Water Imagery and the War against Nature

The troubling features of the border environment—its teeming untreated, illegally discharged effluent, both industrial and human—echoed characterizations of immigrants themselves, who, prior to the emergence of NAFTA as a concern for the media, had dominated reporting on the border. In fact, in the 1970s and 1980s, a "border" story was almost always an immigration story,[24] with the exception of a handful of stories that appeared in the late 1980s, which focused not on illegal immigration of Mexicans to the U.S. but on the effects of American firms that had migrated the south of the border to set up shop to produce goods for the U.S. market and in so doing frequently took advantage of Mexico's anemic enforcement of pollution regulations.

So what did these immigration stories looked like? In his book-length study of magazine cover stories on immigration, Leo Chávez found a thickening anti-immigrant sentiment not only in the visual imagery representing immigration, but also in the metaphoric language and the actual tone of magazine reporting from 1965 to 1999. Thus, even though magazine covers in the month of July (the month of America's "birthday") of any given year tended toward more favorable depictions of immigrants, the general tenor of immigration coverage since 1965 has steadily but persistently moved toward ways of sanctioning and bolstering nativism. This all has bearing on how the border came to be a cultural space defined by immigration, but perhaps the most important trope in doing that work has been the use of water imagery. In my view, this water imagery has three principal effects. First, its crude sensationalism helps present illegal immigration as an urgent crisis. Typically, in the 1970s and 1980s, immigration features pictured "invading" Mexicans easily traversing boundary rivers, "flooding" across the border in "incalculable waves."[25] They "surge" in streams that become "torrent[s]" and "deluge[s]."[26] At the same time the natural boundary between the two countries is but a poor defense — a "skimpy barrier" — against the nature of immigrants. The Border Patrol, by its own admission, "is all but powerless to do more than hinder the swelling tide."[27] Like water from some mysterious underground source "communities of sorts . . . spring up in the staging areas for illegal crossers."[28] A Border Patrol spokesman complains that the efforts of "Customs, D.E.A., Immigration and others" are "just a drop in the bucket against them."[29]

Neither the timing nor language in immigration features were incidental or accidental, as Tim Dunn has shown. Stories typically appeared when immigration enforcement agencies sought increased budgets and expanded policing mandates. Dunn also observed that the Immigration and Naturalization Service provided the nearly exclusive sources that journalists used in the early days of immigration reporting.[30] Indeed, agencies' ambitions led not only to the sensationalist and hyperbolic language of their press releases and congressional testimony but also to their intentional efforts to whip up anti-immigrant fervor: In the 1970s, INS reportedly doctored immigration estimates in order to produce a national sense of urgency.[31] Their efforts to produce a popular sense of immigration as a national security threat worked especially well when immigration stories appeared during downturns in the U.S. economy.

The second effect of the recurring water imagery in immigration stories is that this trope has helped to characterize what is often described as a "battle" against immigrants as a struggle against *nature*. In other words, water imagery suggests that immigrants possess a natural essence that threatens American culture and civilization. This, in turn, has helped characterize the border as a zone unlike the rest of the United States, one that is *naturally*—by virtue of the Mexican immigrant presence there—not American. In the ensuing years, media reports have only further reinforced the conflation of Mexican/immigrant culture with nature. And that kind of thinking, anthropologist Franz Boas long ago observed, reveals a racist impulse to characterize members of some cultures (e.g., Mexican) as unassimilable.

Scholars of Mexican immigration have long observed that while most immigrant populations in the U.S. have suffered outsider status for a period of a few decades at most, Mexicans in the U.S. have withstood this characterization largely without stop since the end of the Mexican-American war.[32] The media have contributed substantially to this phenomenon.[33] For example, during the run-up to the hotly debated Immigration Reform and Control Act of 1986, media coverage of Mexico, Mexicans, and the border turned Mexican immigrants into "aliens"—the new preferred term for immigrants lacking legal status to be in the U.S.—and characterized the border as an alien space, populated by humans who are described in other-than-human ways. According to Immigration and Customs officials, the border was a "horror" and "a monster, growing, feeding on itself." On the border, stolen vehicles were "cannibalized" and youth gangs "who could come from the American or Mexican side" "pounce on their prey" and the weaker among their own numbers.[34]

One sustaining feature in descriptions of Mexican immigrants' alienness has long centered on their purported lack of hygiene. The popular epithet "greasers," for example, a term used for Mexicans in the nineteenth century, provided a coded term to signify the inherent dirtiness of Mexicans.[35] In fact, the suspiciously subjective official view of Mexicans as dirtier than other immigrants helped give birth to the U.S. Public Health Service, as Alex Stern has documented in her history of El Paso's bath riots in 1917. Immigrants from Europe who landed at Ellis Island at this time were famously treated to the poking and prodding of physicians and, if found ill, subjected to a delousing or to other sanitizing treatments.[36] By contrast, *all* Mexicans walking across El Paso's Santa Fe bridge in 1917 were stripped and sprayed with disinfectant, and sometimes had their clothes destroyed, in general a much more rigorous inspection that *presumed* Mexicans were infected by "filth diseases" before inspection began.[37] This difference is notable and durable, and as we shall see shortly, vital to the normative idea of the border environment, by the early 1990s.

The third by-product of water imagery stems from how it contributes to the idea that the borderlands are boundaryless; in other words, as long as a steady stream of immigrants flows across the political boundary, the immigrant space of the "border" will keep seeping (northward). Indeed, some Mexican American intellectuals and political activists have celebrated the inherent elasticity of the border as a place: they claim that wherever Chicanos/Mexicanos are found—as in Chicago—the "border" is found as well.[38] But in the 1980s such elasticity became one of the threats routinely invoked by advocates of immigration restriction who called immigration an "invasion" that will "tak[e] over our [entire] nation" if "we don't control these borders."[39]

In combination, the three features of immigration water imagery helped shape a popular notion of the border as a polluted place: American soil contaminated by Mexicans, and therefore—by implication—in need of containment before further spreading takes place. These three features of water imagery in turn contributed significantly to how the border environment became so easily imaginable when the anti-NAFTA forces called attention to industrialization's impacts in Mexico's northern corridor once NAFTA negotiations were announced. Before turning to that media coverage, let us briefly explore the character of stories on what is more conventionally understood as "pollution" at the U.S.-Mexico border. These, as we shall see, also reinforce the commonsensical nature of Mexican immigration as a pollutant.

Pollution: It Comes from Mexico

Occasionally in the late 1970s through the mid-1980s, journalists ventured far into Mexico. Tellingly, however, a stock theme in any lengthy coverage of Mexico included primarily "immigration," and rarely "emigration."[40] This tendency to focus on the impact in the U.S. of the cross-border movement of people (rather than exploring how Mexico was affected) resonated in the early pollution reporting generated in response to U.S. industrial relocation to northern Mexico. In this reporting, local health personnel in El Paso, San Diego, and Brownsville reportedly described health conditions in border cities in terms of immigration: They noted that "pollutants" which "are being transported across the border in the wind" invade, like illegal immigrants, "[without] a green card [i.e., a residency permit]." An "18-mile-long open sewage ditch in Ciudad Juárez" is troubling because "disease-carrying mosquitoes . . . don't know north from south. And they don't carry green cards." "Air [pollution] doesn't stop at the border." And the Tijuana River, which receives "12 million gallons of raw sewage a day," "does not recognize the U.S. border" and consequently contaminates San Diego beaches.[41] Almost without exception, references to transboundary health problems in the late 1980s began, like immigrants, in Mexico and migrated with their ill effects to the U.S. side of the border. According to this logic, "pollution knows no border," as one *Christian Science Monitor* headline put it, but that logic was firmly grounded in U.S. concerns, as if to say, "*Mexico's* pollution does not respect boundaries."

Many of these accounts also stressed that what emanated from Mexico was fundamentally different than what is ordinarily found in the U.S. So, on the one hand the two sides of the boundary seem starkly different, as different as the "first world" is from the "third world," as many articles put it. At the same time, however, the accounts suggested that what's in Mexico does not stay there. So the "squalid living conditions," "putrid open sewers," "reeking contaminated canals," "squatter camps," "shanty towns," and even the "filthy, unsafe plants" that characterize the Mexican side of the border always seemed poised to spill over onto the U.S. side, following the logic that "pollution knows no boundaries." The commonplace Mexican practices of "indiscriminate and widespread dumping of . . . garbage and industrial wastes" that "trash . . . the landscape" also thus "poison" the implicitly cross-boundary "water and soil."[42] These repetitions of "different" but "merging" conditions suggested that the border's pollution rules took shape by heightening the sense that what Mary Douglas calls a "system" (the environmentally clean U.S.) had come under attack by literal dirt from Mexico.

One way in which pollution (literal and symbolic) seemed to dissolve the boundary between the U.S. and Mexico while simultaneously creating the commonsense notion of "the border" as a shared space was through a rhetorical juxtaposition that many of the border stories employ. Border stories, even more so than the previous generation of immigration stories, needed to cover a lot of diverse settings in order to produce a coherent narrative of the border. Thus "border" stories typically hop-scotched around different boundary cities—from Brownsville to Tijuana—presenting each as characteristic of a larger, seamless geography with discernible features: illegal immigration, poverty, booming industrialization, and filth (with negative valences) and Spanish language, Mexican food, and lively music (with neutral to positive valences). Repetition of the form provided the building blocks from which the whole—"the border"—was eventually constructed. For example, after extolling the accomplishments of manufacturing in northern Mexico, a 1989 *Wall Street Journal* article[43] paused briefly to describe a factory-worker settlement outside of the booming industrial city of Nogales, Sonora. Using the settlement as illustrative, the article explained that the success of foreign-owned factories in Mexico has "turned the border region into a sinkhole of abysmal living conditions" because a "huge, continuing migration of people looking for work has simply overwhelmed the already-shaky infrastructure." Such "shantytowns" where the squatters live "spring up overnight." Not only did these shantytowns echo the descriptions of waves of unstoppable illegal immigration that overwhelm the Border Patrol; they also drove home the point that the border has common features, all up and down—and on both sides of—the 2,000-mile line. For example, because "the border region" referred to in the article entails both sides of the boundary, conditions in Mexico (a factory-worker shantytown) could apparently just as easily show up on the north side of the boundary line. Like the movement of immigrants, border pollution does not stay put.

The Border Environment: Cesspools and Love Canals in the Making

The use of "shocking" visuals and the rhetorical mobility of discrete events and conditions that formed the basis of border reporting and, in turn, border pollution reporting became increasingly reckless during the NAFTA debates: Any remote—and unflattering—feature of Mexico could portend the U.S.'s free-trade future and came to signify the expanding border. Reporters quite deliberately erased distance and social and regulatory differences in order to project a seamless environmental disaster that was but a heartbeat away from spreading across the continent. In one characteristic example, Mike Wallace on *60 Minutes* asked viewers to "take a look" "across the border from Texas at the garbage dumps of Mexico City," as if Mexico City were six miles—rather than six hundred—from the nearest point in Texas and as if conditions in Mexico City were synonymous with those on the border.[44] Like the Mexican aliens in the older immigration reporting, who purportedly "threaten the entire nation," the border itself now presented "a growing environmental nightmare that if left unchecked, could spread to the rest of our nation," according to U.S. Senator Howard Metzenbaum.[45] As popular opinion turned against NAFTA, this kind of hysteria came to seem quite logical. It repeatedly appeared in the border's evidence of the unrestrainable forces of migrancy that NAFTA would unleash: Factories would migrate to Mexico, taking American jobs with them, while more Mexican illegal immigrants and toxic wastes would flood north. In short, unwanted movement became the means by which the border environment became comprehensible to the American public.

However, it was not simply unwanted movement but particular components of the border environment's pollution that helped linked Mexican immigration to environmental problems. Several tropes routinely appeared in the characterization of the border environment's threatening capacity to grow and grow. One was the routine characterization of the border as a "2,000-mile garbage dump."[46] But the most interesting images were a pair of metaphors that were often deployed in conjunction with one another: the "cesspool" and "Love Canal." The image of the cesspool became nearly required language in border reporting following the publication of an editorial in the *Journal of the American Medical Association* in June 1990, shortly after the fast-track vote. The article stated that "the border area is a virtual cesspool and breeding ground for disease."[47]

In light of the numerous factories along the border, press reports of industrial dumping, chemical spills, and the like, it might seem strange that the AMA would employ an essentially excremental/bodily metaphor to call attention to the border's health conditions. In fact, the cesspool metaphor logically refracted the light cast by the immigration lens through which the border had been traditionally projected. Because the border had been rendered believable through images of migrancy and immigration, it is logical that one of the key metaphors to define the border environment should rest, at least implicitly, on a presumed social characteristic of immigrants—their intimacy with excrement. The cesspool became a compelling metaphor for the border environment precisely because it assigned blame: Producers of a cesspool, a repository of human wastes, are eminently human. Because the border itself is created out of Mexican immigrants, it is only *natural* that the principal perpetrator of the cesspool should be the Mexican immigrant.

The cesspool and its associations with immigrants resonated not only with long-standing Euro-American stereotypes of Mexicans as dirty but also with more recent media accounts of the border's public health problems. For example, Dr. Laurence Nickey, longtime director of the El Paso City-County Health District and arguably the most quoted of border environmental authorities,[48] suggested to a *New York Times* reporter in 1988 that

Mexican immigrants lack an essential aversion to their own wastes. In the *colonias* of El Paso County, which are populated by "Americans of Mexican heritage," Nickey noted that the absence of sanitation "has polluted ground water to the point that many residents are literally drinking their own wastes."[49] Similarly, an EPA regional director reported that in poor settlements in Texas, new residents—described as "Mexicans"—"show up, build a house and then drink their own sewage."[50] During two days of preliminary meetings between Presidents George Bush and Carlos Salinas to discuss "free trade, immigration and drugs," *CBS Morning News* aired a brief segment showing how "towns near the Mexican border . . . are paying a high price for low-wage immigrants who are staying and building squalid villages in the canyons of suburban neighborhoods." Pam Slater, the mayor of Encinitas, California, complained, "These people are performing all the sanitary activities necessary for human survival in the open."[51]

The second trope that routinely appeared in border environmental accounts, the Love Canal, by contrast situated blame not on individual migratory Mexicans, but on the emigrant firms that had relocated to Mexico. By invoking Love Canal, these accounts called to mind U.S. corporate crime and disregard for citizen welfare. The images of cesspools and Love Canal were often deployed in conjunction with one another to indicate environmental conditions of the U.S.-Mexico border, although they linked ideas that worked in opposition to one another. On the one hand, images of Love Canal call up a pivotal moment in American history—when hazardous wastes became an abiding household concern. Most associations of Love Canal (which according to environmental historians Colten and Skinner "has been seared into the collective memory of the country")[52] center on corporate abuse of the middle-class families whose neighborhood was poisoned by an industrial giant, Hooker Chemical. The concerns embodied by the signifier "Love Canal" are democratic and middle-class. Love Canal is the tragic but triumphant story of victims of industrial hazardous waste dumping who fought back, bringing a corporation to its knees and helping generate the political will to pass the Superfund legislation. Even for those unfamiliar with housewife-turned-grassroots-environmentalist Lois Gibbs and her Citizens' Clearing House for Hazardous Wastes, Love Canal evokes frightening images of industrial irresponsibility and chemical hazards. The heroes in the mythic image of Love Canal are average Americans, the villain a greedy corporation.

By contrast, cesspools signal individual irresponsibility and inattention to hygiene and cleanliness. Love Canal was a community poisoned by the wanton disposal practices of a large, powerful agent far removed from the consequences of its actions. But cesspools are the small, domestic, failed repositories of household wastes. A cesspool is the product of poorly constructed and/or maintained low-tech plumbing typical of rural poverty. Cesspools threaten to subject a household to the dangers of its own excrement, a perpetual concern signaled by border public health and environmental personnel. Love Canal as a metaphor implies villains and victims who are distinct from one another. In contrast, the victims and perpetrators of cesspools gone foul—households sickened with diseases borne in fecal matter—overlap much more completely than do their counterparts in a Love Canal. And herein lies the suggestive power of cesspools. Cesspools readily allow the designation of blamable victims. Perhaps unsurprisingly, during the free-trade era, the cesspool image appeared much more frequently in the press than the Love Canal image did. In the instances where cesspools and Love Canal were deployed side by side, the suggestive power of the cesspool eclipsed the suggestive power of Love Canal by showing that industrial contamination could in fact be blamed on self-soiling Mexicans.[53]

For example, a widely read article on the border that appeared in *The Atlantic* in 1991 spent some time on industrial pollution: The opening paragraph suggests that industry has contaminated the border: "This much I knew already: the border is a chemical mess. The ground, the water, and sometimes the air have been poisoned. Miscarriage, birth-defect and cancer rates are high. The situation is worse on the Mexican side, where dangerous wastes are dumped haphazardly." However, the following paragraph, which adds a description of what goes on inside a factory, shows how the cesspool narrative takes over: workers, not a powerful corporation, are to blame: "The dumping is not necessarily intentional: at a General Motors plant in Matamoros which makes bumpers, workers are provided with tanks for emptying their cleaning guns. Instead they simply purge the guns into the drains, which empty into a nearby canal."[54] The article did not explore why General Motors might be interested in neglecting to facilitate the disposition of wastes in the legally mandated manner. Rather, readers are left to imagine that Mexican working-class habits—Mexican customs, culture, or nature—are the root cause of the border's befouled waters. In a separate account (in *U.S. News and World Report*), managers complained that any attempts to operate a maquiladora "up to EPA standards are sometimes stymied by the slovenly practices of workers." One manager explained why: "There's a lot of ignorance on the shop floor and *old habits* die hard."[55]

Conclusion

No doubt many Americans who feared the border environment in the early 1990s did so because they feared industrial pollution and transnational corporate malfeasance. Nonetheless, it is impossible to dismiss the associations drawn between self-soiling Mexicans, mired in their own excrement, and the larger projection of the expanding border, seeping like a swamped septic system's drainage field across the greater American landscape. Whether or not this is really what Americans thought would happen with NAFTA, the images of excrement certainly reminded them to consider Mexican immigrants as less-than-fully civilized, due to their self-soiling habits.

We might push the argument a bit further. Mary Douglas suggested that excremental imagery, cross-culturally, symbolizes an incomplete separation of the self from its surroundings and an inadequate understanding of the boundaries of the individual. Like Douglas, Julia Kristeva argued that antipathy toward human effluvia (including fecal matter, blood, and mucous) stems not so much from concerns about hygiene as from fear of *fundamental* boundary transgression—the failure to distinguish between the subject and object, or the self and its others.[56] In allowing a porosity of the boundaries of the body, Mexicans, in such imagining, appear both more natural and less so. They are closer to nature (as they are less civilized), but they are distant from their basic human nature. In failing to recognize the subject/object or the self/surrounding boundaries, Mexican subjects pollute the environment. In so doing, they spread matter that threatens to breach the bodily boundary of American subjects who share the border environment.

Immigrants, in most conventional American perceptions, are largely out of place, especially if they lack legal entitlement to be in place in the United States.[57] Nonetheless, when associated with excrement—as Mexican immigrants often putatively are—Mexican immigrants become inherently polluting, and the environment around them becomes itself inherently polluted. According to Anna Meigs, in her refinement of Douglas's theory, polluting substances are those that attempt uninvited contact between bodies.[58] This makes sense as far as the border environment is concerned.

All the U.S. media reporting that contributed to the groundswell of opposition to NAFTA either implicitly or explicitly suggested that Mexican effluvia threatened to enter the body—symbolic and literal—of Americans.

While the border environment no longer captures the media attention the way it did during the NAFTA debates, the border's presumed porosity and Mexican immigration have become even more exploited by nativists; in recent years, "pollution" continues to appear in the litany of offenses committed by immigrants as they breach the border with their "assaults"[59] on the U.S., "cleaving" American society into two unbridgeable halves, with the Anglo-Saxon side, as Samuel P. Huntington suggested, gravely imperiled.[60] It could be argued that the border environment no longer needs to appear in the media, as it has already performed its work in further naturalizing, on the one hand, a public health logic of exclusion, and on the other, the inherent illegality of Mexican immigration itself. And, ultimately, as it appears now that the environmental problems of NAFTA, during the NAFTA debates, were only a means (albeit an ineffective one) to the larger end of Mexican exclusion from U.S. soil, their relevance as a media issue can vanish, although many of the conditions reported during that period persist.

Notes

Many patient souls read earlier iterations of this essay over a number of years. While of course the errors within are mine alone, I acknowledge the helpful interventions of Adriana Rosas, Boone Shear, Jane Juffer, David Gutiérrez, Bruce Braun, Christopher Niedt, Kristin Hill Maher, James McCarthy, Timothy Dunn, and Eduardo Barrera.

1   John Audley, *Green Politics and Global Trade: NAFTA and the Future of Environmental Politics* (Washington, DC: Georgetown University Press, 1997); Michael Dreiling, *Solidarity and Conflict: The Politics of Sustainability in the NAFTA Conflict* (New York: Garland, 2001); Barbara Hogenboom, *Mexico and the NAFTA Environment Debate* (Utrecht: International Books, 1998); Arturo Zárate-Ruiz, *A Rhetorical Analysis of the NAFTA Debate* (Lanham, MD: University Press of America, 2000).

2   Tomás Almaguer, *Racial Fault Lines: The Historical Origins of White Supremacy in California* (Berkeley: University of California Press, 1994); Steven W. Bender, *Greasers and Gringos: Latinos, Law and the American Imagination* (New York: New York University Press, 2003); Arnoldo De León, *They Called Them Greasers: Anglo Attitudes Towards Mexicans in Texas, 1821–1900* (Austin: University of Texas Press, 1983); Mario T. García, *Desert Immigrants: The Mexicans of El Paso, 1880–1920* (New Haven: Yale University Press, 1981); Howard Markel and Alexandra Minna Stern, "Which Face, Whose Nation?: Immigration, Public Health and the Construction of Disease at America's Ports and Borders, 1891–1928," *American Behavioral Scientist* 42.9 (1999): 1314–31; Mae M. Ngai, *Impossible Sub-*

jects: Illegal Aliens and the Making of Modern America (Princeton, NJ: Princeton University Press, 2004); Charles Ramírez-Berg, *Latino Images in Film: Stereotypes, Subversion, Resistance* (Austin: University of Texas at Austin, 2002); Rolando Romero, "Border of Fear, Border of Desire," *Borderlines* 1 (1993): 36–70; Alexandra Minna Stern, *Eugenic Nation: Faults and Frontiers of Better Breeding in Modern America* (Berkeley and Los Angeles: University of California Press, 2005).

3   See especially the debate over immigration within the Sierra Club that ensued, in 1996, in numerous online fora and on the Sierra Club's on Web site. T. M. Maher, "How and Why Journalists Avoid the Population-Environment Connection," *Population and the Environment* 18.4 (1997): 339–72. Also: www.cis.org/articles/1998/IR33/sierra_club.html (accessed December 14, 2005).

4   Leo R. Chávez, *Covering Immigration: Popular Images and the Politics of the Nation* (Berkeley and Los Angeles: University of California Press, 2001); Leo R. Chávez, "Immigration Reform and Nativism: The Nationalist Response to the Transnationalist Challenge," in *Immigrants Out!: The New Nativism and the Anti-Immigrant Impulse in the United States*, ed. Juan Perea, 61–77 (New York: New York University Press, 1997); Nicholas De Genova, "Migrant 'Illegality' and Deportability in Everyday Life," *Annual Review of Anthropology* 31 (2002): 419–47; Nicholas De Genova, "The Legal Production of Mexican/Migrant 'Illegality,'" *Latino Studies* 2.2 (2004): 160–85; David Gutiérrez, *Walls and Mirrors: Mexican Americans, Mexican Immigrants and the Politics of Ethnicity* (Berkeley and Los Angeles: University of California Press, 1996).

5   Mary Douglas, *Purity and Danger: An Analysis of the Concepts of Pollution and Taboo* (London: Routledge, 1966), 35.

6   It should be noted that the research conducted for this essay can no longer be exactly replicated as I undertook the bulk of it in the fall of 1998, when my two primary tools, *Readers Guide to Periodical Literature* and Lexis-Nexis Academic were quite different than what they are now. At that time the *Readers Guide* was only available in a nonsearchable print edition and Lexis-Nexis contained full-text articles of a number of newspapers and magazines that now have their own, subscriber-only, databases. In 1998, to find articles on the border in the *Readers Guide*, I was restricted to subject terms, while in Lexis-Nexis, I could search under a variety of key-word terms, such as "NAFTA," and "border" and "environment" and so forth. (My recent effort to reproduce these searches yielded significantly different data sets than when I first conducted the research.) I also reviewed the transcripts of several hundred broadcast news programs, indexed on Lexis-Nexis. Although electronic media no doubt played a significant role in what Americans consumed by way of images during NAFTA, methodologically it was (in 1998) and still is difficult to track thematic coverage of a topic through the electronic media. (For an argument on the relation between electronic media and contemporary subjectivity, see Arjun Appadurai, *Modernity at Large: Cultural Dimensions of Globalization* [Minneapolis: University of Minnesota Press, 1996].) Nonetheless, because of the enormous overlap between print and electronic media, print media serves as a valuable barometer of overall media coverage, especially the prestige and mainstream periodicals which often provide source material and set the standards for stories that warrant coverage for other media outlets. See John Bailey, "Mexico in the U.S. Media, 1979–1988," in *Images of Mexico in the United*

States, ed. John H. Coatsworth and Carlos Rico, 55–90 (La Jolla: Center for U.S.-Mexican Studies, University of California, San Diego, 1989).

7   I mean politics in a broad sense of how environmental ideas came to inform political sensibilities, though not necessarily specifically in the form of environmental organizations or lobbying.

8   Walter Benjamin, "The Work of Art in the Age of Mechanical Reproduction," in *Illuminations* (1936; reprint, New York: Schocken, 1968).

9   I am borrowing from Butler here. See Judith Butler, *Bodies That Matter: On the Discursive Limits of Sex* (New York: Routledge, 1993).

10   Bruce Braun, *The Intemperate Rainforest: Nature, Culture and Power on Canada's West Coast* (Minneapolis: University of Minnesota Press, 2002).

11   Raymond Williams, *The Country and the City* (New York: Oxford, 1973). See also David Harvey, *Justice, Nature and the Geography of Difference* (Oxford: Blackwell, 1996); Don Mitchell, *The Lie of the Land: Migrant Workers and the California Landscape* (Minneapolis: University of Minnesota Press, 1996); Neil Smith, *Uneven Development: Nature, Capital and the Production of Space* (New York: Blackwell, 1984); Bruce Willems-Braun, "Buried Epistemologies: The Politics of Nature in (Post)Colonial British Columbia," *Annals of the Association of American Geographers* 87.1 (1997): 3–31.

12   Frederick H. Buttel, "Environmentalism: Origins, Processes, and Implications for Rural Sociology," *Rural Sociology* 57.1 (1992): 1–27; Arturo Escobar, *Uneven Development: The Making and Unmaking of the Third World* (Princeton, NJ: Princeton University Press, 1994); Wolfgang Sachs, ed., *Global Ecology: A New Arena of Political Conflict* (Halifax, Nova Scotia: Fernwood Books, 1993).

13   Buttel, "Environmentalism"; James McCarthy, "Environmentalism, Wise Use and the Nature of Accumulation in the Rural West," in *Remaking Reality: Nature at the Millenium*, ed. Bruce Braun and Noel Castree, 126–49 (London: Routledge, 1998).

14   Eeva Berglund, *Knowing Nature, Knowing Science: An Ethnography of Local Environmental Knowledge* (Cambridge, England: White Horse Press, 1997), Dorothee Schneider, "'I Know All About Emma Lazarus': Nationalism and Its Contradictions in Congressional Rhetoric of Immigration," *Cultural Anthropology* 13.1 (1998): 82–99.

15   Audley, *Green Politics and Global Trade*, 46.

16   Phyllis Pease Chock, "'Illegal Aliens' And 'Opportunity': Myth Making in Congressional Testimony," *American Ethnologist* 18.2 (1991): 280.

17   Author interview, January 2006.

18   De Genova, "Migrant 'Illegality' and Deportability in Everyday Life"; De Genova, "The Legal Production of Mexican/Migrant 'Illegality.'"

19   Audley, *Green Politics and Global Trade*, 49.

20   Guy Gugliotta, "North American Free Trade Pact Could Shorten Clinton Honeymoon," *Washington Post*, November 14, 1992.

21   Dreiling, *Solidarity and Conflict*, 77.

22   Audley, *Green Politics and Global Trade*, 102–3.

23   See, for example, Steve Charnovitz, "The NAFTA Environmental Side Agreement: Implications for Environmental Cooperation, Trade Policy and American Treatymaking," *Temple International and Comparative Law Journal*, no. 257 (1994): 3–62. Of more significance has been the Border Environmental Cooperation and the North American Devel-

opment Bank, which together address specifically infrastructure deficits in border cities and towns.

24 Chávez, *Covering Immigration*; De Genova, "Migrant 'Illegality' and Deportability in Everyday Life," 436–39.

25 Carl J. Migdail, "Invasion from Mexico: It Just Keeps Coming," *U.S. News and World Report*, March 7, 1983; "Troubled Neighbor," *MacNeil/Lehrer Newshour*, July 11, 1986.

26 Wayne King, "Mexican Money Crisis Impels New Surge of Aliens to Texas," *New York Times*, March 10, 1983.

27 Joel Brinkley, "U.S. Set to Act on Mexico Border Drug Flow," *New York Times*, June 26, 1986; George Russell, "Trying to Stem the Illegal Tide," *Time*, July 8, 1985, p. 54.

28 Lawrences Coates, "Crossover Dreams: Impoverished Mexicans Find It Still Pays to Enter the U.S. Illegally, Risk or No Risk," *Chicago Tribune Magazine*, April 3, 1988, p. 12.

29 Brinkley, "U.S. Set to Act on Mexico Border Drug Flow."

30 Bailey, "Mexico in the U.S. Media, 1979–1988"; Christine Contee, "U.S. Perceptions of United States-Mexico Relations," in Coatsworth and Rico, *Images of Mexico in the United States*, 17–54; Dunn, *The Militarization of the U.S.-Mexico Border, 1978–1992*; Frank D. Bean, Barry Edmonston, and Jeffrey S. Passel, "Perceptions and Estimates of Undocumented Migration to the United States," in *Undocumented Migration to the United States: IRCA and the Experience of the 1980s*, ed. Bean, Edmonston, and Passel, 11–31 (Washington, DC: Urban Institute Press, 1990).

31 Bean, Edmonston, and Passel, "Perceptions and Estimates of Undocumented Migration to the United States," 16.

32 Gutiérrez, *Walls and Mirrors*.

33 Chávez, *Covering Immigration*; Daniel B. German, "The Role of the Media in Political Socialization and Attitude Formation toward Racial/Ethnic Minorities in the U.S.," in *Nationalism, Ethnicity, and Identity*, ed. Russell F. Farnen, 285–94 (New Brunswick, NJ: Transaction Publishers, 1994); Rita Simon and Susan Alexander, *The Ambivalent Welcome: Print Media, Public Opinion and Immigration* (Westport, CT: Praeger, 1993).

34 Brinkley, "U.S. Set to Act on Mexico Border Drug Flow"; John Borrell, "Journey Along the Border," *Time*, October 24, 1988; Brinkley, "U.S. Set to Act on Mexico Border Drug Flow"; Coates, "Crossover Dreams: Impoverished Mexicans Find It Still Pays to Enter the U.S. Illegally, Risk or No Risk," 11.

35 De León, *They Called Them Greasers*.

36 Alan Kraut, *Silent Travelers: Germs, Genes, and the "Immigrant Menace"* (Baltimore: Johns Hopkins University Press, 1994); Howard Markel and Alexandra Minna Stern, "The Foreignness of Germs: The Persistent Association of Immigrants and Disease," *Milbank Quarterly* 80.4 (2002): 757–88.

37 Alexandra Minna Stern, "Buildings, Boundaries, and Blood: Medicalization and Nation-Building on the U.S.-Mexico Border, 1910–1930," *Hispanic American Historical Review* 79.1 (1999): 41–81.

38 Alurista, "Myth, Identity and Struggle in Three Chicano Novels: Aztlán, Anaya, Méndez and Acosta," in *Aztlán: Essays on the Chicano Homeland*, ed. Rudolfo A. Anaya and Francisco Lomelí, 41–81 (Albuquerque: University of New Mexico Press, 1989); Ana Castillo, *Massacre of the Dreamers* (Albuquerque: University of New Mexico Press, 1994); Sergio D. Elizondo, "ABC: Aztlán, the Borderlands and Chicago," in *Missions in Conflict: Essays on*

U.S.-Mexican Relations and Chicano Culture, ed. Renate Schmidt-Von Bardeleben, Dietrich Briesemeister, and Bruce-Novoa, 13–24 (Santa Barbara: Santa Barbara Center for Chicano Studies, University of California, Santa Barbara, 1986).

39 "Border Clashes," *Macneil/Lehrer Newshour*, July 8, 1985.

40 John M. Crewdson, "Border Region Is Almost a Country Unto Itself, Neither Mexican Nor American," *New York Times*, February 14, 1979; Anthony Parisi, "Economic and Political Concerns Could Slow Tide of Mexican Oil," *New York Times*, February 13, 1979; Alan Riding, "Mexico Angry at U.S. As Carter Visit Nears," *New York Times*, February 11, 1979; William K. Stevens, "Millions of Mexicans View Illegal Entry to U.S. As Door to Opportunity," *New York Times*, February 12, 1979; "Troubled Neighbor."

41 Howard LaFranchi, "On Rio Grande, Pollution Knows No Borders," *Christian Science Monitor*, December 12, 1988; Lisa Belkin, "Separated by Border, 2 Cities Are United by Needs," *New York Times*, December 17, 1988; William Branigan, "Pollution under Scrutiny at U.S.-Mexico Border," *Washington Post*, October 24, 1989; Howard LaFranchi, "On Rio Grande, Pollution Knows No Borders," *Christian Science Monitor*, December 12, 1988; Sonia Nazario, "Boom and Despair," *Wall Street Journal*, September 22, 1989.

42 J. Michael Kennedy, "Border Has the Worst of Both Worlds," *Los Angeles Times*, October 2, 1989; John Dillin, "Mexico's Pollution Threatens Free Trade," *Christian Science Monitor*, May 13, 1991; Anne Reiley Dowd, "Viva Free Trade with Mexico!" *Fortune*, June 17, 1991; J. Michael Kennedy, "Border Has the Worst of Both Worlds," *Los Angeles Times*, October 2, 1989; Michael Satchell, "Poisoning the Border," *U.S. News and World Report*, May 6, 1991.

43 Nazario, "Boom and Despair."

44 "Overpopulation in Mexico's Cities Causes Problems," *60 Minutes*, November 3, 1991.

45 Dillin, "Mexico's Pollution Threats Free Trade."

46 Joe Old, "How Do You Clean up a 2,000 Mile Garbage Dump?" *Business Week*, July 6, 1992.

47 "A Permanent U.S.-Mexico Border Health Commission," *Journal of the American Medical Association* 263.4 (1990): 3319–21. Almost immediately references to the "AMA report" and the border as a cesspool began to appear in the press: Ana Arana, "The Waste," *San Francisco Chronicle*, Image section, August 30, 1992; Phillip Elmer-DeWitt, "Love Canals in the Making," *Time*, May 20, 1991; Linda Roach Moore, "AMA Urges Action on Severe Pollution along U.S.-Mexican Border," *Los Angeles Times*, June 27, 1990; "NAFTA and the Environment," *New York Times*, September 27, 1993; Old, "How Do You Clean up a 2,000 Mile Garbage Dump?"; Satchell, "Poisoning the Border"; "U.S. Companies Move to Mexico Because of Cheap Labor," *CBS Evening News* (1992); "U.S.-Mexico Border Zone near Ecological Disaster," *Journal of Commerce and Commercial Bulletin*, March 14, 1991; Larry Williams, "Fears of a Trade Deal 'Cesspool,'" *Chicago Tribune*, January 13, 1992. The media also continued to refer to the border as an "open sewer": Branigan, "Pollution under Scrutiny at U.S.-Mexico Border"; Dillin, "Mexico's Pollution Threatens Free Trade"; Nazario, "Boom and Despair." In so doing, they employed a stock motif found in media accounts of the generic third world; see Donald Reid, *Paris Sewers and Sewermen* (Cambridge, MA: Harvard University Press, 1991). But "cesspool" during this time became nearly synonymous with that corner of the third world that was the U.S.-Mexico border.

48 Nickey was a key congressional witness in hearings that brought the border's problems

to Washington's attention. For example, U.S. House, Subcommittee on Water Resources, *Inadequate Water Supply and Sewage Disposal Facilities Associated with "Colonias" along the United States and Mexican Border* (Washington: U.S. GPO, 1991) and U.S. Senate, Committee on Environment and Public Works, *Economic and Environmental Implications of the Proposed U.S. Trade Agreement with Mexico* (Washington: U.S. GPO, 1991).

49 Belkin, "Separated by Border, 2 Cities Are United by Needs."

50 "The Mexican-American Border: Hi Amigo," *The Economist*, December 12, 1992.

51 "California Border Towns Pay High Price for Low-Wage Immigrants," *CBS Morning News*, November 26, 1990.

52 Craig E. Colton and Peter N. Skinner, *The Road to Love Canal: Managing Industrial Wastes before the EPA* (Austin: University of Texas Press, 1996).

53 In comparison to "cesspool," Love Canal, a potentially powerful trope, appeared far less frequently: Elmer-DeWitt, "Love Canals in the Making"; S. C. Gwynne, "From Yukon to Yucatán," *Time*, June 3, 1991; Nazario, "Boom and Despair."

54 William Langewiesche, "The Border," *The Atlantic*, June 1992.

55 Satchell, "Poisoning the Border," 36, emphasis added.

56 Julia Kristeva, *The Powers of Horror* (New York: Columbia University Press, 1982).

57 De Genova, "The Legal Production of Mexican/Migrant 'Illegality.'"

58 Anna S. Meigs, "A Papuan Perspective on Pollution," *Man* 13.2 (1978): 304–18.

59 At this point most of these characterizations appear not in the "old" media, but rather on blogs and Web sites devoted to nativism. Some of the characteristic language can be found on www.limitstogrowth.org (accessed December 14, 2005), or on many of the Web sites of local chapters of the Minuteman Project, a growing nativist organization.

60 Samuel P. Huntington, "The Hispanic Challenge," *Foreign Policy*, no. 141 (2004).

Laura A. Lewis

Home Is Where the Heart Is:
Afro-Latino Migration and Cinder-Block
Homes on Mexico's Costa Chica

The Museum of Afromestizo Cultures (Museo de las Culturas Afromestizas "Vicente Guerrero") was inaugurated in Cuajinicuilapa, Guerrero, Mexico in 1999. Cuaji, as locals call it, is located on Federal Highway 200. This two-lane paved road is the only major artery on the Costa Chica, a historically black region of Mexico's rural southern Pacific coast. When I visited the museum in 2001, I purchased a Valentine's Day card from its small collection of gifts. The cover is a cutout heart; the interior has a blurred color photograph of a round structure of wattle-and-daub. A few dark-skinned people are outside the structure, sitting on a bench under an open shelter made of palm fronds (*ramada*). The caption describes the structure as a *redondo*, a round house, from the village of San Nicolás. One of the coast's "black villages" (*pueblos negros*), San Nicolás is a community with some 3,500 members and a subsistence base in small farming. It is located about 30 kilometers south of Cuaji, which is its municipal seat.

Directly above the photo is a verse referring to the town: "My mother told me not to go to San Nicolás; I'm going to San Nicolás even if I die tomorrow."[1] These words might be a general

South Atlantic Quarterly 105:4, Fall 2006
DOI 10.1215/00382876-2006-002   © 2006 Duke University Press

warning to avoid San Nicolás, or perhaps a more specific caution to the subject that his problems will only get worse if he follows his plan. The verse and the cutout heart also suggest, however, that the individual is drawn to this place so strongly that not even his own death will keep him from getting there.

Today, the houses most desired in San Nicolás are not redondos. They are—in striking contrast—boxy, unadorned structures made of cinder block. These are financed mainly through personal remittances sent by San Nicoladenses living in Winston-Salem, North Carolina, who frequently couch their motivations for migrating in terms of "building my house" (*hacer mi casa*) in San Nicolás.[2] Because both migrant and nonmigrant San Nicoladenses are caught up in the transnational flows that have become characteristic of this moment, their lives can no longer be contained within national boundaries.[3] San Nicoladenses living in the United States are intensely tied to the Mexican community, making the village space a prominent symbol of the connections between migrants and nonmigrants.[4] As I examine these processes, particularly in San Nicolás itself, I focus on how houses "there" indicate the ways in which migrant San Nicoladenses recall a place many have not seen for years, represent their aspirations for upward mobility, and express ongoing attachments to a community where family members remain and where most will return to be buried.

Throughout the article, I stress the paradoxical ways in which houses speak to senses of place, history, and notions of community and kin. Redondos highlight the disconnect in Mexico between an emphasis on the Third Root, or an "African" heritage, and local people's lack of interest in that heritage, in part because of their migration experiences and global restructuring, and in part because, as they see it, they are "Mexicans" for whom the past is not only *not* African, but gone. Cinder block highlights the ironies of the migrant experience, as people cement themselves to a place that changes day by day, in large part due to the accelerating transformations that migration engenders as aspirations for stability and upward mobility transform the community's physical and social landscape.

San Nicoladenses began to establish a community in the metropolitan area of Winston-Salem about fifteen years ago, after a decade of migrating to Santa Ana, California, where some still remain. A trickle turned into a stream as the southern United States offered work, inexpensive living accommodations, and relatively few Latinos with whom to compete for jobs.[5] Today the Winston-Salem community numbers close to one thousand people, most of whom hold low-wage jobs in the service industry, construction, and light manufacturing. Largely undocumented, most live in substandard and crowded housing, often in areas where drug dealing and violence are common. For many U.S. San Nicoladenses, sending remittances to family members in San Nicolás for the purpose of building a house there is a top priority. Such remittances are financially draining, as immigrants struggle to make ends meet, with obligations both in the United States and in Mexico.

Margarita, one of my *comadres*[6] living in Winston-Salem, and her husband Maximino have been able over the past five years to build a large five-room house in San Nicolás, with a wide breezeway that runs its length. I generally stay there when I go to San Nicolás, and have contributed in small ways to the home's construction. One day I called Margarita to ask her about the card I had just brought back from Mexico. After I read to her the verse, she said that it reminded her of the ballads (*corridos*) from her youth.[7] It is from the past, she told me, a time when the community was rife with violence, explaining the reference to mortality, a common theme in many Mexican ballads, not just ones from the coast.[8] But the verse on the card was specific to San Nicolás, and its content as well as its placement above the redondo suggested an abiding connection to this place. One might read the connection as a rootedness in the past, when redondos and ballads were the norm. Margarita described it with a hint of shame as a time when people did not know how to read, were "ignorant," and were more prone to settle disputes through violence. As in many rural Mexican areas, there were frequent agrarian disputes with wealthy landowners and neighboring communities, as Margarita pointed out. But many outsiders attribute the Costa Chica's violence to a local ethos bound to what they construe as its people's African roots, while others, in a different racist move, attribute to blacks a *bravo* (fierce or uncivilized) character.[9]

San Nicolás has long been seen by outsiders as hostile and unwelcoming. However, over the past two decades, Mexico's drive for multiculturalism has produced a set of artifacts and discourses identifying and valorizing African cultural survivals in Mexico. Black villages have become attractive to a variety of cultural investigators, who consider San Nicolás a community where the "old" traditions survive and are drawn there in search of the African bits of the Mexican mosaic. In the context of this discourse, and as the note card implies, redondos have become emblems of a distinctive local culture and identity.

This identity rests on what some researchers refer to as "vestige[s] of African inheritance,"[10] with which majority Mexicans have an ambivalent relationship. "Afro" Mexico is said to have a place alongside the Indian and Spanish roots of the nation and is thus lauded as a cornerstone of modern Mexico. Yet it is also associated with a primitive past and a time when national culture had not yet penetrated the Costa Chica. The discrepancy between outsider perspectives that anchor the past in "wild" African things and give value to their benign survival in the present, and the perspectives of local people who do not self-identify as "Afro" Mexican or even as black, has become clear over my years of fieldwork. San Nicoladenses look back on the past with a mixture of nostalgia and shame; they see themselves as modern Mexicans looking toward a future that distances them from the past. Most find that future in the United States, which they refer to as "the north" (*el norte*) or "the other side" (*el otro lado*). Over the past few decades, migration from San Nicolás to the United States has all but emptied the community of the physical presence of its middle generation and their older children.

Transnationalism, Place, and the Mundane

San Nicoladenses such as Margarita articulate their rationale for leaving San Nicolás through reference to the village itself by linking migration to their desires to build cinder-block houses for their families in San Nicolás. For them, redondos and other dwellings made of earth, such as adobe, are not "real" houses. But redondos do draw attention to San Nicolás's past, for until about thirty-five years ago they were common in the village, and many people remember living in them. More than signifying the past, however, redondos have a central place in the cultural calculus of the present as cultural promoters—anthropologists, local intellectuals, and politicians— "rescue" (*rescatar*) local traditions to draw out the exotic. As they do, however, local people replace the earth of the past with the cinder block of the modern.[11] Because cinder block belongs to the modern, however, it is never part of the cultural promotion that rests on the buried differences of the past. Contemporary houses are thus made invisible in scholars' contemporary accounts of local culture on the Costa Chica.

The sheer ordinariness and ubiquity of cinder-block homes in San Nicolás demands an ethnography of the mundane that contextualizes such homes in the more extraordinary experiences of people's lives, in this case the parallel processes of migration and global restructuring that simultaneously foster displacements *and* reconnections in new and affective ways. Over the last decade or so, these processes in Mexico and elsewhere in Latin America have generated new theoretical insights into migration, all but replacing traditional models resting on unidirectional movement and assimilation.[12] Today scholars stress that many Latin Americans and immigrants to the United States from other parts of the world live "simultaneously in two countries" multilocally through "transnational migrant circuits" or "social fields."[13]

The theoretical scholarship on migration often fails to address directly the issue of undocumented versus documented immigrants. For the former, simultaneity might in fact not be characteristic. For instance, the majority of U.S. San Nicoladenses exist in a kind of liminal space that makes it almost impossible for them to fully "live" in the United States even though they spend their time there. They cannot participate in U.S. society in the ways that legal residents and citizens can. Most people older than fifteen do not speak English and thus cannot communicate with landlords, employers, the electric company, and so on. They are also stymied by state and federal laws that make it all but impossible to move about.[14] Furthermore, due to their legal status and their relatively recent history of migration, most San Nico-ladenses do not participate easily in border-crossing processes because the return journey costs too much and is too dangerous. All of this conspires against their cultural fluidity or bifocality, a description that assumes an equal sense of belonging in two places at once.[15] Instead, their orientation is generally toward the village of San Nicolás and the country of Mexico, which motivates the current generation of San Nicoladenses with hopes for a future return.

Without downplaying the fissures and dislocations that characterize migration, or losing sight of the economic, social, and political conditions that compel it, I believe that, perhaps counterintuitively, it is *because* of their undocumented status that U.S. San Nicoladenses do not experience migration as *disrupting* ties to their home communities. Indeed, rather than being "radically pulled . . . apart from place,"[16] they seem to be constantly pulled toward it through actions and words. By attending to their Mexican connections, I therefore highlight the meaningful sentiments and obligations that orient them to their village and make them always (affectively) present there.[17]

That presence and those sentiments are evident in the marks they leave on the place they left behind. Those marks and that place are central to the logic compelling San Nicoladenses to leave, but they are also evidence of their ongoing identification with home. Most pointedly, the cinder-block houses of San Nicolás speak to the violence of a modernity that ruptures family ties and to other social changes engendered by migration. Yet they also and equally speak to the enduring importance of place, kin, and belonging, and to the paradoxes of being labeled black in Mexico, where blackness is historically tantamount to ongoing displacements.

Cinder block might not at first glance seem to inspire culturally thick ethnographic description. We associate it with the blandness of suburban utopias dotted with strip malls; it is denigrated by elites in those parts of the world where the maintenance of the quaint or exotic feeds tourist economies.[18] But cinder-block dwellings are texts for reading how San Nicoladenses, both at home and abroad, are embedded in a transnational world. That embeddedness is inscribed not just in the houses that people build and often do not occupy for years as they struggle to make it in the United States, but also in the tombs in San Nicolás's cemetery, which personal remittances also pay for and which also index the persistence of place and kin even as they make apparent the scope of the transformations that finally send San Nicoladenses home.

The Past in the Present

San Nicolás's majority population is descended in part from sixteenth-century free and enslaved blacks brought to the coast by Spanish landowners. The free and enslaved population was joined by maroons who settled on the coast after fleeing other parts of Mexico.[19] Along with most of what are referred to today as Costa Chica's *pueblos negros*, San Nicolás is located on the coastal plains, where the land is relatively fertile and where cattle raising—largely by elites—has been part of the economy since colonial times.[20] The community's agrarian history is marked by conflicts and boundary disputes with large landowners. During the 1930s agrarian reform, San Nicolás became an *ejido*,[21] with land carved out of the white American engineer Carlos Miller's 100,000-hectare estate, on which San Nicoladenses had tended his cattle and grown cotton for his cottonseed oil factory. Today, San Nicolás contains about six hundred small farmers who raise cattle, corn, and chile for subsistence and sesame and mangoes for local and regional markets. Unfortunately, these markets have seen dramatic price drops as international policies remove supports and agrarian assistance while opening markets to free trade in commodities and leaving geopolitical borders closed to the free movement of people.

To the north of the coastal plain and its black villages lie the region's small cities—Ometepec, Pinotepa Nacional, and Cuaji. These are still dominated by an economic elite of merchants, politicians, and professionals who would be "mestizo" in national parlance but who are locally referred to as "whites" (*blancos*). In the hills and mountains farther north are indigenous communities of mostly Amuzgo and Mixtec speakers. San Nicoladenses refer to them as "Indians" or as "Indian Indians," depending on how assimilated they perceive them to be. They have poorer land and tend to be more impoverished than whites and African-descent Mexicans, who hire them to work as unskilled laborers on their own holdings.

In recent decades, San Nicolás has become home to several hundred people from an arid and hilly northern zone of the Costa Chica. These relative newcomers are designated "Indians" by majority San Nicoladenses. This is because of their phenotype and geographical origin rather than because of their dress and language, the usual national markers of indigenousness; these individuals suppress "Indian" dress and language or leave them behind. When San Nicolás's Indians began to arrive thirty years ago, land was plentiful and had not yet been privatized, and the Indians became community members with rights to community land. Today, population growth and market demands have put pressure on landholdings, and San Nicolás's Indians often voice fear of ejection from the village while simultaneously disparaging "blacks" as "not from here." These Indians tend to be less well off than the community's African-descent residents, who sometimes still refer to the Indians in a colonial idiom as *gente sin razón* (people without reason, i.e., uncivilized people).[22]

Scholars have long referred to the Costa Chica's African-descent people as "black" (*negro*). This racial label is still maintained, but over the past decade and in the context of cultural preservation initiatives funded largely by the Mexican federal Office of Popular Cultures, "black" has come to overlap with "Afromestizo" and "Afromexican" as politicians, anthropologists, artists, and other culture workers shift their language to accommodate people they identify as the "Third Root"—after Indians and Europeans—of the Mexican nation. San Nicolás's "blacks" are caught up in complex ways in the politics of cultural production. They count as ancestors the African-descent people who have populated the region since colonial times, but they are largely unaware of the history of slavery in Mexico, know nothing about Africa, and ascribe Mexico's status as a "free" country to Indian heroes who "broke the chains of slavery."[23] As with other Mexicans, central to their consciousness is a Mexican national identity that has traditionally rested on ideologies reconciling a romanticized Indian past with an elusive modernity achieved through whitening. Such an identity is therefore a deeply mestizo one, and it has always erased blackness from the face of the nation while including both Indians and whites. That "blacks" are considered people "without a country," as I was once told by a mestizo cab driver from one of the coast's small cities, captures the state of *not belonging* with which African-descent Mexicans have grappled and which have excluded them from the nation.

This historical and ongoing exclusion is part of the reason that majority San Nicoladenses do not self-identify as wholly black (*negro*), a term they reserve for their ancestors, for insults, for people in *other* villages, and for what outsiders say about them. Still less do they see themselves as Afromexican or Afromestizo, in part because "African," like "black," makes them *different* from other Mexicans. Instead, African-descent San Nicoladenses, like majority Mexicans, see Indians as integral to their own identities. Referring to themselves as *criollos* (native-born) and to Indians as *naturales* (primordial natives), they combine what James Clifford calls "diaspora cosmopolitanisms," which draw on historical contexts of displacement, with indigenous claims to continuity, which rest on "natural" connections to places.[24] They refer to themselves as a "race" (*raza*) of "black-Indian" *morenos*, contrasting themselves not only to the *negros* of the past but also to the African Americans with whom they have contact in the United States. *Morenos* make Indians central to San Nicolás's agrarian struggles and filter black-Indian experiences and perspectives through local rituals, stories, histories, politics, kinship, and supernaturalism. Significantly, the authentic statue of the village's dark-skinned eponymous patron saint—San Nicolás Tolentino—is guarded and worshiped in an Indian community 300 kilometers from the coast.[25]

Redondos similar to the one depicted on the museum note card were still common on the Costa Chica in the 1940s, when the late Mexican anthropologist Gonzalo Aguirre Beltrán conducted the several weeks of fieldwork in Cuaji that formed the basis for the only ethnographic monograph focused on Mexicans of African descent. He emphasized what he saw as the isolation of the region's "blacks" as well as their differences from both national (mestizo) and indigenous populations. For him, redondos were "cultural retentions of African origin, more specifically, Bantu."[26] The Mexican scholar Gutierre Tibón drew a much different conclusion, however, when just a bit later he visited the "black" Costa Chican village of Collantes, Oaxaca. Tibón noted that round houses were characteristic of the precolumbian Cauca region of Colombia, as well as of areas of Mexico to which blacks never arrived. He subsequently questioned the logic of Aguirre Beltrán's argument. "Are [Mixtec round houses] precolumbian?" he asked rhetorically, or "a cultural loan from the Africans?" "If some ancient tradition survives in Collantes," he continued, "it is not African but rather Indoamerican." He referred to locals as "Afromixtecos" because of their "mixed" African and Indian heritage.[27]

Although the problem of origins cannot be definitively answered, it is not a question of academic musing or a pointless exercise in outsider essentialism. For Aguirre Beltrán's rather than Tibón's assessment was seized on in the 1980s and 1990s by scholars of black Mexico, and the idea that redondos and other cultural forms are vestiges of Africa and have their origins in "black" culture guides much outsider interest in—and interactions with— local communities on the coast, including San Nicolás.[28] "[Redondos] are now all over the place," I once heard a schoolteacher from Cuaji remark, "even up in the Mixteca (an indigenous part of Guerero and Oaxaca states). This is blacks' influence."

What is happening in Mexico is similar to what has happened in other Latin American locales, where a "black" culture is identified by outsiders and then equated with African survivals depicted as isolated and leftover fragments of a tangible past to which the value of the present is seen to adhere.[29] Within this discourse, the meanings local people give to their "roots" are overlooked in favor of the priorities of outsiders.

Like other local traditions, such as the music known as *sones de artesa* (also coded as African), redondos are folklorized in ways that spatially and temporally decontextualize them. Redondos are turned into portable pictures and replicas and made available for national and even international consumption.[30] During my first visit to San Nicolás in 1992, I was brought directly to a redondo that turned out to be a replica built in the 1980s at the urging of a visiting Mexican anthropologist.[31] It stood on the outskirts of the village on borrowed land, next to a carved wooden trough used as a dancing platform for performances of *artesa* music. Ernesto, the San Nicoladense who took me to the spot, contended that it was the "African center" of the village. This comment caught my attention because the space was at some remove from the village's demographic heart. But I later came to understand that I was invited to visit this site and it was presented to me in the way that it was because Ernesto, an *artesa* musician familiar with the discourse of cultural promotion, was personally caught up in the politics of Africanness. The site he brought me to represented what he saw as of interest to outsiders, who typically seek out "lost" traditions.

The model of the redondo Ernesto identified as African, the one built at the urging of an anthropologist in the 1980s, appears on the note card I found in the museum. The image is therefore twice removed from the authenticity that it seeks to convey. Over the years, the replica has crumbled following a move to a new location: the outskirts of the village next to the shuttered *casa de cultura* (cultural promotion center). No one attends to either of these structures, which are surrounded by overgrown brush. Yet whenever there is a new cultural initiative, outsiders move to have a redondo rebuilt, and the *casa de cultura* again becomes a topic for discussion. Redondos otherwise still surface in contexts controlled by outsiders, who emphasize the past as the repository and fount of racial and cultural difference. Thus, models of redondos cast in concrete are found outside the main building of the museum, control of which has been a source of contention between local "blacks" and "whites." An image of a redondo appeared on the badges made for participants in the 1997 First Meeting of Black [*negro*] Communities, organized by a Trinidadian priest who lives in a nearby Oaxacan Costa Chican village. The attendees—mostly local intellectuals and schoolchildren—seized on redondos as evidence of African influence in the region. Redondos were also depicted—along with palm trees, the ocean, and a black woman in a short skirt carrying water on her head—on the backdrop created for the First Traditional Fair organized by cultural promoters and held in San Nicolás in January 1998.

San Nicoladenses collectively refer to culture promoters as *la cultura* (the culture).[32] As Arlene Torres and Norman Whitten have noted in their work on African-descent Latin Americans, pairing the Spanish article *la* (the) with *cultura* in situations similar to the one I describe here has the effect of elevating culture to a level of "refinement" and "civilization" that contrasts with "low" culture.[33] That San Nicoladenses collectively refer to cultural promoters in the singular and with the article "la" speaks to the distance they perceive between themselves and those who have come to study them. For while cultural initiatives are meant to draw "Afro"-Mexicans into a Mexico that unites its people through their differences, many San Nicoladenses see what one scholar calls the "Africa thesis" as emphasizing their *difference* from other Mexicans while inventing and valorizing the past in ways that are meaningful mostly to outsiders.[34] As one elderly man pointed out to me, "[*La cultura*] is concerned with dated things, but we are in the modern world."

Nostalgia and Shame

San Nicoladenses are cautious about those who profess to act on their behalf. In part this is because cultural promoters and political activists impose identities without addressing the community's experiences or concerns, which include migration and access to basic infrastructure—drainage, paved roads, consistent running water, decent schools—and to the material wealth that late modernity holds out as a promise. In part it is because the interests of the cultural promoters focus on a few local residents, particularly the musicians who were taught *sones de artesa* music in the 1980s and who now perform it mostly for outside audiences. And in part this caution is because many in the community see themselves giving away their cultural capital without getting anything in return. Modesto put it rather bluntly one day as we chatted under the shade of an almond tree in one of my *comadre*'s yards in San Nicolás: "The round house doesn't interest the people here," he said. "That's why [people] don't take care of it. They need someone to pay them. Who's going to pay someone to work in the casa de cultura?" Maximino told me much the same thing in North Carolina. "Miguel Angel [the anthropologist] paid them to make [the redondo]. They don't want to do it anymore. They don't want to cut the wood. They just want to be paid."

For some San Nicoladenses, especially for elderly ones, my questions about redondos brought out wistfulness and ambivalence, as well as descriptions of the more "rustic" but also more generous environment of the past. The recently deceased Margarito, who was born in the wilderness at the height of the 1910 Revolution, during which San Nicolás burned to the ground because its houses were so flammable, described the old San Nicolás as "pure sticks . . . no streets, just redondos, just trails; the village was full of brush." His daughter Lupe, who is Maximino's mother and now in her midsixties, described how redondos would be bunched together during her childhood. People made bonfires and everyone would bring their sleeping mats outside to smoke tobacco. "Men and women would come out to chat," she continued in a long chain of associations. "There weren't any streets. People ate deer, beans, fish, pigeons, iguana, wild pig, badger. [But] then the jungle disappeared," she continued. "The vegetation ended. They began to take down the trees—to remove the brush, you know, agriculture. . . . People used to have a few cattle for the milk, their own chickens, they would grow chiles, tomatoes, and beans and get their salt from seawater, they'd make soap too, but now everything is bought—people want to buy things."

When Sirina, my close friend and *comadre* of three years, was growing up in San Nicolás, her grandparents lived in a redondo. "[Redondos] were made of long fronds [*bejuco*], with earthen walls," she explained. "People would put more grasses on the roof and then would mark off the area with their feet. The beds would be inside and people would make a raised platform out of sticks to keep their clothes off of the ground." She added and laughed: "Cows lived among the people. They would be milked on the patio in front of the house, and come and go by themselves." Like Sirina, Manuel linked redondos to "the time of his grandfather." Back then, he also added, in a raced assessment of progress, the village was "really, really black and there was nothing here."

With the exception of Ernesto, who is familiar with the rhetoric of "la cultura," when local people discuss the origins of redondos they link them not to Africans but to Indians and to a past that was simpler, more deprived, and more rural than the present. "Generations of Indians made houses like [redondos]," Maximino told me. "They can still be found in the hills and mountains . . . who knows where." Even elderly people can be negative about redondos. "Redondos were for poor people," Domingo told me. "Rich people—those who had cattle—built square houses (*casas largas*)." The ninety-year-old Catalina expressed it this way: "Before, there weren't any good houses—just redondos. . . . Now there are only good houses."

If you walk through San Nicolás today, you will notice endless neat rows of "good houses": square and rectangular cinder-block dwellings (and a few red brick ones) in various stages of construction. Yet you will also notice a smattering of unreinforced adobe houses, and even more rustic *bajareque* wattle-and-daub, which are mostly abandoned. Like the ancestral redondos, adobe and *bajareque* are made principally of earth mixed with plant materials. Adobe is sometimes sided with plaster and, like "modern" homes and the historical homes of local elites, earthen houses are rectangular or square.[35] Many of them are transformed into storage or kitchen extensions as their owners move into new cinder-block houses. But many people in

San Nicolás still live in adobe homes. Such homes have pitted walls and dirt floors and, like redondos, have come to be associated with poverty and low status. Sirina told me that it "shames" people to live in a house made of earth and to be perceived as the poorest members of the community. "If you construct a house out of earth," she said, "people will say you are poor and can't make it." Once she derisively described such houses as of "muck" (*lodo*). Lupe once asked me whether Sirina and her family—whose home is brick and added onto year after year with money sent by their son in North Carolina—had a dirt floor in their home as she attempted to gauge how wealthy they were. Sirina, for her part, pointed out that Angela, an "Indian" resident of San Nicolás who lives in an adobe house with exposed walls, "should have had 'her house' a long time ago, but Pedro (Angela's husband) drinks." In Sirina's mind, then, Angela did not yet have "her" house, a "real" house, because she still lived in one made of earth and her family was not unified.

Angela's two grown children and her husband are currently in North Carolina, while she remains in San Nicolás with her young daughter-in-law Chela. She lives among San Nicolás's other Indians in what is considered to be "their" neighborhood on the outskirts of town. On the whole these Indian latecomers have fewer resources—including land—than *morenos*. But due to increases in the Indians' wealth and in intermarriage between *morenos* and Indians, migration and cinder-block homes have taken hold in this neighborhood as well. Angela is therefore even more self-conscious about her adobe dwelling, with its "rustic" walls and dirt floor, fearing not just that *morenos* but also her own kin and neighbors pity her for her material circumstances and for her husband's drinking. Her house might not be a "nice" house, she once said to me, but she always has food and I am always welcome to eat there. She then segued into a discussion of the redondos still favored by indigenous people in the uplands.

Angela's adobe house is surrounded by piles of building materials purchased over the years with funds sent mostly by her son Oscar, as her husband has trouble holding a job. Oscar works in construction in North Carolina and at home, and he will build Angela's "real" house when he returns from the United States. "Oscar is an excellent bricklayer," Angela remarked. "He's going to make us a house in a [city] style. Everyone will like it; he'll then get a lot of work in San Nicolás and he'll never have to go back to the U.S." In fact, construction in San Nicolás provides many opportunities for builders, electricians, and even plumbers as drainage capacities expand and people want the flush toilets and indoor kitchens they became accustomed to in the United States. These workers also wait for the migrant remittances that provide their livelihood in San Nicolás. Although what people make in the United States far outweighs what they could make in San Nicolás or even in Mexico City, economic downturns or too much competition among workers in the United States does sometimes cause migrant San Nicoladenses to send less money home, bringing construction in San Nicolás to a halt.

Stable Attachments and the Tense Mobilities

Indians such as Angela live on the outskirts of town in part because they are relative newcomers and in part because property is expensive in the center, which is tightly packed with houses or plots of land awaiting houses. In the past, the plant materials and earth for redondos were freely available from the surrounding wilderness (*monte*), even when the land that today belongs to the community belonged to Carlos Miller, and San Nicoladenses were peasant tenants and workers on Miller's *latifundia*.[36] The prefabricated cinder block of today is referred to as *material*. This, of course, must be purchased, and most is purchased with remittances. As Lupe's cousin Chico put it rather succinctly, "Lots of dollars, lots of houses."

People go to the United States for those dollars because in San Nicolás "there is no way to make money to build a house for your children," Sirina told me. "If there weren't opportunities in Carolina, there wouldn't be any houses." Such sentiments challenge racist local and national discourses that represent "blacks" as lazy, violent, uninterested in improving themselves, and really "not Mexican" at all. San Nicoladenses not only migrate like other rural Mexicans; they also desire to be upwardly mobile in order to reinscribe themselves as Mexicans in generic Mexican houses that are far removed from the ethnicized *redondos* of the past.

With that past perceived as rooted in Indianness, poverty, dirt, and rurality, *morenos* also link progress and upward mobility to their "mestizoization," an identity that retains an emphasis on Indianness and mixedness but is closer to the romantic Mexican ideal of a glorified Indianized past and a "whiter" future. "The people [here] are modernizing themselves; now they are 'mestizo,'" Lupe told me. She also noted that now people wear shoes because they move about in cities rather than in the countryside. For her, then, "mestizoization" moved people beyond "morenoness," but it was not simply or even primarily a race-based term. Rather, it indexed a move from rurality and poverty, tangentially associated with "darkness," to urbanity and wealth, tangentially associated with "lightness."

The twin processes of "dollarization" and mestizoization engage both geographical and economic mobility. These processes drive and result from migration to the United States, where *gabachos*—white people—hold political and economic power. In the United States, rural San Nicoladenses move to urban areas, develop new aesthetic and ideological tastes, and, like other Mexican immigrants, turn into "eager shoppers" with the means to acquire things unavailable in San Nicolás.[37] Perceptions of deficits in San Nicolás keep some from returning home. As Margarita's sister Alicia once told me while we sat around Margarita's dining-room table in Winston-Salem, "If I went back to San Nicolás, well, I would have money, but there would be nothing to buy!" Her son lives in San Nicolás with his extended family, while Alicia, who is single, sends money to support him and to build her own home.

The United States is not just a place where things can be acquired. It is also seen as cleaner, more orderly, and more comfortable than Mexico. The highways are smooth and wide, I was told admiringly by the elderly Ernesto, who had visited his adult sons in California. My friend Judit's young son, who was born in Winston-Salem and returned to San Nicolás with his parents when he was three, repeatedly told Judit he wanted to go back to North Carolina because "the floors are cleaner there." My former neighbor in San Nicolás, Ismael, who left for Winston-Salem eight years ago when he was seventeen, does not want his own son, who was born in Winston-Salem and has never been to Mexico, to grow up "in the dirt" as he and his younger brothers did.

Despite Ismael's sentiments, even he on occasion checks in with me to see if I can take his son to San Nicolás to visit his grandmother, my *comadre* Rosa. Although Ismael has always changed his mind, most people would go back and forth frequently if they were not undocumented. But home grows ever more distant, as it is nearly impossible for most people to regularly attend the rituals that characterize village life in San Nicolás. Those who have left children and other family members behind wonder when they will have a chance to see them, and telephone calls and videos of missed events are lifelines. People long for the tastes and smells of their home community. Sirina's brother Teo once demonstrated this dramatically while we were riding around Winston-Salem in my car: He suddenly rubbed his belly in an exaggerated way, threw his head back, closed his eyes, and moaned about the iguana he would like to eat. In her Winston-Salem kitchen Margarita cooks the same tamales, barbecued beef, and cheese that she would make in San Nicolás, some of which she sells to San Nicoladenses in Winston-Salem to supplement the family income. After my visits to Mexico, I haul large suitcases and boxes filled with dried meat and shrimp, country cheese, and fresh herbs for San Nicoladenses in Winston-Salem. These foods are not simply about people's gastronomical preferences. They fall somewhere between "ways of being" and "ways of belonging," as people identify through food as Mexicans and as San Nicoladenses.[38]

Perhaps more profound than food choices are the senses of connectedness to the village, which remain deeply and unconsciously ingrained in San Nicoladenses' very gestures. I realized this one day as Margarita and I conversed *in Winston-Salem* about where a particular family lived in San Nicolás. At one point Margarita quite spontaneously and naturally waved her arm and gestured with her hand as she said, "Over there, by the main road" to point me in the right direction, as if we were orienting ourselves in San Nicolás itself.

Going Home, Going Mexican

Houses of *material* have become "symbols of progress," as the Mexican journalist and political commentator Juan Sánchez Andraka writes with reference to northern Guerrero. In contrast, he also writes, "huts and mudbrick have become symbols of social and economic failure." He sees such "progress" as the by-product of a paternalistic state that effects "criminal reconstructions of Catholic churches, covering [even] colonial jewels with cement."[39] Yet while cement might jar the aesthetic sensibilities of intellectuals, and while San Nicolás's unadorned and boxy abodes with their flat slab roofs become all but uninhabitable ovens in the tropical heat, local people consider cinder block more visually pleasing and infinitely more stable than earth.

Nineteen-year-old Amalia, my godchild (*ahijida*) and Ismael's younger sister, has lived for the past two years in Winston-Salem with her husband. She once told me, as we swung in a hammock in the backyard of the two-bedroom, dilapidated house she shares with her husband and his male cousins, brothers and uncle, that "houses made of earth are from the past." "Who would want a house made of dirt?" she asked. She stayed home to look after Ismael's son, who was not yet in school, and to cook for the men while her husband worked to save for what Amalia described as a square or rectangular house with "straight" (*plano*) walls and floors. Back in San Nicolás, Sirina pointed out that while cinder-block houses "might be hot, they survive earthquakes." "[They] do not [fall down]," she said. "They do not get damaged." This part of Mexico also sees its fair share of floods and the high winds and hurricanes that still sometimes blow away corrugated tin roofs. Redondos would "fall to pieces because of the wind and the water," Sirina explained to me. They also easily went up in flames from candles; San Nicolás and Cuaji were both burned to the ground during the Mexican Revolution. In one account the disappearance from the village of its patron saint is linked to a storm that lasted fifteen days and destroyed many redondos, including his. The earth out of which such dwellings were made thus symbolizes the ephemeral, the missing, and the insecurity of the past that people struggled with, even as they now struggle equally to anchor themselves to the ground.

By some accounts, cement was first introduced into rural Mexican communities when the federal government began to build primary schools in the 1960s and 1970s. Instead of constructing local schools with local materials, as Sánchez Andraka writes of northern Guerrero, "schools were made of prefabricated materials and their construction implied specialized knowledge of how to utilize those materials."[40] For San Nicoladenses, the government-built primary school is in fact the turning point in their own collective memory, and they link it to migration. Sirina, for instance, remembers exactly when it was that "good" houses entered the consciousness of San Nicoladenses: after a cyclone in the mid 1970s, when the state founded San Nicolás's first primary school. "From the beginning," Sirina went on, "the schools were made out of *material*." Local people watched as the building progressed, learning the building techniques and modeling their desires for more secure houses on the school. But they did not have the economic wherewithal to buy *material*. Some went off to Acapulco to work and send money back to build a house. "Little by little, people started going off to Mexico City," Sirina said. "Now they go to *el norte*." This indicates that the larger-scale processes wrought by migration to the United States are continuations of changes that were already under way before such migration became the norm.[41]

The strength of gender roles and gender segregation in San Nicolás has historically meant that *women* are closely associated with the community's history of migration. In the past, husbands typically worked the land and cared for the livestock while wives found positions as domestics in Mexico City and sent money home for expenses, including house building. Women separated from their husbands were generally not permitted to return to their father's house, which is still inherited by the youngest son and his wife.[42] Traditionally, these women also went to Mexico City to make a living.

Sirina told me that "from the beginning women have been the ones to pay for the houses." "Amparo's daughter was the first to go" to the United States, she said. The daughter sent money to build the house that Amparo now lives in. Sirina continued, "People would pass by Amparo's house and say, 'Look at the nice house Amparo has.'" Today, although men migrate and couples often cross the border together, single women occasionally go too. Like single men, they live with relatives in the United States while working and sending money home to purchase their own house plot and build their own house. Variations on the kind of home Amparo's daughter built for her are now the norm in San Nicolás, where "even *señoritas* (young women who are virgins and not yet married) can build their own houses," Sirina's husband and my *compadre* (co-father) Rodrigo once exclaimed to me. His own daughter, who separated from her husband soon after marrying him, will be permitted to stay in her father's house for only a short time before she is expected to join her brother in the north. When she goes, her infant will stay behind with Sirina.

In order to build a house, individuals first purchase house plots (*solares*), which are typically fenced off in order to keep other people's wandering pigs—and other people—from encroaching. As a house is built, window openings and breezeways will typically be protected with wrought iron gratings. If the owner can afford it, outside walls will be erected to protect the whole property, as is typical in Mexico, and those walls might be embedded with glass bits or barbed wire for additional security. Most houses are one story, but they have flat rather than pitched roofs in order to accommodate a second floor that adobe could never support. While finished second stories are becoming more common, most houses have protruding metal rods that *anticipate* a future second floor and thus continued upward mobility.

In the past, twenty or so people could lift a redondo and move it to another locale. This meant that extended family could always take in a member who was in trouble. "I had a cousin," Margarito told me before he died. "She got married and lived on the edge of town, where she had her house. They killed her husband, though, and she moved closer in. They brought her house from there. About twenty people tied it up, someone stuck their head inside [to lift it], and they brought it here." "People could move much more easily back then," Sirina said, "because there was a lot more space and now there is none. You could move and build another house."

That redondos were movable meant that disputing parties could separate easily. But new notions of ownership and the sheer immobility of cinder block have increased social tensions because feuds can no longer be resolved by one party moving a dwelling to another location. "Now," Juan told me in San Nicolás, "if you want to change locations] you have to sell." Conflicts arise around interpersonal issues, fruit trees, drainage, rain runoff, and passageways. Sirina used her son's remittances to build a massive brick wall to block her home off from that of the sister-in-law she despises; Delfina once accused me of eating the mangoes that fell from her tree onto my roof, and during the rainy season the runoff from the palm-frond shack that her family used to relieve themselves would drain into Sirina's outdoor kitchen; Lupe did not think she should have to leave room for cars and pedestrians as she built a wall to enclose the house that belongs to one of her emigrant sons; Felipa insists that her neighbor built his wall on her house plot while she was gone; and so on. Such conflicts over property sometimes result in full-blown hostilities that are resolved only through the intervention of the village mayor.

"Before," Sirina explained to me one day, "the people were poorer; with the opportunities that exist in Carolina now, people can go make money to live well, more or less." While new sources of wealth from migration have allowed people to improve their standard of living in ways that are meaningful to them, such sources have also escalated tensions between households. These tensions are linked to emerging class differences. As a middle-aged woman named Yolanda pointed out, "In the past we were all humbler and poorer. Now those who go to 'el norte' send money and we are growing more distant from one another because of jealousy. Now the person who has a lot of money is proud." Rosa put it this way: "Here the person who has money does less [than a poor person] and doesn't even speak to those who do not have [anything]—to poor people."

Reconfiguring Kinship

The processes that have reconfigured dwelling spaces also index changes in kinship, including the potential destruction of the very unity of the families for whom cinder-block houses are built. The fact that, as Rodrigo told me, even unmarried girls have the wherewithal to purchase their own homes is one indication of this. So is the fact that San Nicolás has become "a nursery and nursing home" for the children and parents of migrants.[43] As Vertovec points out, the lives of such nonmigrants are also transformed by migration.[44] Lupe, one such nonmigrant, feels abandoned because four of her six children, and most of her grandchildren, are in North Carolina. She has no one to help her with the demands of the land and cattle she inherited from her husband, who was killed many years ago in a local land dispute. She links her abandonment and subsequent isolation to the widespread obsession with houses. "Before," she told me, "no one bothered about their house. Now it is all anyone thinks about—building additions, this and that. . . . They go to *el norte* and forget about us." She oversees several house plots and several houses for her absent children. One of her grandsons was already dreaming of "his house" by the time he was fifteen. He left for Winston-Salem as soon as he looked old enough to find work in North Carolina, and he just got married there. Her other grandsons have also left to join their parents.

The reconfiguration of living spaces reflects changes in family structure as well. According to one source, in the not-so-distant past, single redondos were inconceivable to local people, who saw redondos in terms of their relation to one another rather than as isolated entities.[45] Redondos, then, were not self-contained living units. Not only did different redondos serve different functions—as Sirina and others have told me, "there would be one redondo for sleeping and one for cooking"—but the kitchen redondo was shared by the women in extended families. Moreover, "there would be one big bed for everyone." As Margarito said, "Before there weren't any house plots . . . people just took them but stayed near their families. Families were united. Everything is changing now." "Before," Rosa lamented, "your family were your neighbors. But that's not the case any longer."

Compounds that used to hold redondos and extended families have given way to individual plots for individual houses and smaller, nuclear households within which separateness is also more of a priority. People still routinely visit friends and family, packs of children dart in and out of one another's homes, and front doors are always open if someone is inside. But shared compounds with a single kitchen are much less common than they once were, houses have more than one room so that people can be both inside and separated, and no one brings their sleeping mats outside to chat or to sleep anymore, in part because people are entertained inside by televisions and cooled by fans as they recline on the store-bought mattresses that have replaced the traditional sleeping mats (*petates*).

Privacy is also more of a concern. Sirina humorously explained the difficulties of making love while living with children or in-laws in a one-room house. Margarita's house has many rooms and partitions. Amalia envisions her house with a large master bedroom, a living room, an indoor kitchen and bath, and separate rooms for her future male and female children.[46]

As some San Nicoladenses grieve the social changes that index widening gaps between the rich and the poor and a breakdown in family ties, they also speak of rising crime that largely affects and is effected by "loose" (*suelto*, unsupervised) young people whose parents are in the United States. Many of these young people have themselves been to *el norte*, and gang graffiti—sometimes in English—can be found on San Nicolás's walls. Sirina explained that when people first started out for the United States, they were responsible and went to work to make a little money. Now, she continued, young people do not want to work. Instead, they want what she called a "hidden" business that will make them a lot of money in a short time. Much local crime is attributed to *marijuaneros* who have been in the United States. "Things weren't like this before," said Rosa. "They brought that [marijuana] from *el norte*. Before it was really really quiet—we could sleep outside." Daria, an elderly woman who had no children and recently died, struggled with her husband for years to scrape together money from crop sales for a one-room cinder-block home with a dirt floor and a flimsy door. Like Rosa, she pointed out that "before, you could sleep [outside] under a *palapa* (shelter) or in a house of sticks. But now you can't" because of the crime. Indeed, while her house is more solid than one made of earth, it is not quite solid enough. She used to leave the little jewelry she owned with a niece, for fear of someone breaking into her home.

Older nonmigrant San Nicoladenses often speak of a breakdown in traditional forms of respect and reciprocity. Margarita's father, for instance, described the past as a time when "people were trustworthy, honorable, and didn't steal from others." It was a "golden era," he insisted; "there were great quantities of fruit." He noted that youth in those days were more respectful. They knelt before their godparents for a blessing, and, in his words, "they greeted older folks with 'uncle,' bowed and tipped their hats." His comments, along with the others, thus characterize the past as an era when residents esteemed one another, crime and class differences did not exist, and the earth itself was more giving.

Carolina Chica and the Persistence of Family and Place

Migration has shifted from being a promising avenue for security and a shortcut to the modern to a move fraught with dangers that come not just from crossing borders without documents but also from social processes that threaten to undermine the very concept of "community." Cinder-block homes might be anchored to the ground, but now the people they are meant to house are scattered all over, and respect and reciprocity have given way to self-centeredness, to a less "communal" set of values. Indeed, San Nicoladenses often refer to themselves as competitive *egoístas* who will not do anything for free, as Modesto indicated in his comment about people wanting to be paid for building redondos.

Yet houses are paradoxical. On the one hand, they do reflect the social displacements that accompany migration, which in a kind of vicious circle make such homes necessary to ensure safety and security, not just because of what nature might bring but also because of the problems that migration has itself engendered, in part through the acquisition of immobile property. Thus, the houses that protect against the "outside" world can exist only because of the processes that simultaneously erode what people perceive to be traditional social rules and bonds as rich people stop talking to poor people, young folks steal, extended families are torn apart, and children stop respecting their parents.

On the other hand, one can see in the very presence and immobility of cinder-block homes an ongoing and profound attachment to place and to kin, an attachment that challenges the idea that global restructuring simply dislocates and one that challenges the displacements that have historically turned African-descent Mexicans into "people without a country," a phrase that becomes even more ironic in the new transnational context. The transatlantic and internal Mexican slave trade, colonialism, land disputes, war, and migration have historically conspired to fragment San Nicolás's families. Yet cinder-block homes now cement in/to Mexico the continuing aspirations and desires of people who have moved quite far afield. Those aspirations and desires are coded by class, as some people are able to literally own more of the village than others. But the fact that they are also coded by absence—a striking number of cinder-block homes stand empty because their owners are elsewhere—attests to the central importance of families and their futures.

Achieving that future requires an ongoing reliance on family. Migrants preparing for departure depend on their kin in Winston-Salem, who often send money to pay for their passage, then find jobs for them, give them a place to sleep, and help them negotiate the complexities of life in a place where the lingua franca is English. Emigrants, on the other hand, have to trust nonmigrant family members to receive remittances and put them to work purchasing the building materials and overseeing the construction of the houses to which the emigrants hope to return. Many of the empty houses, and even the ones that are occupied, are constructed in stages as money trickles in from "the other side." And those who stay behind often live in houses that they are essentially building up around themselves. That people who are not there regularly send money to family to construct sturdy houses which they cannot yet live in, and to which they might in fact never be able to return, suggests that even San Nicolás's most displaced migrants retain abiding ties to—and an abiding confidence in—this place. Indeed, even Ismael has bought a house plot, which suggests a kind of "cognitive tension" between "home" and the "foreign."[47]

Perhaps most tellingly, whatever else happens, virtually every San Nicoladense is buried in the local cemetery. Indeed, even if migrants die before they make it home, their resting place will be in San Nicolás. The burial plots that migrants young and old sooner or later occupy reflect the house aspirations they left in the first place to fulfill, for the preferred form of interment is in elaborate concrete tombs that stylistically resemble houses. These have detailed edifices, some of them are tiled, and most of them are individually enclosed with fencing and sturdy gates, much like house plots themselves.[48] Surviving family members cultivate plants in the enclosed and protective spaces where the dead reside, and many of the plaques that adorn the tombs speak of family and of the deceased, who will "dwell" in the hearts of the living forever.

Sirina's comments speak to the ways in which the "modernity" that is perceived to have destroyed family ties also manages to reaffirm them in the cemetery's tombs. "They have roofs," she said of these residences for the dead, "and the entire family is buried there. People grab their burial plot and enclose it, just like now they grab a house plot." She then spoke of the past and the very transience of the earth. "Before, when people died they were not entombed; they were just buried in the ground. Family members were not buried together. Now everyone is united as a family. If the grave-site is not enclosed and there isn't a tomb," she added, "people will grab a bit of the land and even dig it up again." She knows this because her second child, Antonino, died of a fever many years ago, when he was one year old. He is no longer where Sirina and Rodrigo buried him—indeed, they cannot find his remains because they had no money to entomb him and his bones have been scattered over the earth.

Migrants send money for the cemetery's tombs as well as for the homes they hope to live in one day. Chela explained that the former were in fact more important than the latter in the long run. "Everything comes from Carolina," she said. "What they say here is 'I'm going to make my house,' but one also says that it is not one's house, that it is simply on loan. One's *real* house is in the graveyard, because [as people say] 'I'm going to be there forever. No one can take me out of there. In my [everyday] house, well, [I'll be there] no more than a short time.'"

In the cemetery, then, families are reunited in fixed dwelling places, which are replicas of the homes that have torn them apart in the first place. It is poignant, of course, that people leave to find work in order to purchase their own tombs, as well as those of kin they might never see again, in a homeland to which they might not return alive. San Nicoladenses, however, joke about the situation and, in their inimitable fashion, give it an ironic twist. I discovered this one day after I had visited San Nicolás's graveyard to see the tombs. Afterward, I went by Rosa's house to chat. I told her I had gone to the cemetery, which is along a country road some distance from town, and I expected her to admonish me for going alone, not because it was dangerous but because, despite changing social norms, people still see being alone as unusual and uncomfortable, especially for a woman. Instead of admonishing me, however, Rosa laughed uproariously. "Ahhh," she guffawed, "[you went to] *Carolina Chica* [little Carolina]!" I must have looked perplexed, because she quickly added—still laughing—"You know, [the graveyard]—it's 'the other side' [el otro lado], but you don't need a pass-port or a coyote to get there."

Rosa's three oldest children are now in *el norte*, along with Ismael's son—a grandchild she has never seen. Amalia and her husband just lent the house money they had saved to an uncle who lives in Winston-Salem and needed a car to get to work. Ismael regularly sends Rosa money to secure her own cinder-block home in San Nicolás and to pay for the telephone she uses to call her children. Rosa once asked me where Africa was and whether there was work there. She would like to go to *el norte* herself to see her children and the grandchild she has never met, but she has no documents and is afraid of making the difficult journey across the border on foot.

To conclude, perhaps we can imagine a new note card like the one with which I began. This one would still have a heart signifying a profound attachment to place, but it would speak to the dangers and promises of migration. Its verse might comprise a mother's futile warning to her child not to go to *el norte* and that child's reply that he or she is going anyway, even if he or she dies trying to make it. Such a note card might be embellished not with a picture of a redondo, in a nostalgic rendition of an imagined past, but instead with an ambiguous Mexican cinder-block structure that could be either a home or a tomb.

Notes

Versions of this paper were given at the University of Virginia, Anthropology Department Colloquium, the Conference on Contemporary Issues in Anthropology, the conference "Between Race and Place" at Tulane University, and at the American Studies Association Meetings. I would like to thank the participants at those venues for their comments, and Brad Weiss, Juliette Levy, and Judith Boruchoff for their close readings of final drafts.

1   The original Spanish is colloquial: "Mi madre me lo decia que a San Nicolás no fuera; a San Nicolás me voy a unque mañano me muera."

2   Steven Vertovec makes a distinction between personal or individual remittances sent to families, and collective ones sent to communities by migrant organizations, particularly Hometown Associations; see his "Migrant Transnationalism and Modes of Transformation," *International Migration Review* 38.3 (Fall 2004): 970–1001, esp. 986–87. Unlike many other Mexican overseas communities, San Nicoladenses do not have a Hometown Association. As almost all remittances are personal, they go to personal family needs, including houses. The result is what has been called "'private affluence and public squalor,' or new homes reachable only over dirt roads" (ibid., 986).

3   Peggy Levitt and Nina Glick Schiller, "Conceptualizing Simultaneity: A Transnational Social Field Perspective on Society," *International Migration Review* 3 (Fall 2004): 1003.

4   With respect to my emphasis on meanings (more so than larger structural conditions) and on nonmigrants, I draw on Vertovec, "Migrant Transnationalism and Modes of Transformation."

5   Competition has increased as more and more Latinos move to the U.S. South, which has become a geographical magnet for Latinos; see Arthur D. Murphy, Colleen Blanchard, and Jennifer A. Hill, eds., *Latino Workers in the Contemporary South* (Athens: University of Georgia Press, 2001). North Carolina's Latino population quadrupled between 1990 and 2004 (http://census.osbm.state.nc.us/lookup/, accessed December 14, 2005); Associated Press, "North Carolina Preps for Latino Boom," www.cnn.com, accessed July 9, 2004). San Nicoladenses often complain that Winston-Salem is so crowded with other

Latinos that work there is now difficult to find. Many have moved to nearby cities such as Greensboro and Charlotte, while a few have moved into southern Virginia, which is still within driving distance of Winston-Salem, so that family members can easily move back and forth.

6   Margarita, like all of the names used in this article, is a pseudonym. A *comadre* is literally a co-mother. It is a ritual kin relationship and one that I have with many San Nicoladenses. I have known Margarita for almost ten years both in San Nicolás and in Winston-Salem. She has been my *comadre* for two years, ever since she asked me to attend and to sponsor part of her son's wedding in San Nicolás. She could not return from Winston-Salem for the occasion.

7   An expert in the music of the Costa Chica told me that the verse was more likely a *chilena*, a type of song structure specific to the coast (John McDowell, pers. comm.).

8   These themes can even be traced back to Spain (John McDowell, pers. comm.)

9   Laura A. Lewis, "Blacks, Black Indians, Afromexicans: The Dynamics of Race, Nation, and Identity in a Mexican Moreno Community," *American Ethnologist* 27.4 (2000): 919, n. 4. For examples, see Gonzalo Aguirre Beltrán, *Cuijla: Esbozo etnográfico de un pueblo negro* (1958; reprint, Mexico City: Secretaria de Educación Pública, 1985); Miguel Gutiérrez Avila, *Derecho consuetudinario y derecho positivo entre los mixtecos, amuzgos y afromestizos de la Costa Chica de Guerrero* (Mexico: Comisión Nacional de Derechos Humanos, 1997); and *Corrido y Violencia entre los afromeztizos de la Costa Chica de Guerrero y Oaxaca* (Chilpancingo: Universidad Autónoma de Guerrero, 1988), 19–20.

10 María Los Angeles Manzano A., *Cuajinicuilapa Guerrero: Historia Oral (1900–1940)* (Mexico City: Ediciones Artesa, 1991), 37, lower caption.

11 Cinder-block homes can be found all over Mexico as well as in other parts of the "third world," where globalization, and ideas about modernity and progress, have made it the material of choice for construction in rural areas. Although I have not yet researched cement companies, no doubt such research would add an important dimension to this discussion. Cemex (Cementos de Mexico) is the third largest cement producer in the world.

12 See, e.g., Leo Chavez, *Shadowed Lives* (Fort Worth: Harcourt Brace, 1998). See also the discussion in Levitt and Glick Schiller, "Conceptualizing Simultaneity," 1002, 1005.

13 "Simultaneously in two countries": Nina Glick Schiller and Eugene Fouron, *Georges Woke Up Laughing: Long Distance Nationalism and the Search for Home* (Durham, NC: Duke University Press, 2001), 3. "Transnational migrant circuits": Roger Rouse, "Mexican Migration and the Social Space of Transnationalism," *Diaspora* 1.1 (1991). "Social fields": Levitt and Glick Schiller, "Conceptualizing Simultaneity," 1008–9. Of the vast numbers of studies of Mexican transnationalism, here are but a few that consciously link the different locales Mexicans inhabit: Kimberley Grimes, *Crossing Borders: Changing Social Identities in Southern Mexico* (Tucson: University of Arizona Press, 1998); Peri L. Fletcher, *La casa de mis sueños: Dreams of Home in a Mexican Migrant Community* (Boulder: Westview Press, 1999); and Jeffrey H. Cohen, "Transnational Migration in Rural Oaxaca, Mexico: Dependency, Development and the Household," *American Anthropologist* 103.4 (2001): 954–67.

14 Part of the difficulty is due to U.S. state laws that refuse undocumented people drivers' licenses, bank accounts, access to public higher education, and other services, making it

difficult, if not impossible, for even children brought to the United States by their parents at an early age to acquire property, find good jobs, and receive higher education.

15 The term "cultural bifocals" is from Jonathan Xavier Inda and Renato Rosaldo, "Introduction: A World in Motion," in *The Anthropology of Globalization: A Reader*, ed. Inda and Rosaldo (Malden, MA: Blackwell, 2002), 20. This essay generally fails to distinguish between documented and undocumented immigrants, instead assuming that the position of not fully belonging to any one place that transmigrants find themselves in is due entirely to the state of living in two places at once. As I suggest here, immigrants' legal statuses must be taken into account in any discussion of transnationalism because such statuses affect people's sense of, and ability to, belong. Hilary Cunningham makes similar points when she argues that anthropologists need to "stay attuned to . . . issues of exclusion, access, and stratification in a context of global interconnections," in "Nations Rebound? Crossing Borders in a Gated Globe," *Identities: Global Studies in Culture and Power* 11 (2004): 332.

16 Inda and Rosaldo, "Introduction," 11.

17 In this respect I look to Glick Schiller and Fouron's ethnographic account of Haitian transnationalism. They try to capture the deeply sentimental experiences of transmigrants, whom they define as people who "remain tied to their ancestral land by their actions as well as their thoughts" (Glick Schiller and Fouron, *Georges Woke Up Laughing*, 3). Although she does not make this explicit, Karen McCarthy Brown does the same in her wonderful ethnography of Haitian vodoun, *Mama Lola: A Vodou Priestess in Brooklyn* (Berkeley: University of California Press, 2001).

18 E.g., Jane Perlez, "Where Pagodas Draw Tourists, Concrete Is Unwelcome," *New York Times*, July 8, 2004.

19 For an early history of the region see Rolf Widmer, *Conquista y despertar de las costas de la Mar del Sur (1521–1684)* (Mexico City: Consejo Nacional para la Cultura y las Artes, 1990).

20 For a later history of the region see Maria de los Angeles Manzano Añorve, *Cuajinicuilapa, Guerrero: Historia Oral (1900–1940)* (Mexico City: Ediciones Artesa, 1991).

21 Historically, rights of access to and use of *ejido* lands belonged to communities. Following amendment to Article 27 of the Mexican Constitution in 1992, *ejido* lands were parceled out to individuals and privatized. They can now be bought and sold, including to third parties.

22 Laura A. Lewis, "Of Ships and Saints: History, Memory and Place in the Making of Moreno Mexican Identity," *Cultural Anthropology* 16.1 (February 2001): 62–82.

23 Lewis, "Blacks, Black Indians, Afromexicans," 898–926.

24 James Clifford, "Diasporas," *Cultural Anthropology* 9.3 (1994): 302–38.

25 For more in-depth treatment of these issues see Lewis, "Blacks, Black Indians, Afromexicans" and "Of Ships and Saints."

26 Aguirre Beltrán, *Cuijla*, 93. In the 1940s some of these redondos still displayed crosses at their apex, as they typically did before the Revolution, which curtailed the authority of the Catholic Church.

27 Gutierre Tibón, *Pinotepa Nacional: Mixtecos, negros y triques*, 2d ed. (1961; reprint, Mexico City: Editorial Posada, 1981), 49, 41. "To speak of a Mexican Congo," Tibón concluded, "is a cheap literary device" (ibid., 49). The anthropologist Frederick Starr's account of his late-nineteenth- and early-twentieth-century travels in the Mixteca Alta region of south-

ern Mexico includes photographs of redondos that look strikingly like the ones that prevailed on the coast; see Starr, *In Indian Mexico* (Chicago: Forbes and Company, 1908), 135, 139. Archival evidence, including a late-sixteenth-century map depicting round dwellings with crosses at their apexes, suggests the same, for the dispute the map was meant to help resolve involves Indian homes and land (Archivo General de la Nación, Ramo Tierras, vol. 48, exp. 6, f 162, 1583). Local people also associate redondos with Indians, for the form can still be found in upland Indian communities.

28   The American historian Richard Thompson even devoted a chapter of a book to Mande-influenced architecture in the Americas, arguing on the basis of comparison, and despite significant differences, for cultural ties between Mexican redondos and western Africa; see Thompson, *Flash of the Spirit* (New York: Random House, 1984), 195–206.

29   Peter Wade, *Race and Ethnicity in Latin America* (London: Pluto Press, 1997), 77–78; Jean Rahier, introduction to *Representations of Blackness and the Performance of Identities*, ed. Rahier (Westport, CT: Bergin and Garvey, 1999), xv–xxi.

30   On the concept and intent of folklorization in general see Greg Urban and Joel Scherzer, introduction to *Nation-States and Indians in Latin America* (Austin: University of Texas Press, 1991), 11; William Rowe and Vivian Schelling, *Memory and Modernity: Popular Culture in Latin America* (New York: Verso, 1991), 58–59. On its effects in San Nicolás see Lewis, "Blacks, Black Indians, Afromexicans."

31   Miguel Gutiérrez Avila, *La conjura de los negros* (Chilpancingo: Universidad Autónoma de Guerrero, 1993), 18.

32   As a non-Mexican my relationship to *la cultura* was at first somewhat uncertain, and I repeatedly had to reiterate that I was not with *la cultura* (and also that I was not an evangelical Christian, or an *alelujah*, as other whites in the village tend to be). The constant questions and comments made me quickly realize that many people viewed representatives of national cultural interests with some hostility (Lewis, "Blacks, Black Indians, Afromexicans").

33   Arlene Torres and Norman E. Whitten Jr., "General Introduction: To Forge the Future in the Fires of the Past: An Interpretive Essay on Racism, Domination, Resistance and Liberation," in *Blackness in Latin America and the Caribbean*, ed. Torres and Whitten, 2 vols. (Bloomington: Indiana University Press, 1998), 4.

34   John McDowell, *Poetry and Violence: The Ballad Tradition of Mexico's Costa Chica* (Champaign-Urbana: University of Illinois Press, 2000). See also Lewis, "Blacks, Black Indians, Afromexicans"; Torres and Whitten, "General Introduction."

35   Although both are made of dirt mixed with plant materials, the building processes are different. Adobe bricks are a mud and straw mixture; wattle and daub consists of interlaced posts covered with mud.

36   Manzano A., *Cuajinicuilapa Guerrero*, 30.

37   Grimes, *Crossing Borders*, 66. Consumption, of course, is also fueled by mass media in Mexico, where material goods are racialized in ways that associate them with "whiteness" and power (ibid., 125).

38   "Ways of being" and "ways of belonging": Levitt and Nina Glick Schiller, "Conceptualizing Simultaneity," 1010. On food and self-identification in the wider context of consumption see Jonathan Friedman, "Globalization and Localization," in Inda and Rosaldo, *The Anthropology of Globalization*, 233–36.

39 Juan Sánchez Andraka *¡Hablemos Claro! ¿Que occurió en Guerrero durante el gobierno de Alejandro Cervantes Delgado? Testimonios* (Mexico City: Costa-Amic, 1987), 26.

40 Ibid., 26.

41 As Vertovec points out, "While not bringing about substantial societal transformations by themselves, patterns of cross-border exchange and relationship among migrants may contribute significantly to broadening, deepening or intensifying conjoining processes of transformation that are already ongoing" ("Migrant Transnationalism and Modes of Transformation," 972).

42 Although outright divorce is all but unheard of, separation for a period of time or even permanently is quite common among couples in the community. Postmarital residence is virilocal, with daughters joining their in-laws' household upon marriage. House inheritance in San Nicolás favors the youngest son, and while older male offspring reside in their parents' home with their new wives for a time, they eventually have to find new house plots and build their own homes. This is generally done in phases as older males save to move out on their own, making way for the next son's wife to become the new *nuera* (daughter-in-law) of the household, and so on and so forth until the youngest son's wife takes over running the household permanently from her mother-in-law as the latter ages. Only daughters who are disabled and hence unmarriageable will stay in the family home.

43 Rouse, "Mexican Migration and the Social Space of Transnationalism," 252.

44 Vertovec, "Migrant Transnationalism and Modes of Transformation," 976.

45 Cited in Thompson, *Flash of the Spirit*, 204.

46 Although Amalia desired separate rooms for her male and female children, she did not indicate that each child would have a separate room. This is in keeping with San Nicoladenses' emphasis on gender segregation and on close relationships between brothers, sisters, and cousins. Children find the idea of sleeping alone completely alien, and they always wander and play in groups. This is a fine example of what Inda and Rosaldo refer to as the "customization of alien cultural forms" as people filter outside impositions through their own deep cultural practices. "Introduction," 16.

47 Vertovec, "Migrant Transnationalism and Modes of Transformation," 975.

48 Most tombs have crosses and therefore also recall small churches. Yet churches themselves are in many ways modeled on houses, as Sánchez Andraka's comments suggest, and even redondos had small crosses at their apex.

Alicia Schmidt Camacho

Migrant Melancholia:
Emergent Discourses of Mexican Migrant
Traffic in Transnational Space

> It is not, then, just a question of mapping social rela-
> tions (economic, sociological, or whatever) *on to* space.
> The fact that those relations *occur over* space matters.
> It is not just that "space is socially constructed"—a fact
> with which geographers have for a while been coming
> to terms—but that social processes are constructed
> over space.
> —Doreen Massey, *Spatial Divisions of Labor: Social
> Structures and the Geography of Production*

> It was a Holiday Inn
> downtown El Paso
> where she crossed the line daily
> paso por paso
> mal paso que das
> al cruzar la frontera

> There was the work permit
> sealed in plastic
> like the smile
> she flashed every morning
> to the same uniformed eyes
> —Marisela Norte, "Act of the Faithless"

Reports of migrant deaths and disappearances in the transnational circuit linking the United States and Mexico should disturb the fiction of the regulated border. The fate of the undocumented reveals the violence with which both

South Atlantic Quarterly 105:4, Fall 2006
DOI 10.1215/00382876-2006-007   © 2006 Duke University Press

states have acted over time to rationalize the boundaries of their territory and citizenship.[1] In recent years, sharp increases in the numbers of undocumented migrants and the concurrent escalation of border militarization have made the journey to the United States more hazardous and the possibilities of return to Mexico more uncertain. Furthermore, as migration increasingly extends outward from the Southwest, it challenges the dominant frameworks for depicting or explaining the Mexican presence in the United States. As the costs of Mexican labor migrations have become more visible, state institutions and communications media in both countries have had to address the hazards, both physical and psychological, of unauthorized entry and settlement in the United States. Disappearances of various sorts are revealed in the growing rosters of missing persons kept by the Mexican Office of Foreign Relations (Secretaría de Relaciones Exteriores) and immigrant organizations; these numbers reveal the instability of those narratives of kinship, class, and nationality that have historically functioned to delimit accounts of migration as loss or rupture for sending communities.

Given the recent developments, the melancholic aspect of the journey north has surfaced with a new urgency, putting the tale of the enterprising migrant "seeking a better life" in crisis. Stories of disappearance and lonely deaths put the flesh back on the bare-bones figure of the "guest worker" at a moment when the Mexican state confers neither a living nor rights to poor citizens and when U.S. officials and civilians alike routinely detain, abuse, and exploit migrants with little regard for international human rights conventions. The two nations collude in producing a class of stateless subjects whose personhood is discursively consigned to mere economic being as disposable labor, or legally reduced to the mere status of criminal trespassers.

In what follows, I examine the discourses that produce what I am calling "migrant melancholia" in order to consider the effects of the decade of Operation Gatekeeper. free trade, and neoliberalism for Mexican migrants and what these changes may signify for current understandings of human mobility and transnational community. Alongside established accounts of transnational labor and remittances, other narratives of loss and wounding have always coexisted in tension with the legitimating discourses of international cooperation, development, and economic opportunity that depict the sojourn in the United States as a matter of elective choice.[2] These narratives can be found across a number of media, including television documentaries on migration, *telenovelas* on Telemundo, Internet photos of missing migrants, and cultural productions by border artists. The narration of migrant sorrows constitutes a political act, cast against the prerogatives of neoliberal development and the global division of labor—in particular, the erosion of substantive citizenship and communal belonging but also the collusion with resurgent forms of racial governance in both countries.

I am especially interested in how women's border literature and testimonials provide a counternarrative to official depictions of migration as temporary economic necessity, just as they disrupt conventional narratives of male migration. In contrast to historic masculinist claims to cross-border unity between Mexico and *México de afuera*, women's testimonies reveal a distinct female imaginary operating in the border space, one that moves with ambivalence and caution through competing claims of family, class, and nation in the transnational arena. Women and children are increasingly protagonists of the border crossing, rather than simply dependents left behind by male breadwinners. Their accounts reveal how social relations structuring kinship and community are not simply reconstructed over transnational space but may also provide insufficient refuge from the perils of the cross-border passage.

Lost Citizens

In the days following the destruction of the World Trade Center, members of El Asociación Tepeyac de New York, an advocacy center for Latino immigrants, found themselves inundated with calls from households across Latin America, asking for news of missing relatives believed to be working in the United States. Eventually, El Asociación Tepeyac identified 113 cases of missing people and 857 displaced workers connected to the 9/11 disaster.³ The organization has been instrumental in documenting these cases and helping survivors obtain relief funds. Just as impressive, however, are the hundreds of petitions for assistance in locating missing family members that may have no direct relationship to the events in New York and that remain unresolved. Esperanza Chacón, Director of Urgent Affairs for Tepeyac, argues that the enforced invisibility of undocumented workers in the United States makes it impossible to clarify the status of these reports of missing persons.⁴ Despite the ready availability of cellular phones and electronic communications media for sustaining communal and familial ties among migrants, it was all too clear in 2001 that migration can still threaten sending households with dissolution and loss.

The events of 9/11 foreclosed on the plans of Presidents Bush and Fox for a binational agreement that would facilitate guest worker programs and provide amnesty to thousands of undocumented Mexicans residing in the United States. For Mexico, the losses at the World Trade Center provoked renewed debate about the implications of mass migrations and economic dependency for the exercise of state sovereignty and the coherence of its national community. In 2003, public pressure forced Gerónimo Gutiérrez Fernández, then Subsecretary for North America to the Office of Foreign Relations (SRE), to admit openly that his office received an annual average of five thousand requests for assistance in locating persons presumed missing in the course of emigration to the United States.[5] Mexican officials consider the actual number to be far higher, since the SRE figure only reflects the fraction of incidents where the state becomes involved. Gutiérrez Fernández reported that his office resolves 20 percent of the cases, but he did not elaborate on the specific outcomes of these investigations. The SRE has since outlined a proposal for creating an electronic database for biogenetic data that would assist the state in tracking and identifying the missing, a proposal made urgent by the rising costs of repatriating the remains of Mexicans who die abroad.

Ghosts of Development

As the United States and Mexico pursued policies of accelerated economic integration in the late twentieth century that exacerbated the demand for Mexican labor in the United States, on the one hand, and decimated communal Mexican agriculture, on the other, the U.S.-Mexican border has lost its peripheral status within national processes for either country. The unstoppable movement of people to the border cities and across the international boundary that began before World War I has exerted considerable pressure on the structures of governance, commerce, income generation, and justice for both nations as they have responded to rising levels of undocumented migration since the 1990s (and had to cope with the new exigencies of national security linked to the U.S. war on drugs and the war on terror). Mexican policies for stimulating economic growth and development have effectively redrawn the compact between the state and its poor, its working class, and its rural citizens. The neoliberal programs that culminated in the 1994 North American Free Trade Agreement were heralded by some as "Mexico's second revolution," not so much for their promise of social advancement as for their stark contrast to the revolution of 1910.[6]

While nation-building reforms of the "institutionalized" revolution pro-moted economic restructuring in the name of redistributive reforms, the market-led restructuring of the Mexican economy following the 1980s sub-ordinated social reform to economic growth at enormous cost to the urban and rural poor.

Although Mexican officials and financiers may argue that the first decade of NAFTA brought Mexico new foreign investment and jobs with the unex-pected dividend of the democratic transition from PRI dominance, the actual economic and political benefits accruing from neoliberal reforms have largely bypassed the poorer sectors of society. The rapid restructuring of Mexican agriculture has only exacerbated the historical process of out-migration from the countryside and small towns. In this period, changes to the Mexican state have failed to extend democratic inclusion to margin-alized populations, just as they have weakened those institutions that pro-vide the substance of citizenship: access to goods and services, justice, secu-rity, and political representation. The forms of exchange and consumption that have underwritten neoliberal development depend on the social rela-tions institutionalized in the border region: in particular, an economic caste system that demands workers well versed in both service and low-skilled labor, whose weak social integration assures that they make relatively few demands on either state.

Increased rates of interdiction at the Mexico-U.S. border, along with un-precedented levels of undocumented migration from Mexico and farther south, have added to the perils of the border crossing and settlement in the United States in the last decade.[7] Migrants confront the travails of the desert and anti-immigrant hostilities along the frontier as a passage through a space of death, or what Luis Alberto Urrea calls "the devil's highway."[8] Migrant fatalities have risen 500 percent over the last decade due to stricter U.S. border policing and the expansion of organized crime in the border region.[9] Mexican consuls apportion ever-greater percentages of their bud-gets to the forensic identification and repatriation of bodies, both of mi-grants who perish in transit and of those who die in the United States; they also face increased demands for assistance from families searching for missing relatives, now numbering in the thousands.[10] The space of death is not confined to the border, however, but incorporates the limited spheres of agency afforded undocumented people in the United States: Migrants occupy the legal minefield between labor and human rights protections, on the one hand, and U.S. immigration policy, on the other.

As a result, established patterns of seasonal migration for work have given way to higher rates of permanent settlement following the inception of Operation Gatekeeper in 1994.[11] Greater numbers of women and children are migrating from Mexico to the United States, both to obtain work and to unify families, despite conditions of increased risk.[12] Contracting with "coyotes," once simply optional, has become vital for successful crossings; traffickers are likely responsible for many of the recent disappearances of migrants now that the movement of people has become so lucrative for criminal entities in the region.[13]

The border crossing has always threatened migrants with disappearance or death, and certainly with dislocation from kin and community. The 2001 catastrophe in New York brought the fragility of transnational ties into focus once more during the same period that migrant remittances reached their peak share of Mexican GDP.[14] Mexican settlements in New York followed patterns established by earlier labor migrations; new arrivals to Manhattan and Long Island in the 1990s were just as successful in forming mutual aid societies and exerting economic and political force in their Puebla hometowns as their conationals in Los Angeles or Houston.[15] Many perils of recent migration are in fact not *new*, but the diffusion of migrant circuits beyond the southwestern United States does reflect significant changes in traditional forms of transnational settlement, even from older sending regions. Emigration has shifted from being a rural phenomenon to encompassing industrialized towns and cities, and every Mexican state now confronts the vast scale of out-migration to the United States. These demographic shifts correspond to stalled economic and political reforms in Mexico as state failure continues to promote mass emigration. Jorge Durand and Douglas Massey comment that in Mexico, "migrant networks are much stronger in rural than in urban areas because rural social networks are stronger and more dense."[16] If so, it remains to be seen whether newer migrants can mobilize the same forms of social capital as their predecessors.

Such transformations in Mexican political economy and state policy have profound implications for how displaced Mexicans, both internal and transnational migrants, may experience and express their nationality in the migratory circuit. Mexicans living abroad form hometown associations in order to provide resources for sending communities, a process the government seeks to co-opt through a program of matching funds for migrant remittances. Federal, state, and local authorities promise to match migrant donations on a three-to-one ratio, with the hopes of diverting private remittances to state expenditures. In Chicago, for example, a group of migrants from Indaparapeo, Michoacán, have pooled resources to establish a scholarship program for the town's youth, resisting the state government's suggestion that monies be set aside for new roads and drainage.[17] Grupo Indaparapeo chose to develop the town's human capital over state-run projects as a direct rebuke to officials for their failure to meet its most basic obligations to the townspeople. While the private contributions for the scholarship are always on time, Grupo Indaparapeo reports that matching funds are always in short supply. Members of the hometown association may be exercising the forms of *postnational* agency described in current studies of migration, but they do so in a concerted effort to recover and reconstitute *national* citizenship.[18] The Michoacán migrants designed the scholarship program so that townspeople will not have to leave home to seek their livelihood. After a century of out-migration, their initiative represents a purchase against loss and estrangement in the next generation.

Mourning and Migration

U.S. immigration policies and border policing have effectively cancelled the option for circular migration, making Mexicans much more likely to pursue permanent settlement in the United States. The coercive aspect of these developments warrants further inquiry. In fact, studies overwhelmingly show that most migrants do not wish to stay: "Left to their own devices, the vast majority would return to participate in Mexico's growth as an economy and a society."[19] The prevailing metric of immigration studies, centered as it is on the economic and social productivity of the migrant, cannot measure the melancholic aspect of the shift from circular migrations to a "national population of settled dependents scattered throughout the country" (12). A focus on the relative economic integration between migrants and sender communities, measured in remittances, may obscure the social upheaval and deformations of kinship that extended migrations impose on sender households. The unacknowledged costs of Mexican mobility find expression in the rumors of human traffic and bondage that circulate within migrant communities. The spectacular horror of these stories may correspond to actual incidents, but in their elaboration, rumors also project the phantasmagoric aspect of migrant imaginaries.[20] Lists of missing persons obtain symbolic significance as an inchoate form of contestation to the way government policies continue to displace the burden of maintaining transnational labor circuits from the state onto private individuals and households.

In his 1917 essay "Mourning and Melancholia," Sigmund Freud addressed the ways individuals contend with the death or absence of a beloved person, object, or idea. He noted that distress leads the mourner to deny the loss but that the healthy person will eventually relinquish the attachment and recover a capacity for everyday life. The melancholic person, he argued, refuses to "relinquish the lost object" and cannot therefore overcome the psychic burden of loss. For Freud, melancholia arises from a pathological or thwarted process of mourning, in which the absent object becomes constitutive of the melancholic self. Recent scholarship has applied Freudian models of mourning and melancholia to forms of subjection or abjection enacted in the political sphere.[21] Here I want to consider how the border crossing implies a psychic wounding for migrants and invests their nostalgic desires for return with political significance.

If current conditions make the option of circular migration unavailable to many migrants, then the notion of "home" may take on the qualities of the beloved object whose loss threatens the integrity of the border crosser's personhood. In the same way, the migrant's departure may constitute a catastrophic separation for the sending family and community. In a recent television documentary about a family in rural Michoacán that sent three sons to Kentucky for work, the mother of the young men describes a sense of desperation at her economic dependence on her children's remittances: "Yo sé que me va a ayudar, pero para mí cada partida es una muerte" (I know that it will help me, but for me every departure is a death).[22] Marcelo, the last son to leave, describes his trip to the United States through the Sonoran Desert as an indelible trauma:

> Yo no sabía si podía aguantar. Pasé tres días sin alimentos, tomando sólo tragitos de agua. El sol era tan caliente. Tenía tanta sed. Mi mamá estaba llorando. Eso me afectó mucho. Créo que me afectó psicológicamente.

> [I was not sure if I would make it. I went three days without food, taking only small sips of water. The sun was so hot. I was so thirsty. My mother was crying. This affected me. I think it affected me psychologically.][23]

This exchange, captured in an episode of *Assignment Discovery*, offers a rare pedagogy for U.S. viewers on migrant subjectivity. Marcelo's reflection on his border passage captures exactly the process of melancholic incorporation that Freud describes: As he recalls the hardships of his desert passage, the son makes no distinction between his mother's grieving and his own. Although his mother remained behind, the son narrates his experience as if his mother traveled alongside him in the desert — as a source not of comfort or protection but of the profound guilt and distress that Freud ascribed to the melancholic person.

By extension, we may consider how undocumented status itself might constitute a melancholic condition for migrants in the United States. In 2004, I participated in a local effort to uncover a confidence scheme to defraud undocumented migrants of thousands of dollars through the sale of false papers. That summer, a friend who migrated to New Haven from Veracruz, Rita (a pseudonym), told me that a woman she worked for had offered to assist her in obtaining legal status for herself and her family. While cleaning the home, Rita had observed her employer operating a business in immigration documents out of her home. This woman, a Latina resident of Hamden, Connecticut, said she was a New York immigration official, offering to process paperwork "under the table" and expedite clients' legalization. Dozens of Latin Americans came from New York, Connecticut, and New Jersey to pay fees of as much as $25,000 for the "green cards" that they thought would permit them to work legally, sponsor family members, and move freely between the United States and their home countries.[24]

Rita paid her employer approximately $2,500 to process paperwork for her husband, herself, and her four-year-old son, who had all entered the United States without authorization a few years earlier. She grew alarmed when I communicated my doubts about the veracity of the woman's promises and my concerns that Rita and her family could get into trouble because of the scam. At the time, Rita was a client of Junta for Progressive Action, an advocacy center that serves the predominantly Latino neighborhood of Fair Haven. Having seen the numbers of migrants falling for her employer's false promises, Rita made the courageous decision to report the criminal operation to the police. Junta's director, the attorney Kica Matos, and I mediated between the migrants and the police so as to secure promises that the police would not pursue the immigration cases of the people caught up in the scam. In January 2006, the alleged perpetrator of the crime, María Agosto, a fifty-five-year-old resident of New York, was arraigned in the Superior Court of Connecticut on charges of first-degree larceny and criminal impersonation. Rita was the chief witness in the proceeding.

As I translated for Rita and other victims during their exchanges with

Hamden police, I came to understand how easy it was for the imposter to persuade her clients that she could help them circumvent the most elaborate and impenetrable apparatus of U.S. law enforcement, that of immigration. The people she stole from were hardly naive—they had experienced theft at the hands of coyotes, employers, immigration lawyers, and other migrants—but they were unwilling to relinquish the fantasy of reunion with the lost objects that haunted their residence in the United States— family and citizenship. As a Puerto Rican migrant herself, Agosto must have had intimate knowledge of her clients' melancholic disposition and just how far it would lead her clients into her trap. Even after she was exposed, having abandoned her Hamden residence without delivering the papers, many of her clients remained unwilling to accept the reality of their situation. Rita continued to confide to me after her testimony that she was certain that the police proceeding was a mistake and that perhaps Señora Agosto would return with her documents if she withheld her charges.

Proponents of anti-immigration measures commonly represent the undocumented as people with no respect for the rule of law. This assumption reflects a total misunderstanding of what "law" means for the unauthorized migrant. One could say that the undocumented come from countries where bribes are routinely paid to expedite state services; however, this explanation is, in my opinion, an inadequate answer to the question of how so many migrants came to pay unimaginable sums for the dream of legalization. It is precisely because of their investment in legality, both in practical and moral terms, that the victims of the Hamden scam could invest so heavily in false papers. The migrants did not deliberately seek to circumvent state authority when they paid the imposter to act on their behalf; rather, they sought incorporation into the state through the only means available. Beyond their desire for the goods of citizenship, freedom of movement, better wages, working conditions, and health care, the migrants were gullible because of their profound desire to be recognized as legitimate subjects, to inhabit the status of citizen. Even in simple economic terms, the theft of migrant earnings represents a terrible crime: Consider for a moment how many people were willing to work an inordinate number of hours under difficult conditions to amass $25,000 in the vain hope of bringing children north from Ecuador or Guatemala and making them into U.S. nationals.

The horror of the Hamden incident, then, comes from the reminder that it is so easy to exploit migrant desire. For many, the costs of entering the United States for work preclude the seasonal visits to Mexico that might placate the sense of loss and isolation. In New Haven, far from the ethnic centers of the Southwest, nationality is easily reduced to a consular card and the vague promises of protection it confers. For Mexicans here, U.S. citizenship or legal residence represents the single best option for securing a livelihood and retaining viable connections to family and hometown over time. And yet, the vast majority of the undocumented are unlikely to obtain such a prize.

The material and psychic hungers that propel migrants to abandon, in their quest for wages, the most basic elements of sociality—residence, kinship, language, culture, and landscape: in short, *home*—exert a violence that immigration scholarship and political discourse have yet to fully address. The condition of being "undocumented" does not simply imply a lack of legal protection or status but rather entails the active conversion of the migrant into a distinct category of stateless personhood. This peculiar status emerges with the contradiction between market demands for mobile labor and consumable goods and the immobility of rights beyond the bounds of the nation-state. Mexican migrants, like other displaced peoples, continually invent forms of agency within that space of opposition. It is a melancholy task. Stories of border mortality and disappearance are a means to narrate the other kinds of death that Marcelo's mother describes, the leave-taking that extinguishes one form of connection to make way for another. In this ritual of departure, the family enacts, in intimate form, the migrant's detachment from the state, a severing of citizenship that is also a death, a death that produces.

Disappearing Migrants

Current anxieties about border hazards also appear in popular media, in texts that narrate significant shifts in how migration is managed both at the level of lived experience and at the level of consumer culture. In December 2003, Telemundo aired the Mexican *telenovela El Alma Herida (The Wounded Soul)*, a serial melodrama devoted to a migrant family shattered at the border crossing.[25] The show earned strong ratings and became known as "una de las novelas más queridas por el público hispano."[26] The storyline followed familiar motifs for reinforcing national identity by depicting the dangers of pursuing material aspirations in the United States:

> Una familia llena de esperanzas toma la difícil decision de cruzar la frontera en busca del sueño Americano, déjandolo todo atrás sin

sospechar que el destino les jugará una mala pasada separándolos trágicamente.

[Full of hope, a family makes the difficult decision to cross the border in search of the American Dream. They leave everything behind, not knowing that destiny is about to play them a bad hand, separating them tragically from one another.][27]

The family does not make it across the border intact: The father and two children meet up with abusive police, while the *pollero* forces Catalina, the mother, across to the United States. The sixty-five episodes follow the daughter and mother's efforts at family reunification, allegorizing the broader process of Mexican migration since 1965. The border imposes total familial separation and threatens its annihilation: The plot turns on the family's question of whether the mother has died or abandoned them. The story ultimately ends in a bloodbath, with the daughter electing between two male partners in two countries, a choice which implies that her honor can be safeguarded only in Mexico. However contrived, *El Alma Herida* nevertheless departs from standard nationalist discourse by anchoring its story in a female, rather than a male, migrant. The status of the family depends on the recovery of the missing mother, not its wage-earning father, while her recuperation comes through the agency of the enterprising daughter Eugenia, who first crosses the border at age eleven. *El Alma Herida* thus fulfills the function of melodrama to nourish a female spectatorship; it does so through a migrant imaginary now thoroughly feminized.

For Mexicans living a precarious permanence in the United States, the border operates as a critical juncture for imagining community and exerting claims on either nation. In this context, the crossing *itself*—in its various legal, economic, cultural, and social aspects—shapes the political disposition of the larger transnational community of unauthorized migrants and noncitizens in the United States and their hometowns in Mexico. Here I refer not only to the political apparatus of the border, as it regulates the mobility of peoples or their access to rights and citizenship, but also to the broader binational space that contains the institutions devoted to national security, immigration, and trade at the boundary checkpoints. The transborder corridor is not only the largest urbanized region in Mexico; it is also one of the fastest-growing settlement sites in the Western Hemisphere.[28] The complex communal ecologies of this space do not simply give the border an internal sense of distinction and shared identity; they also influence the form broader transnational linkages and communities may take. So, too, border cities socialize migrants in their passage from citizenship to noncitizenship, authorized status to unauthorized status. As greater numbers of people find themselves stranded in the border space because of failed crossings or deportation, or the availability of jobs in service work and export manufacturing created by neoliberal development, the normative force of this movement to the transnational corridor increases.[29]

This passage may exact different political costs for the federal government from those facing sender communities: Despite new legislation permitting migrants to cast absentee ballots in the upcoming presidential elections, the expatriate vote is likely to disappoint.[30] The stagnation of democratic reform in Mexico means that migrants may opt to retain hometown connections while resisting their interpellation as national subjects. According to Rodolfo Rubio, a researcher at El Colegio de la Frontera Norte, fewer than 10 percent are likely to register out of an estimated 4 million eligible voters, making it less possible for the migrant vote to sway the presidential election.[31] The cost of absentee voter registration effectively functions as a poll tax, repeating a long-standing process whereby the state discourages poor voters. Daniel Solis, director of the Alliance for Community Development in El Paso, argues that eligible voters, even those residing in the border, are "losing hope of better prospects at home and putting stock in their future as new immigrants."[32] The intense nationalism of migrants, in this context, may not extend to a sense of political obligation to the nation-state.

The new hazards and congestion of the border crossing may thus ultimately alter the social networks observed in studies of migrant communities.[33] The proliferating reports of migrant disappearances reflect the uncertainties of this period for sending communities in Mexico. It is impossible to examine the ephemeral Web sites devoted to the missing without considering the weight of the disappearances on the fragile linkages of kin and conationals in transnational space. Family photographs, passport pictures, and identification cards posted to sites operated by the Mexican consulate adopt both the form of official immigration documents and more personal narrative to describe the disappeared. "Odilon Vera Mendez, 32," listed by height, weight, hair and eye color, complexion, and facial features, appears online in a photograph depicting the young man at a track meet (figure 1). The race tag on his chest, "L959," stands in for the official imprint of the state identification number, the mug shot, passport, or perhaps the Bracero

Figure 1. Odilon Vera Mendez, missing since
November 13, 2001. Protección a Mexicanos,
Consul General de México, online resource for
missing persons.

registration number of past migrations. The photo caption reads: "Lugar de
Origen: Huauchinango, Puebla. Últimos datos conocidos: Salió de Tetela de
Ocampo, Puebla el pasado 13 de noviembre de 2001, con destino a Estados
Unidos para trabajar, pero hasta la fecha su familia no tiene noticias de él."[34]
Between the precision of Tetela de Ocampo, Puebla (population 25,859,
304.89 square kilometers in area, and 3,000 meters above sea level), and
the uncharted route to work in the United States, the vast terrain of transna-
tional space presents its threat to identity, to kinship, to territoriality itself.

The interrupted biographies of the disappeared represent a rupture in
time and space for sending families and towns. For the bereft, not knowing whether the missing are alive or dead disrupts the narrative of transnational community, both in its symbolic unity and in the material sense of
economic survival and the futurity of family lines. One image in particular,
from the Consul General Web site, invites analysis: Azucena Quezada Olea,

Figure 2. Azucena Quezada Olea,
missing since 2002. Protección
a Mexicanos, Consul General de
México, online resource for missing
persons.

of Morelos, last seen in 2002 (figure 2).[35] The young woman in the photograph stands in a parking lot that could be anywhere in the north/south
circuit of migrant travels. Her shirt bears the tourist logo for Kentucky, perhaps a sign of her connection to this new outpost of Mexican labor, or perhaps a souvenir of her tourist travel. The nondescript background is nonetheless an occasion for a portrait, for memorialization of the moment, of her
being there. Azucena Quezada Olea smiles as she gazes out at the camera,
one hand shyly at her face, another hand holding a young child. She occupies
the whole of the image: The child next to her is only partly in the picture.
The child looks so much like Azucena that the image can only imply their
relatedness, yet the border of the photograph splits the child in half. What
Roland Barthes would call the *punctum* of the image lies in this bisection of
the child's figure.[36]

The photograph of the missing woman captures what seems ineffable in
narratives of border crossing: the sense that the migrant occupies a place

and no place at once. Disappearance does not only imply the loss of the woman herself, but the destruction her death or departure means for the child. Familial dislocation, occurring across national boundaries, puts children's identities and protection in crisis. Children lose their minimal political status once separated from their parents in the migrant circuit. In a larger sense, the photograph illuminates the profoundly unsettling ways in which transnational migration remakes kinship and reveals how kinship cannot mitigate against loss. In this instance, the vanishing of Azucena makes a ghost of her child.

The formal institutions that enshrine Mexican citizenship seem equally strained by the uncertainties of the border passage: the Office of Foreign Relations (SRE), which oversees Mexican consulates, vacillates between a discourse that interpellates migrants as full nationals and something approaching an official language of mourning. "Tu calidad de indocumentado no te convierte en delincuente," reads a Web site for the Consul General of New York, which goes on to explain the human rights protections that cover migrants in the United States.[37] Within this assertion is a latent recognition of the threat of loss—of personal sovereignty for the migrant, of national sovereignty for the Mexican state—inherent in the unauthorized border crossing. The transit from citizenship to unauthorized status in the United States is, in fact, a process of conversion, effected *through* violence—the sanctioned interdiction of the state, which may seize and remove migrants by its use of force or by the extralegal, informal aggressions of nonstate actors like the Arizona Minutemen.

The Instituto Nacional de Migración (INM/National Institute of Migration) generated controversy in recent years by issuing pamphlets to potential migrants that delineate the hazards of the border crossing. The guides contain emergency telephone numbers, the details of consular services and immigration documents, and information about migrants' protections under international law. With their graphic depictions of migrant deaths, the books become an inventory of *passing* as well as passage in pages devoted to the many ways the border can kill. In a section devoted to the Sonoran Desert, the *Guía del Migrante Yucateco* lists the symptoms of dehydration, only to conclude: "Si tienes estos síntomas, estás en peligro de morir lentamente."[38] The irony is, of course, that the Mexican government cannot do more than forecast this death. Mexican sovereignty does not extend to providing gainful employment to nationals at home, nor does it provide safe passage for those leaving the country.

This point came home to me in an interview with officers from the Grupos Beta de Protección a Migrantes (Beta Group for the Protection of Migrants), the Mexican border patrol in Ciudad Juárez, in 2003. C. Roberto Gaytan Saucedo, the interim director for the INM in Juárez, reported that the scale of migration makes the task of policing the desert region impossible. Officially a humanitarian operation of the INM, Grupos Beta claimed just seven officers for the vast Juárez metropolitan region in 2003. Like generations of border officers before him, Gaytan Saucedo admitted that every seizure of a migrant merely delays the eventual crossing.[39] Grupos Beta has resorted to posting signs in the desert about the perils of migration, advising women to purchase pepper spray as a defense against male aggressors. The empty gesture makes it clear that women alone are responsible for their personal safety. The state functions of security do not extend into this denationalized border zone, nor do they cover the bodies of women moving through this space. Mexican sovereignty and state power are so compromised in the border region that the Grupos Beta does not dare to venture into the path of armed criminal groups operating in the desert; the absurdity of pepper spray here makes a cruel joke of the state's disinterest in women's suffering. In March 2005, Claudia Smith, president of the Coalition in Defense of the Migrant, presented the statistic that one in ten women report being raped in the attempt to cross the border.[40]

In this context, the INM warning "Hay caminos sin regreso" doubles as an admonition and an admission of state complicity in migrant suffering.[41] Neoliberal governance has only exacerbated the government's role as a broker for cheap labor. The failure of market-led development has forced individual states to compete with one another for migrant remittances. Various states now issue their own localized migrant guidebooks, which combine the national discourse on the border crossing with promotions of regional identity and loyalty. The *Guía del Migrante Yucateco* offers information on Yucatecan clubs and mutual aid societies in California, stressing the interest of the state government in helping migrants organize abroad. "Yendo o viniendo Yucateco sigue siendo," it reads, displaying an official regard for how local Mayan ethnicity offers a vital resource for group survival in the United States.[42] Of course, those Yucatecos who perish or vanish do not remain Yucateco. On average, five migrants from southern Mexican states die every month trying to reach the northern border, and many more disappear. The state's invocation of human rights or cultural unity as a supplement to citizenship collapses under the pressure to obtain migrant remittances at any cost. The final assertion, "Cuida tu vida," underlines how life, in this instance, gets reduced to a vehicle for income generation.[43] In their ambivalent discourse of nationalism and mourning, migrant guides articulate contradictions in Mexican development: The links between nation building and migration mark the state's intimacy with death.

Women's Border Imaginaries

On May 10, 1948, "Concepción Zapata" presented her retablo to the Santísima Virgen de San Juan de los Lagos as a testament to the saint's protection during her sojourn in the United States (figure 3).[44] The retablo, or votive painting, is a popular form of devotion that renders compensation for the miraculous intercession of the patron saint. The votive practice records a private act of supplication and gives witness to the person's deliverance from illness or danger. For Mexican migrants, the retablo combines a holy image with a visual rendition of perils faced in the border crossing, forming a closed narrative of departure and return once the painting is deposited in its shrine. As the patroness of Los Altos de Jalisco, La Virgen de San Juan de los Lagos has heard many stories of emigration and has made many border crossings of her own.[45] Alongside accounts of averted deaths and wondrous cures, this guardian of migrants knows the particular gender terror of the passage northward.

In her account of divine protection, Concepción Zapata relates:

> Dedico el presente RETABLO a la Sma. V. de San Juan de los Lagos por aberme salbado de un TEXANO que me llebara, me escodi [sic] debajo de un arbol con mi hermanito ala orilla de la carretera.

> [I dedicate the present retablo to the Holiest Virgen of San Juan de los Lagos for having saved me from a Texan who tried to carry me off. I hid under a tree by the side of the road with my little brother.][46]

Unlike conventional votive paintings, this retablo does not depict the traumatic encounter itself, but Concepción's act of devotion after the fact. The image places the kneeling figure of Concepción just beyond a drawn curtain, as if the viewer is looking in on a confessional. Staged this way, this public disclosure of the young woman's experience reinscribes the private, unspeakable nature of sexual aggression. The anonymous artist painted the nationality of the aggressor in capital letters, "TEXANO," as if to locate the threat of gender violence *en el otro lado*, on the other side. The story describes

Figure 3. Retablo of Concepción Zapata. San Luis Potosí, May 10, 1948. Oil on metal.
14 × 19.5 cm. Taken from the Durand-Arias collection. Reproduced from Jorge Durand and
Douglas S. Massey, *Miracles on the Border: Retablos of Mexican Migrants to the United States*
(Tucson: University of Arizona Press, 1995), 138–39. Reproduced by permission.

the peril of a young woman traveling alone, her younger brother too small
to act as her guardian or chaperone. Concepción's narrative leaves open the
question of what might have happened: She describes the male threat in
the verb *llevar* (carry off) ("un TEXANO me llebara"), a taking that is both
rape and capture. The verb shows how the sexual violation is discursively
linked to disappearance, a taking from which there is no return. The story
ascribes the agency behind the young woman's evasion of harm to the saint
rather than to her own resourcefulness. Concepción's escape under the tree
anticipates her enclosure back at home. The narrative figures the border as
the open road, "la carretera," in opposition to the protective closeness of the
interior space rendered in the painting.

In its reticence toward depicting Concepción as a fully autonomous
agent in her border crossing, the retablo presciently anticipates current
concerns about Mexican women's mobility through transnational space.
Women's perceived sexual availability and vulnerability incite social anxi-

eties about the nation's exposure at the northern frontier. The question of women's autonomy of movement takes on greater urgency at the international boundary, where disappearance can also be a matter of a change in political status altogether. The story of Concepción Zapata's miraculous deliverance speaks to us from midcentury San Luis Potosí as a testament to the ways sex has historically been constructed as a woman's price for a successful border crossing.[47]

Zapata traveled north to Texas at the height of the Bracero Program, a period of mass emigration in which women's mobility remained invisible in public discourse, rendering women migrants doubly undocumented. Some fifty years later, we might inquire into the strategies of rendering visible these journeys—artistic strategies for elucidating the complex relationships linking women's bodies, processes of deterritorialization, and the fabric of social bonds.

I'm Just Passing Through Here

By way of conclusion, I want to draw out the possibilities for locating alternate imaginaries of the border space in recent literary productions by women emerging from the transnational migrant circuit. For this, I turn to Los Angeles author Marisela Norte, whose spoken-word composition "Act of the Faithless" narrates the relationship between a young Chicana girl and her uncle's girlfriend, a Juárez woman who crosses the border for daily work in a luxury hotel in El Paso.[48]

> The story would have to begin with her.
> She worked as a maid
> in the El Paso Holiday Inn.
> El Paso
> Mal paso que te das
> al cruzar la frontera
> I mean
> I'm just passing through here.

Chicana poet and performer Marisela Norte is an "Eastside Girl," a voice for urban Los Angeles. Born in 1955 to Mexican parents who immigrated to Southern California in the 1930s and 1940s, Norte grew up in a community with strong kinship and cultural ties to Ciudad Juárez.[49] "Act of the Faithless" first appeared in recorded form in 1991, on the poet's album

Norte/Word. Rather than publish her compositions in book form, Norte chose to circulate her work in a format that would make it available to a broader audience and would also retain the texture of her voice. Norte's work exploits shifts in narrative time and perspective in order to convey the multiplicity of female subjectivity in the border space; her poem appropriates a working-class, migrant vernacular to delineate the complex alteration of female agency and perspective taking place in the border crossing.

In Norte's poem, the urban environs of Ciudad Juárez and El Paso appear as sites of economic and personal transactions that convert Mexican women into commodified beings. Norte's story of a young Chicana girl's relationship to her uncle's girlfriend, whom she calls her "aunt," embeds the relationship in a longer narrative on family, danger, and desire at the U.S.-Mexican border. But Norte tells us that if she were to tell her story straight, it would begin with the aunt cleaning rooms in the luxury hotel, "twenty stories high" above the squalor of the urban frontier. Their crossing into El Paso, narrated as a momentary departure from the confines of class, is described as "a bad step" or a "wrong move." For the protagonist, the border crossing doubles as a change in cultural identity and a passage from girlhood to maturity. The story links the formation of the girl's critical consciousness to her separation from the maternal figure of her aunt.

Border crossing is doubly hazardous, both because *mexicanas* are pressed into the service of a foreign and punishing racial system in the United States and also, for the young narrator, because it signifies loss:

> El paso con la frontera
> Por vida
> con safos
> mas vale
> as it is written
> up and down that border
> that runs up and down our backs
> like a bad tattoo

The severing of national ties symbolized in the border forces an understanding of migrant identity as a violation, "the bad tattoo" marking emigrants to the United States in difference. The racial inscription of the migrant's body is analogous to the division of social space by the national boundary. "Por vida / con safos," the tags of graffiti that adorn the crossing, are ironic articulations of presence and ownership written into the interstices of nation and property that exclude migrant subjects. "The acceptance of difference," writes Ramón Saldívar, "does not diminish the pain of separation that difference implies," a loss that resides at the heart of identity.[50] Norte's poem turns on jagged inflections of loss within the gestures of intimacy between family and workers, on the particular forms of nonidentity produced in the border crossing.

"She was an aunt / I would know too briefly," Norte warns us from the beginning. Norte's poem enacts the dialectic of identification and disidentification that Saldívar prescribes, as she continually delivers an affirmative statement, "she cleaned up / decorated their home" only to more effectively communicate its negation, "with objects of rejection." As Norte's narrator visits the Holiday Inn with her aunt, her trip features an ascent "in the hotel elevator / from the basement / to the honeymoon suite," a crossing of class boundaries that far exceeds the physical distance of her journey from home. The young girl quickly perceives that this visit has significance beyond her entertainment, as her aunt shows her the workings of leisure and bourgeois values:

> A slow curtain is pulled
> by the delicate hand
> holding the heavy gold cord.
> Slowly and deliberately
> she will expose,
> letting out a little sigh.
> She cannot believe it herself.
> This is what it could all look like,
> this view from twenty stories high.

Like a magician, the aunt ceremoniously presents her niece with a glimpse of a world of privilege wholly distinct from life as it is lived on the ground floor. The view signifies not only the romantic temporal disengagement from worldly cares promised by the tourist industry, however; here it is described in spatial terms as the deliberate construction of an insular social landscape. As the "delicate hand" that services this fantasy, the maid experiences the crossing of class boundaries as a kind of cognitive dissonance—even as she reveals it to her niece, "she cannot believe it herself."

The view alternately figures a space of possibility beyond the social restrictions of the border and reinscribes the aunt and niece's outsider status within this cosmopolitan realm. The statement "This is what it could all look like" reminds us that the landscape can only reflect the gazers' own social position. Looking out, the narrator situates herself in relation to the luxury that encloses her by reading the storefronts:

> There was a dance hall
> called El Peor es Nada,
> Better than Nothing,
> and then there was
> that narrow stretch of nothing,
> the remains of a dried-out sewer.
> She told me it was El Río,
> El Grande grande.
> Surely these were the things
> bad dreams were made of.

The place-names signify the absolute negation of the social mobility manifested in the gilded ornaments of the luxury suite. Even the river, made heroic in border legend, betrays its name by serving as the washed-out basin for pollution and waste generated in the tourist trade and the maquiladora industry. The repetition of "nothing" inscribes the landscape with a fatalism sharply divergent from Chicana feminist constructions of the border as a crossroads.[51] This nothingness exerts a material force on its subjects, expressed as the substance of nightmares. Norte's border insistently spatializes the racial and gender formations that make up the neocolonial tourist economy.

At first, the narrator wishes to experience her ascent to the luxury suite as an escape, to close her eyes:

> I only wanted to lay down
> and shut my eyes
> to the annoying Texas sun
> in the sky
> and make these feet
> leave the ground
> for one moment
> and imagine the afterlife,
> eternity at twenty stories high

Abandonment of her place under the "annoying Texas sun" connotes not only relief but also a kind of death. The ability to evacuate her subject position for that of the tourist is figured as immobility and stasis, not mobility or freedom of choice. The girl's lesson continues in a trip to the rooftop swimming pool. "If there's no one up there," the maid tells her, "you can take your shoes off / and put your feet in the water." This episode speaks to the innumerable hidden acts by which migrant women contest the dehumanizing control of their labor in forms of resistance that feminize class struggle. The act of putting her feet in the pool alleviates tiredness from long hours spent standing; it also signifies a transgression of the boundaries between the domestic worker and the customer. For the niece, getting her feet wet is an experience of what it means to be a tourist.

The inscription of race within a class hierarchy serves as the occasion for a struggle over the meanings of the girl's transnational identity:

> You are not from here,
> nor are you from over there,
> you understand m'hija?
> Entiendes?

The aunt understands her niece's identity as a condition of homelessness, of estrangement from both Mexican and U.S. national unities. She ascribes a particular cognitive advantage to the girl's ambivalent national status, but also an utter lack of a coherent identity. The narrator counters with a recitation that reclaims the border as the "sitio y lengua" which both authorize and give form to her utterance.[52]

> Los dos idiomas?
> Claro que sí.
> Que no soy de aquí
> Que no soy de allá
>
> But I can speak
> the language, I insisted,
> both of them.
> Entiendes?

One important detail of this exchange is the way the aunt distinguishes between her own border identity and her niece's. The niece belongs to both worlds on either side of the border; "she speaks both languages," though her aunt does not. The maid merely travels to render her services at the hotel. The whole of the girl's adventure in the pool is staged as a foreshadowing of her future travels beyond the confines of her border existence. This tran-

sient destiny is shaded with both pleasure and danger: "mal paso que das /
al cruzar la frontera," she warns, "I mean, I'm just passing through here."

Norte's narrator takes pleasure in transgressing the boundaries of privilege. But as she imagines her immersion in the luxury pool, she is pulled
back to the present by the sight of her aunt performing her duties as a maid,
wiping down the patio furniture: "I watched her body move inside the uniform / . . . / the sound of her nylon stockings." Immediately she senses her
separation from her aunt's status as a worker and wishes to repudiate her
fantasy. Her aunt, observing the girl in her dark glasses, laughs at her pan-
tomime of the role of U.S. tourist: "Ahora sí pareces turista americana." Her
niece, threatened with the gulf of difference opening between them, hands
the sunglasses back:

> She began to laugh, but I shook my head.
> I don't belong here and neither do you.
> I'm just passing through here, remember?
> I'm not from here and neither are you.

The niece recognizes that her play creates a separation between her aunt
as a worker and her own mobility of identifications. She refuses to identify
as a tourist, seeking instead to make her aunt share in her own position of
"passing through." But the aunt knows better.

Rather than assume that kinship unites the girl and her aunt within a
shared class position, Norte allows us to see precisely how the labor of the
maid figures in the production of her niece's cognitive desire as a writer. In
a moment of great poignancy, the maid reveals how the lesson she gives her
niece plays a part of her own gendered class struggle:

> She gave me a pair of sunglasses to wear
> "Toma, cuidate los ojos
> take care of your eyes.
> There's so much you should see."

The sunglasses signify both the trappings of class privilege and a shield
against the potential harm of exposure that the girl faces in her formation as
a writer. The aunt prepares her niece to bear witness and also, in a moment
of great generosity, to protect herself. Here the poem contrasts the relative
social mobility of the Chicana niece and the Mexican maid.

The poem articulates the divides of class and citizenship instantiated in
the border, revealing how the girl's transient status at the border ("passing

through") is simultaneously a matter of wounding and of agency. In the final scene of the poem, the narrator relates the conclusion to her poolside fantasy. As the maid pushes her cart toward the door back to the elevator, the voice of a U.S. tourist calls her back:

> Excuse me. Señorita, can you come here, por favor?
> . . . .
> He waves an empty glass at her.
> The wife looks up at him smiling
> The "He's all mine" smile.

The drama of the formation of the girl's critical consciousness thus takes place within an ongoing conflict over the terms of sale for migrant women's labor. Opposed to the maid and her niece are a white tourist and his wife, who play out their heterosexual travel adventure against the neocolonial backdrop of the luxury hotel.

This final scene instructs us in the way the struggle over signification shares space with the class struggle over production:

> I tug at her arm.
> I point at the man now silent.
> "There is too much to see," she said.
> "Too much to remember."

By leaving open the problematic of seeing and narrating, *Norte* "problematizes women's discursive practices" in the border space: "There is too much to see / too much to remember."[53] The girl's formation as a border subject separates the cognitive agency of "knowing" and "seeing" from the security of kinship and rootedness. Her "passing through" is a process both of personal transformation and of leave-taking, dislocating her from the resourceful aunt she "would know all too briefly."

"Act of the Faithless" narrates the border traffic in Mexican women in terms that banish any fantasy of the border's dissolution or permeability. Through her protagonist's fond recollection of the aunt she has lost, Norte gives voice to the "longing for unity and cohesion" that critic Rolando Romero ascribes to Chicana/Chicano narrative, even as her story of fractured kinship refutes any notion of an organic class or kinship unity among Mexicans, migrants, and Mexican Americans across the boundary.[54] In this piece, Norte details the intimate and often conflicted relationships among women in this clandestine labor economy, relationships complicated by the constant presence of sexual danger, transgressive erotic relations, and personal violence accompanying the binational sale of women's labor.

===

Norte's work exists alongside the consular lists of the disappeared that preserve accounts of the missing as parents, children, partners, friends—they are a form of desperate contestation to the binational state apparatus that converts the undocumented into people without status, without a place. Yet the disappeared are nonetheless *present*; their stories of loss remake the narratives of kinship, community, and belonging that sustain the transnational circuit.

In closing, I want to consider the significance of other vanishings. Ciudad Juárez is not only the place of arrival and departure for thousands in the migrant circuit; throughout this period of increased migration, the city has been a final terminus of utter brutality for the victims of *feminicidio*.[55] The northern boomtown, whose principal function is to support the mobility of capital, goods, and labor, has been the site of unprecedented killings of girls and women, residents of the Juárez colonias.[56] Many more young women are missing. For more than a decade, state and federal officials have permitted the murders to continue with impunity. The nation that sends thousands of its people into the migrant labor circuit has little to offer as protection for the female citizens whose vitality and labors sustain the fragile social ecology of the border space. Images of the missing girls travel the same networks as the pictures advertising the names of disappeared migrants. Currently, El Paso and Ciudad Juárez are the sites of ardent campaigns against both the *feminicidio* and the death of migrants in the border crossing. The success of these local mobilizations will depend on effective witness to migrants' stories of bereavement and absence. There is much to admire in the melancholic will to deny loss, to refuse to surrender the lost object, to refuse to go quietly. The political forms we devise in this moment of global transformation must partner the melancholic work against the violence that bring the circuits of human mobility into traffic with death, an immovable death, a departure with no return.

Notes

The author thanks the editor of this volume, Jane Juffer, along with *SAQ* managing editor Christi Stanforth for their contributions to this article. Special acknowledgments are also offered to the staff at Junta, to "Rita," and to Elizabeth Alexander, Jorge Durand, Jonathan Fox,

Kellie Jones, Alondra Nelson, Stephen Pitti, Arthur Schmidt, and María Aurora Camacho de Schmidt.

1   I use the term *undocumented* to refer to migrants who either enter the United States without proper documents or overstay their visas. Jeffrey S. Passel offers a useful discussion of the term. See Jeffrey S. Passel, "Estimates of the Size and Characteristics of the Undocumented Population" (Washington: Pew Hispanic Center Project Report, March 21, 2005), www.pewhispanic.org (accessed November 18, 2005).

2   See, for instance, the works of Jorge Durand and Patricia Arias, *Experiencia migrante: iconografía de la migración México-Estados Unidos* (Mexico DF: Altexto, 2000), and María Herrera Sobek, *Northward Bound: The Mexican Immigrant Experience in Ballad and Song* (Bloomington: University of Indiana Press, 1993).

3   Asociación Tepeyac, "Missing But Not Counted," November 2002, compiled in 9/11 digital archive, *911digitalarchive.org/collections/asntepeyac* (accessed November 15, 2002).

4   Ibid.

5   See press communications of the Secretaría de Relaciones Exteriores—México, sre.gob .mx (accessed January 5, 2006).

6   See Manuel Pastor and Carol Wise, "State Policy, Distribution, and Neoliberal Reform in Mexico," *Journal of Latin American Studies* 29 (1997): 419–56.

7   Passel, "Estimates of the Size and Characteristics of the Undocumented Population."

8   Luis Alberto Urrea, *The Devil's Highway: A True Story* (New York: Little, Brown, 2004).

9   This figure comes from Amnesty International, "United States of America: Human Rights Concerns in the Border Region with Mexico," May 20, 1998. Further details are available in statistics compiled by the Mexican Foreign Relations Office for the past decade. The figure is corroborated by various nongovernmental agencies, including the California Rural Legal Assistance Foundation of El Centro, California (www.crla.org). At the time of this writing, the U.S. Border Patrol has acknowledged the December 30, 2005, shooting of Guillermo Martínez Rodríguez, an eighteen-year-old Mexican national, who met his death just north of the San Ysidro crossing point in San Diego County. President Vicente Fox is under political pressure in Mexico for his weak response to the incident. The killing occurred just days after the U.S. House of Representatives had approved the installation of 700 miles of new walls along the border as part of the punitive immigration reform bill H.R. 4437, which would make undocumented entry into the United States a felony.

10 Miguel Escobar Valdez, consul for Mexico at Douglas, Arizona, interview by the author, Tempe, Arizona, April 9, 2004. For an illustration of consular functions related to the disappearance of Mexican migrants, see the Web site for the Mexican Consulate of New York, www.consulmexny.org/esp/proteccion_tabla_desaparecidos.htm (accessed November 20, 2005).

11 Durand and Massey, *Crossing the Border.*

12 Jeffrey S. Passel, "Unauthorized Migrants: Numbers and Characteristics" (Washington: Pew Hispanic Center Project Report, June 14, 2005), www. pewhispanic.org (accessed November 2, 2005).

13 For data on the migrants' use of coyotes or *polleros*, see Jorge Durand and Douglas S. Massey, "What We Learned from the Mexican Migration Project," in Durand and Massey,

Crossing the Border, 1–14. On human traffic, see Peter Andreas, "The Transformation of Migrant Smuggling across the U.S.-Mexican Border," in *Global Human Smuggling: Comparative Perspectives*, ed. David Kyle and Rey Koslowski (Baltimore: Johns Hopkins University Press, 2001), 107–28. See also John Bailey and Jorge Chabat, eds., *Transnational Crime and Public Security: Challenges to Mexico and the United States* (La Jolla: Center for U.S.-Mexican Studies, University of California at San Diego, 2002).

14 See Roberto Suro, "Remittance Senders and Receivers: Tracking the Transnational Channels," Pew Hispanic Center Report written in partnership with the Multilateral Investment Fund (Washington: Pew Hispanic Center, November 24, 2003), available at www.pewhispanic.org/page.jsp?page=reports (accessed November 15, 2005).

15 Robert C. Smith, "'Los ausentes siempre presentes': The Imagining, Making, and Politics of a Transnational Community between Ticuani, Puebla, and New York City" (Ph.D. diss., Columbia University, 1994).

16 Durand and Massey, "What We Learned," 10.

17 Carrie Kahn and Lourdes García Navarro for National Public Radio, "Immigrants Run Scholarship Program for Mexicans," aired January 6, 2006, on *Morning Edition*. See npr.org.

18 The term *postnational* describes the exercise of political agency outside the migrant's country of origin. The term also references a range of loyalties, social networks, or political claims that extend beyond the boundaries of national citizenship. See Linda Basch, Nina Glick Schiller, and Cristina Szanton Blanc, *Nations Unbound: Transnational Projects, Postcolonial Predicaments, and Deterritorialized Nation-States* (Langhorne: Gordon and Breach, 1994); Linda Bosniak, "The State of Citizenship: Citizenship Denationalized," *Indiana Journal of Legal Studies* 7.2 (2000): 447–510; Saskia Sassen, "The Repositioning of Citizenship: Emergent Subjects and Spaces for Politics," *CR: The New Centennial Review* 3.2 (Summer 2003): 41–66; and Yasemin Nuhoǒlu Soysal, *Limits of Citizenship: Migrants and Postnational Membership in Europe* (Chicago: University of Chicago Press, 1994).

19 Durand and Massey, "What We Learned," 13.

20 Accounts of human traffic, organ trafficking, and slavery are not only limited to the border cities, where narcotrafficking and the *feminicidio* in Ciudad Juárez have raised the specter of other forms of predatory violence. Spanish-language media catering to new immigrants commonly carries stories of superexploitation and crimes against migrants. Both Univisión and Telemundo maintain Web sites devoted to immigration. In addition, Telemundo carries the syndicated program *Sin Fronteras*, which is devoted to immigrant concerns.

21 See Judith Butler, *The Psychic Life of Power: Theories in Subjection* (Palo Alto: Stanford University Press, 1997); David Eng and David Kazanjian, eds., *Loss: The Politics of Mourning* (Berkeley: University of California Press, 2002); and Ann Anlin Cheng, *The Melancholy of Race: Psychoanalysis, Assimilation, and Hidden Grief* (New York: Oxford University Press, 2001).

22 "Battling Beyond U.S. Borders," *Assignment Discovery*, 2005.

23 My translations and transcription.

24 Details of the case appear in Mary E. O'Leary, "Scam Cost Illegal Aliens $150G," *New Haven Register*, January 6, 2006.

25 *El Alma Herida* (The Wounded Soul) was a coproduction of Telemundo and Argos in Mexico. The program completed shooting in 2003 and aired in the United States throughout 2004.

26 "One of the most beloved novelas of the Hispanic public": Organic Broadcast Project, http://broadcast.organicframework.com (accessed November 18, 2005).

27 My translation. Story synopsis and cast information are available at http://tdmnovelas .tripod.com/elalmaherida/ (accessed November 18, 2005).

28 See Daniel D. Arreola and James R. Curtis, "Cultural Landscapes of the Mexican Border Cities," *Aztlán* 21.1–2 (1992–96): 1–48.

29 In fact, many of those stranded or deported are children. María Eugenia Hernández Sánchez, "Deported Children in Ciudad Juárez," paper presented at the Center for Latin American and Iberian Studies, Yale University, New Haven, CT, October 12, 2005.

30 "Mexican Expatriate Voter Registration Falling Flat," *Frontera NorteSur* (online newsgroup circulated by Center for Latin American and Border Studies, New Mexico State University at Las Cruces), November 21, 2005.

31 Ibid.

32 Ibid.

33 See especially Smith, "'Los ausentes siempre presentes'"; Roger Rouse, "Mexican Migration to the U.S.: Family Relations in a Transnational Migrant Circuit" (Ph.D. diss., Stanford University, 1989), and Luin Goldring, "Diversity and Community in Transnational Migration: A Comparative Study of Two Mexican U.S. Migrant Communities" (Ph.D. diss., Cornell University, 1992).

34 "Place of birth: Huauchinango, Puebla. Last known: He departed from Tetela de Ocampo, Puebla, on 13 November, 2001, on route to work in the United States, but to this date, his family has received no news of his whereabouts." Protección a Mexicanos, Consulado General de México, www.consulmexny.org/esp/proteccion_tabla_desaparecidos .htm (accessed November 12, 2005).

35 Protección a Mexicanos, Consulado General de México, www.consulmexny.org/esp/ proteccion_tabla_desaparecidos.htm (accessed November 12, 2005).

36 Roland Barthes, *Camera Lucida*, trans. Richard Howard (New York: Hill and Wang, 1981). "The punctum *punctuates* the meaning of the photograph (the studium) and as a result punctures or pierces its viewer" (27).

37 "Your undocumented status does not make you a criminal." Protección a Mexicanos, Consulado General de México, www.consulmexny.org/esp/proteccion_migratorios.htm (accessed November 12, 2005).

38 "If you have these symptoms, you are in danger of dying slowly." Gobierno del Estado de Yucatán, *Guia del Migrante Yucateco* (Yucatán, 2004), 32.

39 The United States instituted an official border patrol unit in 1924. C. Roberto Gaytan Saucedo, interview by author, Ciudad Juárez, November 13, 2003.

40 Claudia Smith, quoted in "Rapes on the U.S.-Mexico Border Up," United Press International, March 18, 2005, www.feeds.bignewsnetwork.com/?sid=2768526633891249 (accessed March 18, 2005). Smith argues that given the low rates of reporting crime, the actual number of rapes may be much higher.

41 "There are paths of no return."

42 "Going or coming, you remain Yucatecan." *Guía del Migrante Yucateco*, 79.

43 "Protect your life."

44 *Retablo of Concepción Zapata*, in Jorge Durand and Douglas S. Massey, *Miracles on the Border: Retablos of Mexican Migrants to the United States* (Tucson: University of Arizona Press, 1995), 138–39.

45 Ibid.

46 Ibid., 138.

47 See Sylvanna M. Falcón, "Rape as a Weapon of War: Advancing Human Rights for Women at the U.S.-Mexico Border," *Social Justice* 28.2 (2001): 31–50.

48 Marisela Norte, "Act of the Faithless," in *Norte/Word* 062/Cro2 (Lawndale, CA: New Alliance Records, 1991).

49 My discussion of Marisela Norte is informed by Michelle Habell-Pallán's definitive work on the poet, "No Cultural Icon: Marisela Norte and Spoken Word—East L.A. Noir and the U.S./Mexico Border," in *Loca Motion: The Travels of Chicana and Latina Popular Culture* (New York: NYU Press, 2005), 43–80.

50 Ramón Saldívar, *Chicano Narrative: The Dialectics of Difference* (Madison: University of Wisconsin Press, 1990), 190.

51 This concept of the border appears in Gloria Anzaldúa, *Borderlands/La Frontera: The New Mestiza* (San Francisco: Aunt Lute, 1987), and Sonia Saldívar-Hull, *Feminism on the Border: Chicana Gender Politics and Literature* (Berkeley: University of California Press, 2000). See also Norma Alarcón, "The Theoretical Subject(s) of *This Bridge Called My Back* and Anglo-American Feminism," in *Criticism in the Borderlands: Studies in Chicano Literature*, ed. Hector Calderón and José David Saldívar (Durham, NC: Duke University Press, 1991), 28–39.

52 Emma Pérez, "Sexuality and Discourse: Notes from a Chicana Survivor," in *Chicana Lesbians: The Girls Our Mothers Warned Us About*, ed. Carla Trujillo (Berkeley: Third Woman Press, 1991), 159–84. Pérez's phrase "sitio y lengua" means "place and language/tongue."

53 The phrase comes from María Socorro Tabuenca Córdova and Debra A. Castillo, *Border Women: Writing from La Frontera* (Minneapolis: University of Minnesota Press, 2002), 64.

54 Rolando Romero, "Postdeconstructive Spaces," *Siglo XX/Twentieth Century II* (1993): 225–33, cited in ibid., 15.

55 Since 1993, some 370 women have been murdered in Chihuahua City and Ciudad Juárez; approximately 137 were sexually assaulted before their death. Of these, 100 fit a pattern of serial killings. Some 75 of the bodies have not been identified or claimed. The mothers' organization Nuestras Hijas de Regreso a Casa (Bring Our Daughters Home) estimates that in addition to these documented killings, 600 women have disappeared from the Juárez/Chihuahua metropolitan areas. Amnesty International, "Mexico: Intolerable Killings: Ten Years of Abductions and Murders in Ciudad Juárez and Chihuahua," August 11, 2003, AI index: AMR 41/027/2003.

56 See my discussion of the *feminicidio* in Alicia Schmidt Camacho, "Body Counts on the Mexico-U.S. Border: *Feminicidio*, Reification, and the Theft of Mexicana Subjectivity," *Chicana/Latina Studies* 4.1 (2004): 22–60.

Tony Payan

The Drug War and the U.S.-Mexico Border: The State of Affairs

The U.S.-Mexico border has long been the set-ting for America's longest war: the drug war. The first shots of the border drug war were fired during the U.S. Bureau of Customs's Operation Intercept on September 21, 1969, not long after President Richard Nixon declared a war on illegal drugs. The border was shut down unilaterally by the U.S. government on that day, deeply affecting the lives and the economy of border residents. In the short run, the border blockade managed to expose the interdependence of cross-border communities,[1] though its actual effect on stem-ming the tide of illegal drugs across the border was negligible. The long-term significance of Operation Intercept resides in a single fact: It inaugurated an era of illegal-drug policy that has resulted in the creation and consolidation of a few large drug cartels and the increas-ing effectiveness of their operations. Moreover, Operation Intercept brought with it a new kind of war based on a logic of escalation between law enforcement and criminal organizations— one that evidence shows U.S. law enforcement has been losing.

The border drug war is now nearly four decades old. It has undergone several reorga-

South Atlantic Quarterly 105:4, Fall 2006
DOI 10.1215/00382876-2006-006   © 2006 Duke University Press

nizations and has expanded its resources and personnel considerably.[2] Its importance in the eyes of the public, politicians, and the media has waxed and waned over time. The public emotionalism that surrounds drug use and smuggling varies. Along the border, however, in a space far removed from the policy-making circles, the relentless dynamic is one in which the border and the drug war shape and influence each other in a never-ending logic of escalation. Departing from a historical perspective, this essay offers an analysis of the interaction between the drug smugglers and the U.S. government's law enforcement efforts to stop the flow of illegal drugs; it explores the dynamics of the day-to-day drug war at the conjuncture where the two distant neighbors meet.[3] What my observations and interviews on the border reveal is the gap between everyday life and the claims made by the U.S. government about the successes of its policies here—in relation not only to drugs but also to free trade and post-9/11 security measures. Ironically, the war on drugs and free-trade policies have consolidated the power of the drug cartels, forcing small-time smugglers out of business. The four major cartels have become increasingly efficient and flexible hierarchies, ready to respond to the contingencies of the drug war and the technological innovations at the border instigated by the Department of Homeland Security.

The Beginning of Today's Game

America's love affair with illegal drugs began in the counterculture of the 1960s. Since then, America's appetite for psychotropic substances has escalated from marijuana through heroin and cocaine to the hardcore chemical drugs consumed in nightclubs throughout the country.[4] Because mind-altering drugs were already illegal in the 1960s, the growing appetite for them increased the risks of dealing in drugs and also the profits of doing so. The profits, however, increased more than the risks, because the incentives for people to deal in drugs grew considerably not just in Mexico but also inside the United States.[5] Many illegal-drug producers and smugglers found it profitable to enter the business. Moreover, because the border was wide open, the costs of smuggling drugs into the United States were relatively low, as were the chances of getting caught. By the 1970s, the illegal-drug smuggling business was booming along the border. There were numerous small ganglike groups in Mexico that operated to smuggle drugs into the United States. The market was large and growing, and willing suppliers were plentiful. Mexico was a major supplier of marijuana and heroin, particularly the Mexican brown heroin. Cocaine came mostly from Colombia via the Caribbean.

During the early 1980s, the United States implemented a series of operations in the Caribbean to stem the flow of cocaine from Colombia.[6] Since the drug war is a strategic game, the Colombians, in response, began to look for different routes to smuggle their cocaine. They discovered Mexico, whose location and open border with the United States were seen as remarkable assets. Two thousand miles of largely unguarded border into the largest drug market in the world did not go unnoticed. The Colombians found a willing counterpart in Mexico, Miguel Angel Félix Gallardo, a well-known Mexican drug smuggler who had consolidated many of the small-time smugglers of the 1960s and 1970s into a single organization and by then controlled much of the illegal-drug trade along the border. His heroin- and marijuana-based organization was already in place and readily served as a conveyor belt for Colombian cocaine. The alliance between the Colombian drug lords and the Mexican Félix Gallardo organization would produce a formidable drug cartel that operated through most of the 1980s. Félix Gallardo, a quiet man who preferred to negotiate and avoided violence for the most part, became the drug lord of the border. He would consolidate the Colombian-Mexican multidrug corridor into a formidable business.

In response to this development, the United States redirected massive antidrug efforts to the U.S.-Mexico border,[7] often with considerable insensitivity, bringing the U.S.-Mexico relationship to some of its lowest points.[8] Félix Gallardo was finally arrested in Mexico in 1989. He continued to run his operations from inside his prison cell, but his collaborators outside were in a constant struggle for control of the organization's operations on the border. From his cell, Gallardo, sent a message to his many lieutenants, who were vying for control of the drug business. They met in a posh hotel in Acapulco to receive his directive. He told them through his messenger to stop quarreling and ordered them to divide the border into territories. Each "lieutenant" would control one smuggling corridor. He then exhorted them to live in peace among themselves and to stay within their own territories. These intraorganizational disputes had to be settled because the U.S. government, "the real enemy," was stepping up its efforts to destroy his organization. It was at this meeting that the modern drug cartels with their respective corridors would emerge: the Tijuana Cartel, the Sinaloa-Sonora Cartel, the Juárez Cartel, and the Gulf Cartel.[9] These are the same organizations that today move at least 70 percent of all the drugs that enter the

United States. The drug war had done little to undermine the Gallardo cartel but had done enough to inspire the 1989 breakdown of his organization into a group of drug-smuggling oligopolies (cartels) that have been even more difficult to fight. The Gallardo cartel, like the Bell Telecommunications cartel of the 1980s, was broken up—except, in the case of the former, it was divided to "rationalize" and maximize its monopoly, not to increase competition.

The Consensus Breaks Down: Intercartel Violence

The formula that Félix Gallardo gave his lieutenants was relatively simple and would have made for a relative peace among the four drug cartels, particularly because Félix Gallardo also taught them how to negotiate with the Mexican authorities so that they would not harass the cartels' operations. The only drug war on the border would be between U.S. law enforcement agencies and the cartels—with some discreet intracartel violence to impose discipline among their members. But the men left in charge of divvying up the Félix Gallardo organization quickly engaged in rivalries. They did not exhibit the quiet demeanor and subdued character of their former boss and were more willing to use violence to solve their disputes. Occasionally one of them tried to gain control of a neighboring, profitable smuggling corridor by eliminating his cartel competitors. This generally led to intercartel violence. At this juncture, extreme violence became manifest on the border. While Félix Gallardo preferred the use of discreet violence, some of the bloodiest of his successors were brazen and employed public executions and dumped dead, tortured bodies in border towns. Drug war–related violence became an integral part of the border landscape.

In addition to the intercartel violence, struggles sometimes occur inside a cartel between two powerful figures for control of the organization, particularly when a capo is killed or captured and jailed. If the jailed capo can no longer control the cartel, even from inside his prison cell, his lieutenants engage in competition to become his successor. This often causes intracartel bloodshed. The members and workers of a cartel take sides and use violence to eliminate the supporters of the competing group. This can result in a heightened level of visible violence, because the bodies of the executed are often disposed of in empty lots or alleys in border towns.

Recently, Mexican president Vicente Fox's determination not to concede anything to the cartels has exacerbated the violence. President Fox's administration (2000–2006) declared an all-out war on the cartels, making it very difficult for any group to establish most-favored status anywhere. The cartels have had to defend their corridors with increased violence, not only against opportunistic violence from their competitors but also from a government that has not let up the fight against the cartels. The capture of several capos by the Mexican federal government has created instability inside the cartels and between them. A recent illustrative period of this kind of intercartel violence was the summer 2005 struggle for control of the Nuevo Laredo–Laredo smuggling corridor in the Rio Grande Valley of Texas.[10] Intercartel rivalries were responsible for a large number of drug-smuggling-related deaths during that high-violence summer. The Nuevo Laredo situation reveals why cartels are today powerful organizations, such that they can put law enforcement efforts and authorities to the test. This case also reveals how violence is sometimes worsened by the drug war's tactical successes.

For drug-smuggling-related violence to be kept to a minimum, there are two requirements. First, the four cartels have to be at a relatively equal level of power, so that no capo feels tempted to take over the operations of another. This balance of power produces a relative peace and keeps to a minimum the level of violence, specifically, down to the violence necessary to discipline the cartel's workforce (eliminating whistleblowers, cheaters, thieves, big-mouths, detractors, traitors, and other undesirables within the organization). The killing or arrest of a cartel capo—a presumed tactical success of law enforcement—can quickly provoke an imbalance of power between competing cartels and lead to opportunistic intercartel violence. Second, there must be at least a tacit agreement between the Mexican authorities at all levels and the cartels regarding the level of protection that the government will offer a cartel—or at least the extent to which the government will look the other way. This generally involves the Mexican government going after the small-time smugglers but looking the other way on the operations of the large cartels—a move that further strengthens the large cartels' hand because it concentrates all the drug business in the hands of the four large organizations.

The Nuevo Laredo violence was due to both of these factors: first, the decapitation of the Gulf Cartel with its subsequent intercartel violence because it provoked other cartels to enter the fray to gain control of the profitable smuggling corridor; and, second, the refusal of the Mexican federal authorities to abide by any agreements not to go after the large drug cartels.

Having beheaded the Gulf cartel by jailing its leader, Osiel Cárdenas, the Mexican federal authorities refused to endorse a successor or allow another cartel to take over the Gulf Cartel operations peacefully. This refusal caused an all-out war between cartels vying for control of the Laredo–Nuevo Laredo corridor operations and between the Mexican authorities and those fighting for control of the smuggling operations. At least 150 people died during that bloody summer, including a local chief of police, who was executed within seven hours after taking office.[11]

The Nuevo Laredo situation reveals that while the popular image of the border is one of random and rampant violence, there are actually certain discernible principles that govern illegal-drug-related violence. Border violence obeys certain patterns that are followed and reproduced by the actors that perpetrate it and suffer it—most important, the laws of the market. When a government makes a commodity, such as psychotropic substances, illegal but the human desire for the commodity remains unabated, the result is the creation of a black market. In a black market, there is always a high level of knowledge of the risks involved in participating in it. Individuals assess the risks and then make a choice to participate or to stay away. But by definition, a black market is denied the same mechanisms for dispute resolution that a legal, well-regulated market has. Instead, those who participate in an illegal market must resort to informal mechanisms to resolve their disputes, including violence. Negotiations among players are not always absent. Often the drug lords first negotiate, then they threaten, and then they resort to violence. Their violence has a purpose and even a meaning: to eliminate the competition and to settle accounts with those who betray them.

In the case of Nuevo Laredo, the balance of power was upset. Accounts had to be settled. In effect, the Mexican government's strategy was indirectly "responsible" for the bloodshed that summer, as was the United States, which has adamantly supported Fox's drug policies. From very early on in both the Fox and Bush administrations, there was complete agreement that the drug cartels were a security concern for both nations. In fact, it became clear very quickly that this might be the only item where the two countries' "security agendas" coincided. President Fox gave President Bush guarantees that he would combat drug trafficking extensively; the latest development is the willingness of President Fox to extradite several drug lords to the United States.[12]

Hence, the border bears the costs of a war that cannot be won.

Backfire: Escalation and Structural Deficiencies

When most Americans talk about illegal drugs, they focus on the number of overdoses that end up in hospitals, the ups and downs of drug use, street-level drug dealing, and law enforcement drug busts covered by the media. Some moralize about drug use. The media's sporadic, incomplete, and largely scandal-driven coverage of illegal drugs contributes to this partial understanding of illegal drugs and the drug war. For the bulk of the population, the border and its relationship with the illegal drugs consumed by some 20 million Americans regularly and many more casually is a problem for policy makers.[13] Many Americans do not generally think of the border and illegal drugs. Even border residents have learned to live with the drug war as part of their communities. They hardly pay attention to it anymore. On the border, the drug war is part of the landscape.

The drug war on the border is a constantly escalating cat-and-mouse game between law enforcement agencies and drug cartels.[14] Law enforcement agencies increase their resources, hire more personnel, and introduce the latest technology to intercept illegal drugs. The drug cartels respond with ever more creative ways to circumvent the latest law enforcement efforts. In this escalation game, the U.S. government is the loser. A diachronic analysis of illegal-drug quality and availability in U.S. streets shows that despite all of America's tactical victories, illegal drugs are just as abundant as they have ever been. There is also evidence that their price is dropping and their quality increasing, signaling a steady, inexhaustible supply.[15]

The drug war not only caused the creation of four large oligopolies but is also turning these organizations into more efficient smuggling machines. In response to the logic of escalation produced by U.S. antidrug strategies, drug-trafficking organizations have proven flexible and adaptable. Because the cartels are constantly responding to U.S. moves, it can be argued that the drug war only makes the cartels even more flexible and adaptable. A review of the modus operandi of the cartels on the border shows how these organizations adapt and change. In the struggle for survival, it is generally the small-time smugglers who do not survive the increased and more sophisticated nature of U.S. antidrug efforts. The four cartels thrive, even in difficult times, because they can change and adapt when faced with these same increased and more sophisticated U.S. drug war efforts. The cartels therefore are nowhere near being destroyed. In fact, the current Homeland Security strategy may actually be strengthening these cartels rather than weakening them, because the effectiveness of U.S. law enforcement efforts turns the four cartels into more flexible, more efficient, more technologically mobile and well-consolidated smuggling units.

Another big advantage of the cartels is the organizational difference between them and the U.S. law enforcement agencies. Even if the cartels' hierarchies are pyramidal, they operate in ways that make them extremely adaptable. There is no handbook. There are no ethical and legal requirements. They are able to respond to contingencies immediately and often creatively.[16] That is precisely the great difference between the U.S. drug war bureaucracies and the criminal organizations they are up against. While the former are saddled with ethics, or administrative or legal rules, the latter are limber and adjust quickly.[17] This is a nearly insurmountable structural difference of U.S. bureaucracies vis-à-vis the cartels. To demonstrate this, I turn to an analysis of the smuggling methods.

Modes of Smuggling

Despite the occasional media hype regarding the intersection between undocumented migration and drugs, the overwhelming majority of undocumented migrants cross on foot between ports of entry and have nothing to do with drug smuggling. Most drugs are brought into the United States at official points of entry (POEs) and hidden in vehicles. According to a source I interviewed in Ciudad Juárez, cocaine, heroin, and methamphetamines are too valuable to risk crossing between POEs, in the wilderness. They can be intercepted by a Border Patrol agent, causing a considerable loss to the organization.[18] Only the small-time smugglers risk crossing drugs between POEs, and they smuggle only marijuana, which is not as valuable, therefore the losses are low enough that the risk of crossing between POEs is worth it.

Those few who do risk crossing the border on foot carrying illegal drugs are mostly novices or people who work for small-time drug dealers. Some may pose as backpackers or attempt to cross drugs hidden on their bodies or clothing at POEs. They are recruited by small-time smugglers and trained to hike certain routes that may or may not coincide with the preferred routes of undocumented workers. This is rare, however. There are, of course, stories of people caught trying to smuggle illegal drugs hidden on their bodies and clothing or in their bags and luggage, but as U.S. officials get better at detecting the nervousness of a border crosser or odd body shapes or their bags, transporting drugs on foot is just too risky. Also, the amount of drugs that a pedestrian can transport is small, compared to the amounts that can be hidden in a vehicle. Those who get caught end up in local courts, rather than federal courts, because they tend not to exceed the amounts that would force them into federal court with higher penalties. These pedestrian drug smugglers are individuals that cannot provide much intelligence, either, because they tend not to work for the large drug cartels but for smaller entrepreneurs and sometimes are hired on the spot for a few dollars. One individual reported that he was offered fifty dollars to transport drugs on his person. Others reported that they did it because they were coerced or threatened. Some reported sheer economic need.[19] What a drug dealer offers is sometimes several times a Mexican resident's monthly salary and can go a long way toward helping their families financially.

A more favored method for smuggling drugs is vehicles (cars, vans, and pickup trucks), and to facilitate this more difficult maneuver, many dealers build "networks" of employees and bureaucrats who are willing to offer protection to the organization's operations through payoffs. This ensures that the cargo crosses safely into the United States. They are willing to pay not only Mexican but also American officials handsome rewards in order to minimize the risk of losing the merchandise. Further protection is gained through the building of special compartments in the vehicles where the drugs can be hidden. A vehicle prepared in such a way is known as a *clavo* (nail). The secret compartments tend to be in the gas tank, behind the dashboard, the spare tire, or some other secret compartment in the body of the vehicle. The drugs are wrapped in tinfoil, Saran wrap, or other packaging material. The packages are sometimes basted in substances such as gasoline, oils, and perfumes to disguise the smell so that the load is not detected by the sniffing dogs during inspection. According to my interviewee in Ciudad Juárez, the drug cartels have sniffing dogs to test the *clavos*. If their sniffing dogs detect the smell, the appropriate steps are taken until they cannot detect it. Only then is the vehicle sent to the POE.

A *clavo* can make it across the border in two ways. The first is by taking a chance. The vehicle shows up in the hope of not being detected. Whether they are detected depends on a number of factors, including the presence of sniffing dogs, the nervousness of the driver, the thoroughness of the inspection, and so on. *Clavos* are sometimes sent in groups that include one easily detectable member, so that agents are distracted by that one "bust" and neglect thorough inspection of the other vehicles crossing at that moment. The busted *clavo* is the price to pay for reducing the risk of the other *cla-*

vos being caught. This works partly thanks to the "spies" posted on both sides of the border by the drug cartels. It is not uncommon to see idle men, often posing as vendors, whose job is to "spot" for the cartel, watching the work patterns of U.S. officials and looking for a "lazy" or "distracted" officer who might not bother to double-check a vehicle. This information is relayed to the cartel operatives, who immediately send a pre-prepared *clavo* to that checkpoint at the POE.

A better way to reduce uncertainty and risk for a cartel is to smuggle a *clavo* in an operation that has been prearranged with a U.S. official working at a POE. This modus operandi involves the corruption of U.S. officials. Every year produces several dozen cases of corrupt U.S. officials who are willing to cooperate with a drug cartel in order to supplement their salaries. An agent makes between $30,000 and $50,000 a year depending on rank and longevity in the job. A drug cartel is willing to pay anywhere between $10,000 and $20,000 to that same agent for allowing a *clavo* to come across by waving it through the POE inspection point. There's more than greed at work, however. A two-day documentary on corruption by National Public Radio showed that blood ties also matter. Many officials are tempted by their own relatives across the border. Corruption by U.S. officials has an enormous impact on facilitating the drug trade and is perhaps more perverse than the corruption of Mexican officials. A corrupt Mexican official may offer protection by overlooking the operations of the drug cartels, but the drugs are still in Mexico. A corrupt U.S. official may allow tons of marijuana and produce millions of dollars in profits by waving dozens of *clavo*s through over time. That official undermines the entire efforts of his organization and constitutes a considerable loophole through which the drug business can profit enormously.[20]

The NAFTA Connection

The favored method of the drug cartels to smuggle their drugs across the border today is not *clavo*s, though these, unlike pedestrians, are still extensively used. The large cartels now ride the formal NAFTA economy. Nearly 5 million trucks cross the U.S.-Mexico border every year.[21] They carry 70 percent of all U.S.-Mexico trade, with a total value of around $260 billion. NAFTA turned out to be a heaven-sent blessing to the drug cartels. Over time, the four large cartels have come to rely on trucking as the primary conveyor belt of illegal drugs across the border. Tons of marijuana, cocaine, heroin, and now methamphetamines ride hidden in the millions of trucks that cross the border. These same millions of trucks also move the drugs on U.S. highways to the major metropolitan areas throughout the country.

What makes this possible can be understood through a simple mathematical reflection. Of the 5 million trucks that cross the border back and forth, only a fraction of them is inspected. It would be extremely costly and time-consuming to run a thorough inspection of every truck. Technology, such as infrared scans, is helping to catch more of the drugs hidden in trucks, but still only a fraction are detected.

U.S. bureaucracies realize the impossibility of inspecting every truck crossing the border and catching every load of drugs hidden in them. To go around this problem—and the potential of a terrorist attack on the border—the Homeland Security Department is building a new system called Customs and Trade Partners against Terrorism (C-TPAT). C-TPAT is largely a trust-based system that consists in building networks of intimate knowledge between U.S. officials, importers and exporters, and truck drivers. The drivers and the trucking companies are registered and precleared with Customs and Border Protection (CBP), as is the merchandise. C-TPAT participants are required to apply for preclearance to avoid delays at inspection points. The trucks are loaded at the warehouse or factory in the Mexican border town, and a seal is placed on the cargo container to expose any break-ins. CBP agents may or may not break the seal upon inspection at the POE, but when they break it, they do not generally replace it. If they don't replace it, this sometimes allows a trucker to load illegal drugs kept in stash houses in U.S. border towns and move them via the major highways into metropolitan areas throughout the United States.[22] Thus, what is billed as essentially a supply chain security program for international businesses often fails because corruption at any point in the system causes its breakdown.[23]

The C-TPAT system has proven to be less than infallible. The rewards the cartels offer to anyone willing to break the rules are just too high. Truckers can be tempted into breaking that trust. A truck operator from Laredo explained that some trucks after leaving the warehouse in Mexico and before arriving at the POE take a "detour." At an appointed place, the seals can be broken, the drugs loaded, and the seals replaced. Sometimes, it is not noticeable that the seals have been violated, although CBP inspectors are gaining experience in detecting whether a seal has been tampered with.[24]

Sometimes the Mexican police, principally the local police, offer protection to these trucks and escort them on their routes in Mexican border towns. My guide in Ciudad Juárez took me to Avenida de las Américas, where a local policeman was standing directing traffic. We approached the policeman and they spoke of the policeman's ability and willingness to "escort" a load of drugs in town so that no one would stop the truck on its route to the POE. Such services are regularly offered by the Mexican local police forces. At a May 2004 conference on border security in El Paso, Texas, a Mexican businessman complained bitterly that their cargo was sometimes "contaminated" by corrupt drivers. Businesses often lose the merchandise, which is seized by CBP if the truck is found carrying illegal drugs. To avoid this, many business owners and managers in Mexican border towns bought small cars and hired drivers to "escort" the trucks all the way to the POE. This effort turned out to be very expensive and has been largely scrapped. Besides, nothing guaranteed that the driver of the escorting vehicle was not in on the take as well.

There is new technology being introduced to keep track of the eighteen-wheelers carrying the majority of trade between the United States and Mexico. GPS devices are being installed in the trucks to ensure that the company knows where a truck is at all times. Even so, there are too many transactions to keep track of. My Laredo interviewee said that often trucks are detected way off their appointed route, perhaps thirty or forty miles south of the border. At that point, the trucking company must decide what to do. If they decide to report it, they risk losing the truck and having the driver jailed. Generally, they first call a lawyer who can deal with the issue before reporting it to the authorities. The intensely risky and extremely legal protocol often leads to informal inquiries with the driver, without involving the authorities at all. No real follow-up may happen at all.[25]

The increasing sophistication of the war on drugs means that the smaller smuggling operations are struggling to survive. Ironically, the Homeland Security strategy of the post-9/11 era is hurting these small-time smugglers in higher numbers. As new technology is introduced, as border law enforcement resources and personnel increase, and as inspectors get savvier at finding the drugs hidden in *clavos*, the small illegal-drug entrepreneurs are being detected and caught in higher numbers.

As the entrepreneurs struggle to stay alive, the drug cartels have the wherewithal to invest heavily in corrupting truckers and U.S. and Mexican officials and to invest in more sophisticated technology to get around Homeland Security tactics. They also invest in building better *clavos*. If caught, they can also take larger losses given the volume of drugs they handle. Unlike the small-time entrepreneurs, they enjoy an economy of scale that affords them higher risks. Thus, Homeland Security effectiveness has contributed to strengthening veritable oligopolies in the drug cartels. This is further evidenced by the kinds of cases that come to the federal court along the border. Most of those arrested and hauled to court for smuggling work for small-time smugglers. Seldom is someone working for a large drug cartel arrested crossing a *clavo*.[26] The testimony of many of those that end up in court shows that they are often inexperienced smugglers hired haplessly through a friend, at a bar, or on the streets. An analysis of court cases and testimony corroborates this consolidation of large cartels along the border because of enhanced Homeland Security tactics.

Corruption at the Border

Corruption is a fundamental component of any illegal industry. Drug trafficking is no exception. Corruption greases the wheels of the drug smuggling business and assures its flow on both sides of the border. Corruption practices have also contributed to strengthen the hand of the large drug cartels because they are increasingly the only ones that can afford the millions of dollars that it takes to keep the wheels of the drug smuggling business rolling. The small-timers simply cannot afford to corrupt officials on either side of the border who increasingly demand more and more of the drug smugglers in a perverse game of reverse extortion.[27]

Mexican illegal-drug-driven corruption is pervasive. It is systemic. It involves thousands of individuals both horizontally and vertically inside the country. A drug cartel may have several thousand direct employees—from buyers to spotters to smugglers to weapons procurers to *sicarios* (executioners for the drug cartels) to accountants—but indirectly it pays off hundreds, if not thousands, of people, particularly law enforcement officials and politicians. Border law enforcement agencies in Mexico are heavily penetrated by the drug cartels because they are indispensable in ensuring that the operations of the drug cartels can be conducted without interference by government operatives, especially those not on the payroll of the drug cartels. Cartels are now becoming more professionalized, hiring highly educated individuals who serve as public relations officers that recruit the help of other professionals, including accountants, businessmen (to launder money), law enforcement officials, doctors, and lawyers.

My interviewee in Ciudad Juárez attempted to disentangle the relationship between the cartels and law enforcement officials in Mexico. He explained that sometimes the cartels are the "victims" of law enforcement officials because the latter often extort criminal organizations attempting to obtain a greater share of the profits than the cartel is naturally accustomed to giving up. Law enforcement officials and even some politicians become extortion entrepreneurs and demand money in exchange for allowing the cartel to operate freely within their jurisdiction or for offering protection. Many do not passively take what the cartel is willing to give. Instead, they set their own price. If the cartel does not deliver, its operations can be made quite difficult. Occasionally, a police officer or even a politician is executed because their demands on the cartel far exceed what the cartel is willing to pay for help or protection.

American officials do not offer this kind of protection to cartels or their operatives. American corruption is considerably less extensive and is nowhere near as systemic as Mexican corruption. However, American corruption has a much larger concentrated impact than Mexican corruption. A single corrupt American official is enough to let through tons of illegal drugs producing hundreds of millions of dollars in profits for a cartel, by a simple act as waving a *clavo* or a truck through a checkpoint. Corrupting a U.S. official pays much more handsomely than corrupting nearly any official in Mexico. Most of the time, a U.S. official's corruption is uncovered when it becomes apparent that their lifestyle appears to surpass their earnings.

Interestingly, the escalation of U.S. antidrug efforts and the increased effectiveness of U.S. officials at POEs have made it increasingly expensive to bribe them. The higher the risk for the corrupt official, the higher the payoffs by the drug cartels. Often, a corrupt official will even demand more money to wave a *clavo* through the inspection point. Cartels now disburse millions of dollars to buy officials on both sides of the border. Both the heightened vigilance and its consequent higher payoffs are squeezing the small-time smugglers out of business.

Drugs and Money: North and South

The American appetite for illegal drugs is so large that in and of itself it constitutes a huge northward pull. The border is caught in the drug war as the passageway for drugs to satisfy this insatiable demand. But what happens to the money gathered in the millions of daily illegal-drug transactions that occur in bars, clubs, restaurants, street corners, houses, etc. throughout the

United States? A ton of cocaine may produce "tons of cash." How is it possible to hide and transport all this money? How does the money make its way down to Mexico and Colombia?

This is a complicated and increasingly dangerous process as well. Cartels send drugs north, accepting the risk of not being paid after delivery, although the chances of this happening are small given the fact that the local dealer would then lose his supplier. Also, disciplinary measures are taken in these cases as well. My Ciudad Juárez interviewee informed me of three women who failed to pay the cartel for the drugs sold to them. These three women were kidnapped and brought to Ciudad Juárez in the trunk of a car to force them to pay.

Most drugs move north across the border and then north to the rest of the United States, an enormous majority of them in trucks and other vehicles. The money collected in those areas is warehoused in homes in major U.S. cities and then carefully packaged to be smuggled south. The money is concealed in trucks and vehicles traveling south. These same vehicles take it across the border into Mexico. Just as drug lords worry about packaging their drugs so that they are not detected, they also worry about packaging the money so that it is not detected by U.S. or Mexican authorities, who can confiscate it. The money must then be warehoused in places scattered along the border and prepared for money laundering. Cartels today have sophisticated finance and accounting divisions that find creative ways to hide the cash and then to launder it. Professionals are hired for that purpose.

Sometimes, the cash makes it to the U.S. border town and then is transported in smaller amounts into Mexico, often by individuals hired to cross the cash into Mexico. They make trips south with cash hidden in various compartments in their vehicles. Moving cash south is increasingly as delicate as moving drugs north. Cheating by cash smugglers is just as punished as cheating by other cartel employees. Treason, shaving cash off the stashes, or stealing is punishable by torture and death as well. A person is paid up to $30,000 for crossing anywhere between $500,000 and $1 million south in his car, truck, or van. Millions of cars cross the border every year, and some of them do so with cash stashed inside. This is partly made easier by the fact that the Mexican customs system relies on random checks, meaning that only about one in ten or twenty vehicles are checked—if they trigger the red inspection light upon crossing. Most vehicles simply cross right through into Mexico without being bothered. This enables the drug lords to cross tons of cash going south.

Efficient money smuggling contributes to the maintenance of the large cartel operations in Mexico and beyond. The cartels can take losses. They can bribe a considerable number of people. They can invest in R&D to out-wit the technology used by U.S. law enforcement officials. In general, the enormous amounts of cash have created veritable oligopolies that can oper-ate massively and turn a profit, even when the United States steps up the pressure on their organizations.

Over time, the U.S. drug war on the border has forced the cartels to con-solidate their operations, to make their practices more efficient, and to make use of the economies of scale. Cartels have become flexible hierarchies, ready to respond to the contingencies of the drug war. And they generally succeed in doing so. The border drug war waged by the United States has consolidated drug smuggling into four large oligopolies that continue to send massive supplies of illegal drugs into this country. There are no stra-tegic successes in the drug war, and the tactical successes of the drug war appear to have the ability to squeeze the small-time smugglers out and make it easier for the large, consolidated drug-smuggling organizations to oper-ate. Such is the paradox of the war on drugs: It reveals itself to be largely ineffective and to produce nothing but monopoly capital that is remarkably flexible, agile, and resourceful in its capacity to circumvent U.S. technology and antidrug tactics. The U.S. government is not likely to win this war in another forty years.

Notes

1   Lawrence Gooberman, *Operation Intercept: The Multiple Consequences of Public Policy* (New York: Pergamon Press, 1974). Entire text found at www.druglibrary.org/schaffer/history/e1960/intercept (accessed on October 4, 2005).

2   Office of National Drug Control Policy, The White House, *The President's National Drug Control Strategy* (Washington: The White House, 2004). Entire publication can be found online at www.whitehousedrugpolicy.gov/publications/policy/ndcs05 (accessed on Oc-tober 4, 2005).

3   An interesting book that does just this from a journalistic perspective is Charles Bow-den's *Down by the River: Drugs, Money, Murder, and Family* (New York: Simon and Schus-ter, 2002).

4   See Peter Braunstein and Michael William Doyle, *Imagine Nation: The American Counter-culture of the 1960s and 1970s* (New York: Routledge, 2002). See also *Pulse Check: Drug Markets and Chronic Users in 25 of America's Largest Cities* (Washington: Executive Office of the President, Office of National Drug Control Policy, January 2004). The publication and previous *Pulse Check* issues can be found at www.whitehousedrugpolicy.gov/drugfact/pulsecheck.html (accessed on September 28, 2005).

5   Several books that analyze the relationship between an illegal product and the consumer market for it—essentially black market economics—are: Lawrence J. Kaplan and Dennis Kessler, eds., *An Economic Analysis of Crime* (Chicago: Charles C. Thomas, 1976); Annelise Graebner Anderson, *The Business of Organized Crime: A Cosa Nostra Family* (Stanford, CA: Hoover Institution Press, 1979); David J. Pyle, *The Economics of Crime and Law Enforcement* (New York: St. Martin's Press, 1983); André Bossard, *Transnational Crime and Criminal Law* (Chicago: University of Illinois at Chicago, 1990); Susan Pozo, ed., *Exploring the Underground Economy* (Kalamazoo, MI: W. E. Upjohn Institute for Employment Research, 1996); and R. T. Naylor, *Wages of Crime: Black Markets, Illegal Finance, and the Underworld Economy* (Ithaca, NY: Cornell University Press, 2002).

6   For a recount of these efforts in the Caribbean see Charles M. Fuss, *Sea of Grass: The Maritime Drug War, 1970–1990* (Annapolis, MD: Naval Institute Press, 1996).

7   See various chapters in Bruce M. Bagley and William O. Walker III, eds., *Drug Trafficking in the Americas* (Miami: University of Miami, North-South Center, 1994).

8   See some of these accounts in Elaine Shannon, *Desperados: Latin Drug Lords, U.S.A. Lawmen, and the War America Can't Win* (New York: Viking, 1988).

9   This story is told at length and quite eloquently by one of the greatest chroniclers of the Mexican illegal drug business, Jesús Blancornelas, in his book *El Cártel: Los Arellano Félix: La mafia más poderosa en la historia de América Latina* (México: Plaza Janés, 2002), 46–52.

10 Alfredo Corchado, "Violence Takes Toll on Nuevo Laredo," *Dallas Morning News*, August 16, 2005.

11 José Antonio Caporal, "Nuevo Laredo: Plaza en Disputa," *Revista Vértigo*, September 29, 2005. Article found in www.revistavertigo.com/historico/2-7-2005/reportaje2.html (accessed on September 29, 2005).

12 See the *Arizona Star* article at www.azstarnet.com/dailystar/dailystar/67273.php.

13 L. D. Johnston, P. M. O'Malley, J. G. Bachman, and J. E. Schulenberg, *Monitoring the Future: National Survey Results on Drug Use, 1975–2004*, vol. 1: *Secondary School Students*, NIH Publication No. 05-5727 (Bethesda, MD: National Institute on Drug Abuse, 2005); and L. D. Johnston, P. M. O'Malley, J. G. Bachman, and J. E. Schulenberg, *Monitoring the Future: National Survey Results on Drug Use, 1975–2003*, vol. 2: *College Students and Adults Ages 19–45*, NIH Publication No. 04-5508 (Bethesda, MD: National Institute on Drug Abuse, 2004).

14 This game of escalation and the logic behind it is explained in Peter Andreas's *Border Games: Policing the U.S.-Mexico Divide* (Ithaca, NY: Cornell University Press, 2000), 3–14.

15 *Illegal Drug Price and Purity Report* (Washington: Drug Enforcement Administration, April 2003), available at www.usdoj.gov/dea/pubs/intel/02058/02058.html#2 (accessed September 28, 2005).

16 Witness, for example, how quickly the warring factions of the Sinaloa and Gulf Cartels responded to the new chief of police of Nuevo Laredo, Alejandro Domínguez, and his strong language against the drug cartels. Within eight hours of his swearing in, on June 8, 2005, they gunned him down summarily to avoid further complications in the ongoing drug war in Nuevo Laredo.

17 Alfonso Urquidi, "Capstone Project," master's in public administration, University of Texas at El Paso, 2005. Alfonso Urquidi's unpublished work compares the flexibility of

criminal organizations with the rigidity of bureaucratic organization on the U.S.-Mexican border.

18   Interview with a former member of the Juárez cartel who wished to remain anonymous. The interview took place in Ciudad Juárez on August 3, 2005.

19   Interview with a federal court employee in El Paso, Texas, who wished to remain anonymous. The interview took place in El Paso on August 18, 2005.

20   John Burnett, "Corruption at the Gates: Series Explores Lure of Money, Prestige among U.S. Border Agents," National Public Radio, September 12–13, 2002, available at www .npr.org/programs/atc/features/2002/sept/border_corruption/ (accessed on October 2, 2005).

21   Bureau of Justice Statistics, *National Transportation Statistics 2005* (Washington: Department of Transportation, 2005). Tables at www.bts.gov/publications/national_ transportation_statistics/2005 (accessed on October 5, 2005).

22   According to an anonymous source, here's how it works: The trucks are sealed when they leave the plant in Mexico. They come to the border. Because they are precleared, they simply are X-rayed on the border and move on. Sometimes, if the customs inspector on the border has a reason to suspect anything, he will break the seal, go in, inspect the merchandise, etc. When the inspector breaks the seal, he will not replace it. The truck, if allowed to continue, will go on with a broken seal. This provides an opportunity for a truck involved in drug transportation from the border to U.S. cities to make a "stop" by some "stash house" and pick up a load of drugs. The truck then moves on loaded with drugs. The seals are important because they are sometimes checked at the secondary inspection points some fifty miles away from the border on major and minor U.S. highways.

23   U.S. Customs and Border Protection, "Securing the Global Supply Chain" (Washington: U.S. Customs and Border Protection, November 2004).

24   Interview with "James," a trucking company operator who asked to remain anonymous. The interview was conducted in San Antonio, Texas, on August 5, 2005.

25   Ibid.

26   Interview with a federal court employee in El Paso, Texas, August 18, 2005.

27   Interview with an anonymous former member of the Juárez Cartel in Ciudad Juárez, Chihuahua, August 4, 2005.

Notes on Contributors

ARTURO DÁVILA is chair of the Department of Foreign Languages and assistant professor of Spanish and Mexican–Latin American Studies at Laney College, Oakland. He is poet laureate in Mexico and Spain, where he was awarded international prizes for the following collections: *La ciudad dormida* (National Prize "Sor Juana Inés de la Cruz," Mexico, 1995); *Catulinarias* (International Prize "Antonio Machado," Baeza, Spain, 1998); *Poemas para ser leídos en el Metro* (International Prize "Juan Ramón Jiménez," Huelva, Spain, 2003).

SARAH HILL recently migrated to the U.S.-Canada border region and now lives in Kalamazoo, Michigan, where she teaches anthropology and environmental studies at Western Michigan University. She is completing a book about a century of cross-border garbage and recycling between the cities of El Paso and Ciudad Juárez and is a director of a regional nonprofit alternative energy start-up, Bronco Biodiesel.

JANE JUFFER is associate professor of English and women's studies and director of the Latina/o Studies Initiative at Pennsylvania State University. She is the author of *Single Mother: The Emergence of the Domestic Intellectual* and *At Home with Pornography: Women, Sex, and Everyday Life* (both New York University Press). She also has published articles on lingerie, Sammy Sosa, Latina/o studies at the corporate university, and various aspects of the U.S.-Mexico border.

LAURA A. LEWIS is associate professor of anthropology at James Madison University. She is the author of *Hall of Mirrors: Power, Witchcraft, and Caste in Colonial Mexico* (Duke University Press), winner of the 2004 Wheeler-Voegelin Best Book Award from the American Society of Ethnohistory. She has also published articles on contemporary black Mexicans in *American Ethnologist, Cultural Anthropology* and *Identities: Global Studies in Culture and Power*. She is writing an ethnography based on fieldwork in San Nicolás and Winston-Salem and was the recipient of a Guggenheim Fellowship in 2002–3.

ALEJANDRO LUGO is associate professor of anthropology and Latina/Latino studies at the University of Illinois at Urbana-Champaign. His photographic essay "Cruces" brings together his theoretical and ethnographic interventions in gender studies and border studies. See Lugo and Bill Maurer, eds.,

Gender Matters: Rereading Michelle Rosaldo (University of Michigan Press); Lugo, "Reflections on Border Theory, Culture, and the Nation," in *Race, Identity, and Representation in Education*, ed. Cameron McCarthy et al. (Routledge); and Lugo, "Theorizing Border Inspections," *Cultural Dynamics* 12 (2000).

ANA MARÍA MANZANAS CALVO is associate professor of American literature and culture at the Universidad de Salamanca, Spain. Currently she is working on a comparative study of the border and its literary reflection in the United States and Spain. Her publications include *Intercultural Mediations: Mimesis and Hybridity in American Literatures* (LIT Verlag, 2003) and collections of essays such as *Literature and Ethnicity in the Cultural Borderlands* (Rodopi, 2002) and *The Dynamics of the Threshold: Essays on Liminal Negotiations* (Gateway Press, 2006). She is now preparing the volume *Border Transits: Literature and Culture across the Line* for Rodopi.

TONY PAYAN is assistant professor of political science at the University of Texas at El Paso, where he teaches international relations, foreign policy, international law, and border issues. He has published two books in 2006: *Cops, Soldiers and Diplomats: Explaining Bureaucratic Agency in the Drug War* and *The Three U.S.-Mexico Border Wars: Drugs, Immigration, and Homeland Security*. He is also coeditor, with Maria Socorro Tabuenca, of *Gobernabilidad o Ingobernabilidad en la Región Paso del Norte*. In 2005–6 he was cochair of the executive committee of the largest border studies conference to date, "Lineae Terrarum," which took place in March 2006.

CLAUDIA SADOWSKI-SMITH is assistant professor of English at Arizona State University. She is the editor of *Globalization on the Line: Culture, Capital, and Citizenship at U.S. Borders* (Palgrave) and has published articles on border theory, literatures of the U.S.-Mexico border, and the internationalization of American studies in such journals as *Arizona Quarterly*, *Comparative American Studies*, and *Diaspora*. Sadowski-Smith is completing a book-length study entitled *Border Fictions: Transnational Writing from U.S. Borders, Globalization, and Inter-American Studies*.

ALICIA SCHMIDT CAMACHO is assistant professor of American studies at Yale University. She serves on the board of Junta for Progressive Action, a community agency serving the Latino neighborhood of Fair Haven. Her current scholarship concerns the *feminicidio* in Ciudad Juárez and the political rights of migrants. Her book, *Migrant Imaginaries: Cultural Politics in the Mexico-U.S. Borderlands*, is forthcoming from NYU Press.

SANTIAGO VAQUERA-VÁSQUEZ is an unrepentant border crosser, writer, painter, former DJ, and academic migrant worker. He has published stories in international literary journals (*Tinta; Los universitarios; El País; Barcelona Review*) and major anthologies dedicated to writing in the Spanish-speaking Americas. He is a senior lecturer in Latin American and Latino literatures at Pennsylvania State University. In 2006, as a Fulbright Scholar in Spain, he lectured at universities in Madrid and Salamanca and worked on completing a collection of short stories, *El libro que nunca te escribí*.

MELISSA W. WRIGHT is associate professor of geography and women's studies at Pennsylvania State University. Her research examines the interplay of culture, social justice, and political economy along the Mexico-U.S. border, particularly in Ciudad Juárez. Her book, *Disposable Women and Other Myths of Global Capitalism*, is forthcoming from Routledge (2006).

Contents of Volume 105

EXTENT AND NATURE OF CIRCULATION: Average number of copies of each issue published during the preceding twelve months; (A) total number of copies printed, 1172; (B.1) sales through dealers and carriers, street vendors and counter sales, 157; (B.2) paid mail subscriptions, 386; (C) total paid circulation, 543; (D) samples, complimentary, and other free copies, 41; (E) free distribution outside the mail (carriers or other means), 0; (F) total free distribution (sum of D & E), 41; (G) total distribution (sum of C & F), 584; (H.1) office use, leftover, unaccounted, spoiled after printing, 588; (H.2) returns from news agents, 0; (I) total, 1172.

Actual number of copies of a single issue published nearest to filing date: (A) total number of copies printed, 1039; (B.1) sales through dealers and carriers, street vendors and counter sales, 65; (B.2) paid mail subscriptions, 487; (C) total paid circulation, 552; (D) samples, complimentary, and other free copies, 48; (E) free distribution outside the mail (carriers or other means), 0; (F) total free distribution (sum of D & E), 48; (G) total distribution (sum of C & F), 600; (H.1) office use, leftover, unaccounted, spoiled after printing, 439; (H.2) returns from news agents, 0; (I) total, 1039.

represent*ations*

SPECIAL ISSUE: Redress

Representations 92 (April 2006) features a number of thought-provoking articles touching on the theme of political redress

Edited by Stephen Best and Saidiya Hartman

www.ucpressjournals.com/rep

 UNIVERSITY OF CALIFORNIA PRESS
JOURNALS + DIGITAL PUBLISHING

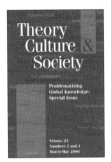

Graduate Faculty Philosophy Journal

The **Graduate Faculty Philosophy Journal**, published biannualy in association with the Department of Philosophy, New School for Social Research, is a forum for historical and contemporary issues in philosophy. The *Journal* regularly publishes special issues dedicated to investigating the historical development of concepts and problems in the history of philosophy and their ongoing relevance to issues in contemporary philosophy.

Vol. 27, No. 1

All communications should be addressed to the Editor, **Graduate Faculty Philosophy Journal**, Department of Philosophy, New School for Social Research, 65 Fifth Avenue, New York, NY 10003. The *Journal* is biannual. Domestic rates: Individuals: $25.00/year; Students: $15.00/year; Institutions: $50.00/year. Libraries and institutions can access *GFPJ* online by subscribing to the *Poesis* database. For more information, please visit www.nlx.com/posp/index.htm